Microsoft®
EXCEL 97
VISUAL BASIC®

Step by Step

Other titles in the *Step by Step* series:

Microsoft Access 97 Step by Step
Microsoft Excel 97 Step by Step
Microsoft Excel 97 Step by Step, Advanced Topics
Microsoft FrontPage 97 Step by Step
Microsoft Internet Explorer 3.0 Step by Step
Microsoft Office 97 Integration Step by Step
Microsoft Outlook 97 Step by Step
Microsoft PowerPoint 97 Step by Step
Microsoft Team Manager 97 Step by Step
Microsoft Windows 95 Step by Step
Microsoft Windows NT Workstation version 4.0 Step by Step
Microsoft Word 97 Step by Step
Microsoft Word 97 Step by Step, Advanced Topics

Step by Step books are also available for the Microsoft Office 95 programs.

Microsoft®

EXCEL 97
VISUAL BASIC®

Step by Step

Microsoft Press

PUBLISHED BY
Microsoft Press
A Division of Microsoft Corporation
One Microsoft Way
Redmond, Washington 98052-6399

Library of Congress Cataloging-in-Publication Data
Jacobson, Reed.
    Microsoft Excel 97/Visual Basic Step by Step / Reed Jacobson.
        p.   cm.
    Includes index.
    ISBN 1-57231-318-8
    1. Microsoft Excel for Windows.   2. Microsoft Visual Basic for
Windows. 3. Electronic spreadsheets.   I. Title.
    HF5548.4.M523J334   1997
    005.369--dc21   97-4203
                                                                      CIP

Printed and bound in the United States of America.

7 8 9   WCWC   2 1 0 9

Distributed in Canada by ITP Nelson, a division of Thomson Canada Limited.

A CIP catalogue record for this book is available from the British Library.

Microsoft Press books are available through booksellers and distributors worldwide. For further
information about international editions, contact your local Microsoft Corporation office. Or
contact Microsoft Press International directly at fax (425) 936-7329. Visit our Web site at
mspress.microsoft.com.

For WASSER*Studio*
Project Manager: Marcelle Amelia
Print Production Manager: Mary C. Gutierrez
Desktop Publishing Lead: Kim Tapia
Desktop Publisher: Arlene Rubin
Copy Editor: Walter Kilbourne
Technical Editor: Michael Brown

For Microsoft Press
Acquisitions Editor: Casey D. Doyle
Project Editor: Stuart J. Stuple

About the Author

Reed Jacobson owns Jacobson GeniusWorks, a company that specializes in creative training, consulting, and custom development services for Microsoft Excel and other Microsoft Office products. Jacobson GeniusWorks is one of the original companies invited to participate in what later became the Microsoft Solution Provider program.

Reed received a B.A. in Japanese and Linguistics and an M.B.A. from Brigham Young University, and a graduate fellowship in Linguistics from Cornell University. He worked as a Software Application Specialist for Hewlett-Packard for 10 years.

Reed is the author of *Excel Trade Secrets for Windows*. He has given presentations on Excel at Tech•Ed and other Microsoft conferences and seminars; he has created training video tapes for Microsoft Excel and contributes articles to *Inside Visual Basic*.

Reed Jacobson
Jacobson GeniusWorks
P. O. Box 3632
Arlington, WA 98223
rj900@msn.com

Table of Contents

Table of Contents

Part 4   Making Macros Easy to Use

*Quick*Look Guide

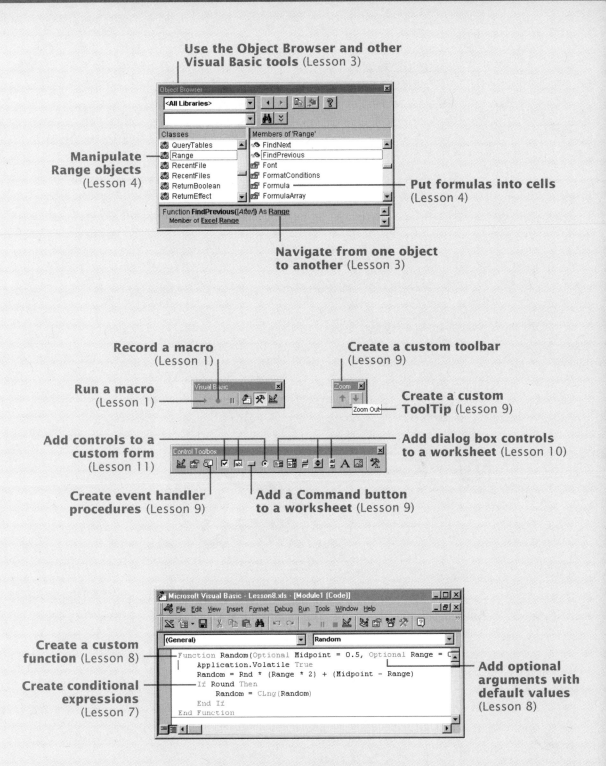

Use the Object Browser and other Visual Basic tools (Lesson 3)

Manipulate Range objects (Lesson 4)

Put formulas into cells (Lesson 4)

Navigate from one object to another (Lesson 3)

Record a macro (Lesson 1)

Create a custom toolbar (Lesson 9)

Run a macro (Lesson 1)

Create a custom ToolTip (Lesson 9)

Add controls to a custom form (Lesson 11)

Add dialog box controls to a worksheet (Lesson 10)

Create event handler procedures (Lesson 9)

Add a Command button to a worksheet (Lesson 9)

Create a custom function (Lesson 8)

Create conditional expressions (Lesson 7)

Add optional arguments with default values (Lesson 8)

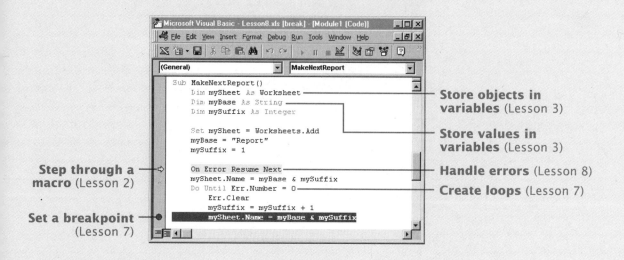

Store objects in variables (Lesson 3)

Store values in variables (Lesson 3)

Step through a macro (Lesson 2)

Handle errors (Lesson 8)

Create loops (Lesson 7)

Set a breakpoint (Lesson 7)

Create an Enterprise Information System (EIS) (Lesson 12)

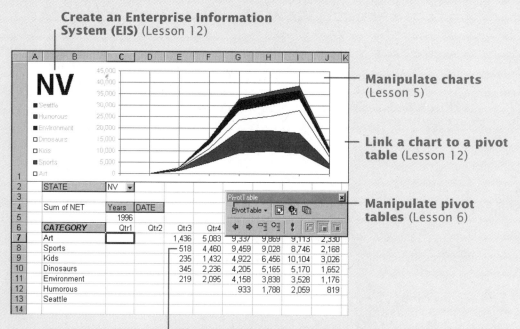

Manipulate charts (Lesson 5)

Link a chart to a pivot table (Lesson 12)

Manipulate pivot tables (Lesson 6)

Retrieve data from an external database (Lesson 12)

Finding Your Best Starting Point

Microsoft Excel is a powerful tool for analyzing and presenting information. One of the strengths of Excel has always been its macro language. Since Excel first appeared, it has always had the most extensive and flexible macro language of any spreadsheet program. Visual Basic for Applications first appeared as part of Excel in version 5. In fact, Excel was the first major application to include this exciting new architecture.

The version of Visual Basic for Applications that is included with Excel 97 is a major improvement over that original effort. The new version of Visual Basic for Applications is a complete development environment, consistent with the stand-alone version of Visual Basic, and shared by all Microsoft Office applications.

When you start writing macros in Excel, you really need to learn two different skills. First, you need to learn how to work with Visual Basic. Everything you learn about Visual Basic will be true not only for Excel, but for other applications that incorporate Visual Basic as well. Second, you need to learn how to control Excel. The more you know about Excel as a spreadsheet, the more effective you can be at developing macros that control Excel. While this book focuses on Visual Basic as Excel's development environment, much of what you learn will help you to be more effective using the spreadsheet as well.

Microsoft Excel 97/Visual Basic Step by Step walks you through tasks one at a time, keeping you on track with clear instructions and frequent pictures of what you should see on the screen. In each lesson, you'll become familiar with another important area of Excel or Visual Basic.

IMPORTANT This book is designed for use with Excel 97 (version 8.0) or Microsoft Office 97 Professional for the Microsoft Windows 95 and Microsoft Windows NT operating systems. To find out what software you're running, you can check the product package, or you can start the software, click the Help menu, and click About Microsoft Excel. If your software is not compatible with this book, a Step by Step book for your software is probably available. Many of the Step by Step titles are listed on the second page of this book. If the book you want isn't listed, please visit our World Wide Web site at http://www.microsoft.com/mspress/ or call 1-800-MSPRESS for more information.

Finding Your Best Starting Point in This Book

This book is designed for Excel users who are starting to write macros, and for programmers familiar with another programming system (such as Visual Basic or COBOL) who want to use Excel as a platform for developing applications. You'll get the most from this book if you're already familiar with the basic capabilities of Excel, such as entering values and formulas into worksheets.

Learning about Visual Basic and about how Excel works with Visual Basic can seem overwhelming. That's why you need this book. This book starts with simple, practical tasks and then takes you on to advanced concepts and powerful applications—*step by step*.

The book is divided into four parts:

Part 1: Automating Everyday Tasks starts you off with practical, straightforward ways to use macros in Excel. It also introduces the macro recorder and the Visual Basic for Applications development environment.

Part 2: Exploring Objects helps you understand how Visual Basic talks to Excel. In this part, you will learn what objects are, how they relate to one another, and how you can find the objects you need when you are writing macros for your own use. You will get practical experience using some of the most important types of objects in Excel: ranges, charts, and pivot tables.

Part 3: Exploring Visual Basic teaches you how to get Visual Basic to move beyond the limitations of a recorded macro. You will learn how to write macros that make decisions and repeat actions in a loop. You will also learn how you can write your own functions that you can use from a worksheet as well as from other macros.

Part 4: Making Macros Easy to Use moves you into the world of a complete application. You will learn how to make applications easy for others to use by adding ActiveX controls to the worksheet and to custom forms. You will learn how to make applications that respond to actions that a user takes, such as clicking on a worksheet. You will also build a complete application that retrieves information from an external database and presents it to the user.

Use the following table to find your best starting point in this book.

If you are	Follow these steps
New...	
to Microsoft Excel	**1** Install the practice files as described in "Installing the Practice Files and Additional Microsoft Excel Tools," later in this section.
to Visual Basic programming	**2** Become acquainted with the basic features of Excel, referring to the online Help system and other documention as necessary.
	3 Learn how to create practical macros by working sequentially through Lessons 1 and 2. Then, as you want to understand more about advanced macros, work through Lessons 3 through 8. If you need to create macros that others can use, continue to Lessons 9 through 12.

If you are	Follow these steps
Switching...	
from Microsoft Visual Basic	**1** Install the practice files as described in "Installing the Practice Files and Additional Microsoft Excel Tools," later in this section.
from another Microsoft product that uses Visual Basic	**2** Work through Lessons 1 and 2 to become familiar with Excel's powerful macro recorder. Work through Lessons 3 through 6 to become familiar with important Excel objects. Skim Lessons 7, 8, and 10, because these are very similar to other versions of Visual Basic. Then, work through Lessons 9, 11 and 12 to learn aspects of creating an application that are unique to Excel.

If you are	Follow these steps

Upgrading...

from Excel for Windows 95	**1** Install the practice files as described in "Installing the Practice Files and Additional Microsoft Excel Tools."
from a previous version of Excel	**2** Complete the lessons that cover the topics you need. Use the table of contents and the *Quick*Look Guide to locate information about general topics. You can use the index to find information about a specific topic or a feature from a previous version of Excel.

If you are	Follow these steps

Referencing...

this book after working through the lessons	**1** Use the index to locate information about specific topics, and use the table of contents and the *Quick*Look Guide to locate information about general topics.
	2 Read the lesson summary at the end of each lesson for a brief review of the major tasks in the lesson. The lesson summary topics are listed in the same order they are presented in the lesson.

Corrections, Comments, and Help

Every effort has been made to ensure the accuracy of this book and the contents of the practice files disk. Microsoft Press provides corrections and additional content for its books through the World Wide Web at

http://www.microsoft.com/mspress/support/

If you have comments, questions, or ideas regarding this book or the practice files disk, please send them to us.

Send e-mail to

mspinput@microsoft.com

Or send postal mail to

Microsoft Press

Attn: Step by Step Series Editor

One Microsoft Way

Redmond, WA 98052-6399

Please note that support for the Excel software product itself is not offered through the above addresses. For help using Excel, you can call Microsoft Technical Support at (800) 936-5700, or visit Excel Online Support on the World Wide Web at

http://www.microsoft.com/MSExcelSupport/

Visit Our World Wide Web Site

We invite you to visit the Microsoft Press World Wide Web site. You can visit us at the following location:

http://www.microsoft.com/mspress/

You'll find descriptions for all of our books, information about ordering titles, notice of special features and events, additional content for Microsoft Press books, and much more.

You can also find out the latest in software developments and news from Microsoft Corporation by visiting the following World Wide Web site:

http://www.microsoft.com/

We look forward to your visit on the Web!

Installing the Practice Files and Additional Microsoft Excel Tools

The disc inside the back cover of this book contains practice files that you'll use as you perform the exercises in the book. By using the practice files, you won't waste time creating the samples used in the lessons—instead, you can concentrate on learning how to write macros in Microsoft Excel. With the files and the step-by-step instructions in the lessons, you'll also learn by doing, which is an easy and effective way to acquire and remember new skills.

 IMPORTANT Before you break the seal on the practice disc package, be sure that this book matches your version of the software. This book is designed for use with Excel 97 (version 8.0) for the Windows 95 and Windows NT version 4.0 operating systems. To find out what software you're running, you can check the product package or you can start the software, and then on the Help menu click About Microsoft Excel. If your program is not compatible with this book, a Step by Step book matching your software is probably available. Many of the Step by Step titles are listed on the second page of this book. If the book you want isn't listed, please visit our World Wide Web site at http://www.microsoft.com/mspress/ or call 1-800-MSPRESS for more information.

Install the practice files on your computer

Follow these steps to install the practice files on your computer's hard disk so that you can use them with the exercises in this book.

1 Remove the disc from the package inside the back cover of this book and insert it in your CD-ROM drive.

2 On the taskbar at the bottom of your screen, click the Start button, and then click Run.

The Run dialog box appears.

3 In the Open box, type **d:setup** (or, if your CD-ROM drive uses a drive letter other than "d," substitute the correct drive letter).

4 Click OK, and then follow the directions on the screen.

The setup program window appears with recommended options preselected for you. For best results in using the practice files with this book, accept these preselected settings.

5 When the files have been installed, remove the disc from your drive and replace it in the package inside the back cover of the book.

A folder called Excel VBA Practice has been created on your hard disk, and the practice files have been put in that folder. A shortcut named MS Excel VBA SBS Practice has also been added to your Favorites folder, to make it easy to switch to the practice files.

NOTE In addition to installing the practice files, the Setup program created a shortcut to the Microsoft Press World Wide Web site on your Desktop. If your computer is set up to connect to the Internet, you can double-click the shortcut to visit the Microsoft Press Web site. You can also connect to the Web site directly at http://www.microsoft.com/mspress/.

Installing All the Excel Tools You Need

To permit you to complete the steps in this book, the Excel installation on your computer must include the Data Access component, which includes tools for retrieving data from external databases. You'll also want to have the Visual Basic Help files. However, these components are not included if you selected the Typical or Minimal option in Setup. Before you begin the lessons, it's best to check your installation by running Setup again.

Fortunately, you don't have to reinstall Excel to check your installation or add the developer tools. When you run Setup, it will detect that Excel is already installed and allow you to add the necessary components.

Install Excel developer components

1   Start Excel 97 Setup (or Microsoft Office 97 Professional Setup).

2   When Setup asks what you want to do, click the Add/Remove button.

3   If you're using Microsoft Office Setup, select Microsoft Excel in the Options list, and then click the Change Option button. (If you're using Excel Setup, you're already viewing Excel options, so you can skip this step and Step 6.)

4   Select Help and Sample Files from the Options list, and click Change Option.

5   Click the Select All button to select all the Help files, and then click OK.

6   If you're using Microsoft Office Setup, click OK to return to the main list of components.

7   Select Data Access from the Options list, and click the Change Option button.

8   Click the Select All button to select all the Data Access options, and then click OK.

9   Click Continue.

Setup installs all the necessary files. If you have previously installed the necessary files, Setup displays a message instructing you to click Cancel and not to make any changes.

Using the Practice Files

Each lesson in this book explains when and how to use any practice files for that lesson. When it's time to use a practice file, the book will list instructions for how to open the file. You should always save the practice file with a new name (as directed in the lesson) so that the original practice file will be available if you want to go back and redo any of the lessons.

Along with the practice files is a Finished folder. This contains a copy of each workbook as it will appear at the end of the lesson. If you have problems with an item in any lesson, you can see how the macro works in the Finished folder to help you understand how to correct the problem.

Here's a list of the files included on the practice disc, along with where each file is used:

You may not see the extensions for the files, depending on how you have configured Windows 95.

Lesson	Filename	Description
1,11	Budget.xls	A workbook containing the annual budget for the fictional Miller Textiles company.
2,6,7,12	Orders.dbf	The Miller Textiles order history database. This file contains the monthly orders for different shirt designs. This file is stored in a format that can be accessed either by Excel or by the database drivers that come with Excel.
2	Ord9711.txt	A text file containing the most recent month's order information.
3	Objects.xls	Simple macros that will demonstrate what objects are and how to use them.
4	Ranges.xls	Macros along with sample data that demonstrate how Visual Basic controls Excel ranges.
5	Graphics.xls	Simple graphical objects that you will create macros to manipulate.
7	Flow.xls	Simple macros that you will enhance using new Visual Basic features.
8	Function.xls	Simple macros that you will enhance using new Visual Basic features.
9	Events.xls	An otherwise empty workbook that contains some simple pre-recorded macros to help you learn how to link macros to events.
10	Loan.xls	Sample values on a worksheet that you will use to create an easy-to-use loan payment calculator.
12	Map.wmf	A picture file containing a map that will be used as the basis of the user interface.
12	Code12a.txt Code12b.txt Code12c.txt Code12d.txt Code12e.txt Code12f.txt	Code that you will enter to create the custom application. Long sections of code are included as importable files so you won't need to type the code in.

Uninstalling the practice files

Use the following steps to delete the practice files added to your hard drive by the Step by Step program.

1 Click the Start button, point to Settings, and then click Control Panel.

2 Double-click the Add/Remove Programs icon.

3 Select Microsoft Excel/Visual Basic Step by Step from the list, and then click Add/Remove.

   A confirmation message appears.

4 Click Yes.

   The practice files are uninstalled.

5 Click OK to close the Add/Remove Programs Properties dialog box.

6 Close the Control Panel window.

Need Help with the Practice Files?

Every effort has been made to ensure the accuracy of this book and the contents of the CD-ROM. If you do run into a problem, Microsoft Press provides corrections for its books through the World Wide Web at

   http://www.microsoft.com/mspress/support/

We also invite you to visit our main Web page at

   http://www.microsoft.com/mspress/

You'll find descriptions for all of our books, information about ordering titles, notices of special features and events, additional content for Microsoft Press books, and much more.

Using Shortcuts

Excel has several different ways of accomplishing almost any action. For most actions, you can select a command from a menu, press a shortcut key, click a toolbar button, and so forth. Different people prefer different techniques. To minimize confusion, for most actions the body of the text describes only a single method. Appendix A, however, gives you all the alternate ways that you can carry out the actions described. You may find that you prefer a different method than the one described in the text.

Resolving Possible Configuration Differences

This book assumes that Excel is configured the way it would be immediately after installing it. You may, however, have customized Excel to your preferences. In most cases, customizing Excel will not affect the way you can use this book. In some cases, however, you could customize Excel in such a way that what you see on the screen may not match the illustrations in the text, or the steps in this book may not work properly. Appendix B describes all the possible configuration settings that may affect the way that you use this book. If something in the book is not working the way it should, and you have customized Excel in any way, compare your settings with those in this appendix.

Conventions and Features Used in This Book

When you use this book, you can save time by understanding, before you start the lessons, how the instructions, keys to press, and so on are shown in the book. Please take a moment to read the following list, which also points out other helpful features of the book.

Procedural Conventions

- Hands-on exercises for you to follow are given in numbered lists of steps (1, 2, and so on). An arrowhead bullet (▶) indicates an exercise that has only one step.

Typographic Conventions

- Text that you are to type appears in **boldface**.

- New terms, program code within body text, and the titles of books appear in *italic*.

- Names of keyboard keys for you to press appear in SMALL CAPITAL LETTERS. A plus sign (+) between two key names means that you must press those keys at the same time. For example, "Press ALT+TAB" means that you hold down the ALT key while you press TAB.

- Program code (on a separate line or lines) appears in monospace type:

```
Me.AllowEdits = False
```

Supplementary Features

The following icons identify the different types of supplementary material:

	Notes labeled	Alert you to
	Note	Additional information for a step.
	Tip	Suggested additional methods for a step or helpful hints.
	Important	Essential information that you should check before continuing with the lesson.

Other Features of This Book

*Run Macro
button*

- You can perform many operations in Microsoft Excel by clicking a button on the toolbar or a tool in the toolbox. When the instructions in this book tell you to click a toolbar button, a picture of the button is shown in the left margin next to the instructions. The Run Macro button in the margin next to this paragraph is an example.

- Screen capture illustrations show sample user interfaces and the results of your completed steps, and frequently include text that calls out the part of the illustration you should notice.

- Sidebars—short sections printed on a shaded background—introduce special programming techniques, background information, or features related to the information being discussed.

- You can get a quick reminder of how to perform the tasks you learned by reading the Lesson Summary at the end of a lesson.

- You can quickly determine what online Help topics are available for additional information by referring to the Help topics listed at the end of each lesson.

Automating Everyday Tasks

Make a Macro Do Simple Tasks

Estimated time
40 min.

In this lesson you will learn how to:

- Record and run a macro.
- Understand and edit simple recorded macros.
- Run a macro by using a shortcut key.

If you haven't yet installed the practice files that come with this book, refer to "Installing the Practice Files," earlier in this book.

Last month we lost the remote control to our VCR. It was awful. I wanted to set the machine to record "Mystery Science Theater 3000" at 1:00 A.M. one night, but I couldn't do it because all the scheduling features were built into the remote control. Fortunately, after about two weeks, my wife detected a bulge in the cloth backing of the recliner and retrieved the precious controller. I am so happy that I can now record old movies. Someday I may even watch some of them.

Microsoft Visual Basic is Microsoft Excel 97's remote control. Sure, you can use Excel without ever using Visual Basic, but not only can the Visual Basic "remote control" make your life more convenient, it also allows you to take advantage of features that you can't get to with the standard "front-panel" controls. And once you become acquainted with Excel's remote control, you will wonder how you ever did without it.

How Visual Basic Talks to Excel

The first spreadsheet macro languages mimicked the user interface. For example, if you typed **R** (for "Range"), **N** (for "Name"), **C** (for "Create") in the user interface, you would enter **RNC** into the macro to automate the process. This approach had inherent weaknesses. Not only were keystroke macros difficult to read, they did not adapt well to the graphical user interface. What do you use to represent dragging a rectangle with the mouse?

To solve these problems, the early versions of Excel contained a new type of macro language that made the macro commands independent of the user interface. For example, in Excel version 4 there were at least three different ways to copy a range: press CTRL+C, click the Copy toolbar button, and click Copy on the Edit menu. All those user interface sequences translated to a single macro function, =COPY(). These function-based macros had two major drawbacks. For one thing, Excel macros were very specific to Excel; the language could not be adapted to other applications. For another thing, the number of functions kept increasing with each new version, and there was no good way of organizing or grouping the thousands of possibilities.

Automation

Excel with Visual Basic for Applications incorporates a whole new way of automating applications called *Automation* (previously known as OLE Automation). Excel version 5 was the first major application to take advantage of this concept. In this new approach, Visual Basic acts as a general-purpose language that is independent of the application. Suddenly, anyone who knows how to work with Visual Basic has a big head start in automating Excel, and anyone who learns how to write Excel macros in Visual Basic can transfer that knowledge to other types of Visual Basic programming.

Even though Excel hosts Visual Basic, Visual Basic does not have any special "hooks" into Excel's internals. Rather, Excel *exposes* its capabilities to Visual Basic by means of a special set of commands called an *object library*. Visual Basic talks to Excel's object library.

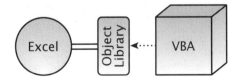

Visual Basic can control not only Excel, but also any application that provides an object library. All Microsoft Office applications provide object libraries, and several other Microsoft and non-Microsoft applications do, too.

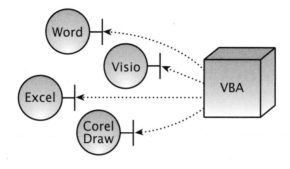

The Visual Basic that comes with Excel is not the only language that can communicate with the object library. Any language that supports Automation can control Excel. You can control Excel not only with the Visual Basic hosted by Excel, but also with the Visual Basic hosted by Microsoft Word, or with the stand-alone version of Visual Basic, or even with C++ or Borland's Delphi program.

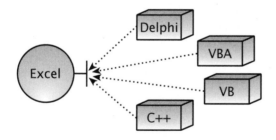

Excel Objects and You

Not only does the object library expose Excel's capabilities to Visual Basic, but even more importantly, the object library exposes Excel's capabilities to you. Once you know how to read and interpret an object library, you can discover new features and figure out quickly how to put them to work. The best way to start finding out about how Visual Basic communicates with Excel's objects is to record some simple macros. Eventually, however, you will want to move beyond the limitations of the macro recorder.

In Part 1 of this book, you will learn how to record and modify simple macros. In Part 2, you will learn how Excel objects work. In Part 3, you will learn secret powers of Visual Basic. And in Part 4, you will learn how to make a macro easy to use.

Start the lesson

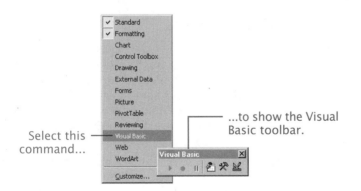

Open button

1 Start Excel.

2 On the toolbar, click the Open button, and in the Open dialog box, click the Look In Favorites button.

3 Double-click the Excel VBA Practice folder. Double-click the Budget workbook.

4 Save the Budget file as **Lesson1**.

Creating a Simple Macro

Excel has a large collection of convenience tools readily available as shortcut keys and as buttons on toolbars. Sometimes the built-in convenience tool doesn't work quite the way you want. Enhancing a built-in tool is a good first macro to create.

Show the Visual Basic toolbar

Before you start creating the macros, take one small step that will make your work with macros much easier.

1 Click any toolbar using the right mouse button. (This is called "right-clicking.")

The toolbar shortcut menu appears, showing most of the available toolbars.

2 Select Visual Basic from the toolbar list.

The Visual Basic toolbar appears. You can change the location and shape of this toolbar just as you can any other Excel toolbar.

Now, when you are ready to record a macro, just click the circle. When you are ready to run a macro, click the triangle.

Format currency with a built-in tool

On the Formatting toolbar, Excel has a button that formats the current selection as currency: the Currency Style button.

*Currency Style
button*

1　In the Lesson1 workbook, select cells D3:F4 on the Budget97 worksheet.

2　Click the Currency Style button on the Formatting toolbar.

Excel reformats the selected cells as currency.

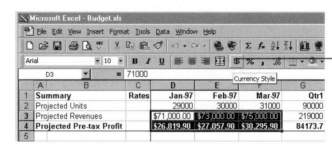

Click here to
format the
selection as
currency.

The currency format Excel applies when you click the Currency Style button has two decimal places. Sometimes you want to display currency with two decimal places—perhaps in your checkbook. But other times you don't want two decimal places—perhaps your budget doesn't warrant that kind of precision. You may want to create a macro to format a cell as currency with no decimal places instead.

Record a macro to format currency

1　On the Budget97 worksheet, select cells D7:F8.

2　On the Visual Basic toolbar, click the Record Macro button.

3　Replace the default macro name with **FormatCurrency**, and click OK.

*Record Macro
button*

*A macro name
can contain
uppercase and
lowercase
letters, under-
scores, and
periods, but no
spaces.*

Type the name
of the new
macro here.

The word *Recording* appears in the status bar, and a Stop Recording toolbar appears. You are recording.

4 On the Format menu, click the Cells command, and then click the Number tab. Select Currency from the Category list. In the Decimal Places box, type **0** to change the number of decimal places to zero, and then click OK.

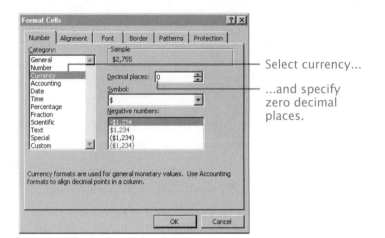

Select currency...

...and specify zero decimal places.

Excel formats the selected cells as currency without decimal places.

5 Click the Stop Recording button.

6 Save the Lesson1 workbook.

Stop Recording button

That's it. You recorded a macro to format a selection with the currency format you want. Now you probably want to try out the macro to see how it works.

Run the macro

1 On the Budget97 worksheet, select cells D9:F10.

2 On the Visual Basic toolbar, click the Run Macro button.

3 Select the FormatCurrency macro in the list, and click Run.

Run Macro button

Your macro gives the selected cells your customized currency format. Running the macro from the Macro dialog box is not very much of a shortcut, though.

Assign a shortcut key to the macro

*Run Macro
button*

1 On the Visual Basic toolbar, click the Run Macro button.

2 Select the FormatCurrency macro in the list, and click the Options button.

The Macro Options dialog box allows you to change the macro's shortcut key assignment and its description.

3 You want to assign CTRL+SHIFT+C as the shortcut key. Select the box below the Shortcut Key label and press SHIFT+C.

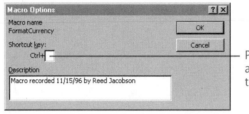

Press **SHIFT+C** here to assign CTRL+SHIFT+C as the shortcut key.

IMPORTANT Excel uses many CTRL key combinations as built-in shortcuts. For example, CTRL+C is Copy and CTRL+Z is Undo. If you assign one of these shortcuts to your macro, pressing the shortcut will run your macro rather than the built-in command. If you always use a CTRL+SHIFT key combination for your macros, you will be much less likely to override a built-in shortcut.

You can also assign a short-cut key at the time you first record a macro.

4 Click OK to return to the Macro dialog box, and then click Cancel to get back to the worksheet.

5 Select cells D11:F13, and press CTRL+SHIFT+C to run the macro.

6 Save the Lesson1 workbook.

Now you have successfully recorded, run, and enhanced a macro—all without seeing anything of the macro itself. Aren't you burning with curiosity to see what you have just created?

Look at the macro

The macro is actually hidden away in the workbook, but you need to open the Visual Basic Editor to be able to see it.

Run Macro button

Excel versions 5 and 7 stored new macros on a sheet in the workbook. Excel 97 also stores the macros in the workbook, but they do not appear as sheets.

1 On the Visual Basic toolbar, click the Run Macro button.

2 Click FormatCurrency, and then click Edit.

The Visual Basic Editor window appears. Visual Basic appears to be a separate program, but it is "owned" by Excel. If you quit Excel, Visual Basic will automatically shut down. Inside the Visual Basic Editor, a window captioned Module1 appears as well.

Maximize the Module1 window so that it fills the Visual Basic Editor, and then resize the Visual Basic Editor window so that you can see the Excel workbook in the background.

If there are any other windows visible in the Visual Basic Editor, close them now.

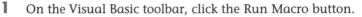

The window captioned Module1, a *module*, is the place where the recorder puts macros. Your macro is in the Module1 module. The macro looks like this:

For details about number format codes, ask the Assistant for help using the words "user-defined numeric formats."

```
Sub FormatCurrency()
'
' FormatCurrency Macro
' Macro recorded 11/15/96 by Reed Jacobson
'

'

    Selection.NumberFormat = "$#,##0"

End Sub
```

The five lines that start with apostrophes at the beginning of the macro are *comments*. In any line, anything that follows an apostrophe is a comment. (The blank line among the comments, without even an apostrophe, is where the recorder would have put the shortcut key combination if you had assigned it when you recorded the macro.) The recorder puts in the comments partly to remind you to add comments as you write a macro. You can add to them, change them, or delete them as you wish without changing how the macro runs. Comments are green to help you distinguish them from statements that do something.

The macro is written in Visual Basic and follows standard Visual Basic rules. The macro itself begins with *Sub*, followed by the name of the macro. Is *Sub* used because a macro is typically hidden, out of sight, like a *sub*marine? Or does it stand for *sub*routine, for reasons you will learn at the end of Lesson 2? Stay tuned. The last line of a macro is always *End Sub*.

The Selection.NumberFormat statement does the real work. It is the body of the macro. *Selection* stands for "the current selection." *NumberFormat* refers to an attribute—or *property*—of the selection. To interpret a Visual Basic instruction, read the statement from right to left, like this: "Let '$#,##0' be the number format of the selection."

NOTE   Some people wonder why the word *NumberFormat* comes after the word *Selection* if you read Selection.NumberFormat as "number format of the selection." In an Excel worksheet, you do not use the English language convention of stating an action first and then the object. ("Copy these cells. Put the copy in those cells.") Instead, on an Excel worksheet you select the object first and then perform the action. ("These cells—copy. Those cells—paste.") Selecting the object first in the worksheet makes carrying out multiple actions more efficient.

Macro statements in Visual Basic work backwards, the same as actions do in an Excel worksheet. In a macro statement, you state what you're going to work on, and then you do something to it.

Changing Multiple Properties at Once

The FormatCurrency macro changes a single attribute of the current selection—the number format. In Excel macros, an attribute is called a *property*. In the FormatCurrency macro, NumberFormat is a property of a cell. Many macro statements assign a value to a property. Whenever the macro recorder creates a statement containing an equal sign, the word in front of the equal sign is a property. Sometimes when you record an action, the macro changes multiple properties at the same time.

Merge text vertically with a command

Excel has a toolbar button that can merge and center several cells in a horizontal row: the Merge And Center button. But sometimes you may want to merge cells vertically along the edge of a report. Excel does not have a toolbar button that merges cells vertically along the edge and adjusts the position of text in those cells, but you can record a macro that does.

To better understand what's required, first walk through the steps to create this format using menu commands.

1 Activate the Budget97 window.

2 Select the range A6:A12.

The label is at the top of the selected range.

Select the cells you want to merge.

3 On the Format menu, click Cells, and then click the Alignment tab.

The Alignment tab has several controls that control alignment, wrapping, orientation angle, shrinking, and merging.

4 Click the Merge cells check box, and drag the red dot in the orientation control up to the top of the arc to set the orientation to 90 degrees.

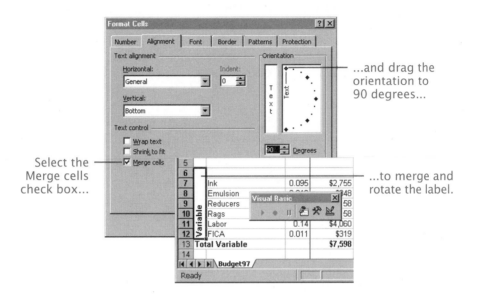

Select the Merge cells check box...

...and drag the orientation to 90 degrees...

...to merge and rotate the label.

5 Click OK to merge and tilt the label.

Putting a label to the side of a block of cells is extremely powerful. You can make it easy to do by recording a macro.

Where Do New Macros Go?

The first time you record a macro, Excel creates a new module. Each time you record an additional macro, Excel adds the new macro to the end of the same module. When you close and reopen the workbook, the macro recorder will start recording macros into a new module. There is no way for you to control where the recorder puts a new macro.

Having macros in multiple modules should not be a problem. When you use the Macro dialog box to select and edit a macro, it will automatically take you to the appropriate module.

Record a macro to merge cells vertically

*Record Macro
button*

1 Rearrange your windows as necessary so that you can see the Module1 window and the Excel window itself. Select the range A15:A20, and click the Record Macro button.

2 In the Record Macro dialog box, replace the default macro name with **MergeVertical**, replace the default description with **Merge cells vertically**, and set CTRL+SHIFT+M as the shortcut key.

> **IMPORTANT** If you assign the same shortcut key to two macros, the one that appears first in the Run Macro list is the one that will run. A shortcut key is only valid while the workbook containing the macro is open.

3 Click OK.

In the module window, you can see that the recorder immediately puts the comment lines and the Sub and End Sub lines into the macro.

4 On the Format menu, click Cells. In the Format Cells dialog box, on the Alignment tab, select the Merge Cells check box, set the alignment to 90 degrees, and click OK.

The recorder puts several lines into the macro all at once.

*Stop Recording
button*

5 Click the Stop Recording button.

6 Save the Lesson1 workbook.

*Run Macro
button*

7 Click Run Macro, select MergeVertical, and click Edit to look at the macro code in the Visual Basic window.

```
Sub MergeVertical()
'
' MergeVertical Macro
' Merge cells vertically
'
' Keyboard Shortcut: Ctrl+Shift+M
'
    With Selection
        .HorizontalAlignment = xlGeneral
        .VerticalAlignment = xlBottom
        .WrapText = False
        .Orientation = 90
        .ShrinkToFit = False
        .MergeCells = True
    End With
End Sub
```

The macro shows six different property settings for the cell alignment. Each property is followed by an equal sign. These properties correspond exactly to the controls you saw in the dialog box.

Each of the property settings affects the current selection, just as the NumberFormat property setting does in the FormatCurrency macro. In the FormatCurrency macro, however, the property name is attached directly to *Selection* with a period, to show that the property affects the cells in the current selection. In this macro, by contrast, each of the property names just "hangs there," preceded only by a period.

A pair of statements beginning with *With* and ending with *End With* is called a *With structure*. It means that every time there is a period with nothing in front of it, pretend that the word that followed the *With* is there. With structures make the code easier to read because you can tell instantly that all the properties relate to the current selection. You will often see With structures in macros that you record.

Eliminate unnecessary lines from the macro

In many dialog boxes, the macro recorder records all the possible properties, even though you might change the values of only one or two of them. You can make your macro easier to understand if you eliminate unnecessary properties.

In the MergeVertical macro, you need to change the values of only the Orientation and MergeCells properties. You can therefore delete the other lines from the macro.

1 Activate the Visual Basic Editor and click as far to the left of *.HorizontalAlignment* as you can within the Editor window. This will select the entire line.

2 Press DELETE.

Undo button

3 Repeat Steps 1 and 2 for each of the properties except Orientation and MergeCells. If you delete too much, click the Undo button to restore what you deleted. The simplified macro (ignoring the comment lines, which can be deleted if you want) should look like this:

```
Sub MergeVertical()
    With Selection
        .Orientation = 90
        .MergeCells = True
    End With
End Sub
```

View Microsoft Excel button

4 Activate the Excel window and select cells A25:A30.

5 Press CTRL+SHIFT+M.

The macro adjusts the label.

15

6 Save the Lesson1 workbook.

Now you have not only recorded a macro, you have also deleted parts of it. And it still works. Next you'll record a macro and make additions to it.

Editing a Recorded Macro

A typical Excel worksheet has light gray gridlines that mark the boundaries of the cells. Sometimes, you may want to remove the gridlines. First walk through the process to remove the gridlines with menu commands, and then record a macro to make the change.

Remove gridlines with a command

1 On the Tools menu, click Options, and then click the View tab.

2 Clear the Gridlines check box at the bottom of the Window Options group.

3 Click OK.

The gridlines disappear.

4 Repeat step 1, and select the Gridlines check box to turn the gridlines back on. Then click OK.

Gridlines are a property of the window. You can select the Gridlines check box so that the value of the property is True and the window displays the gridlines, or you can clear the check box so that the value of the property is False and the window does not display the gridlines. Now see how the recorder turns off the gridlines.

Record a macro to remove gridlines

Record Macro button

1 Click the Record Macro button.

2 Replace the default macro name with **RemoveGrid**, and click OK.

The recorder puts the shell of the macro (the comments and the Sub and End Sub lines) into the module.

3 On the Tools menu, click Options, click the View tab, clear the Gridlines check box, and click OK.

The gridlines disappear.

Stop Recording button

4 Click the Stop Recording button, and then save the Lesson1 workbook.

Run Macro button

5 Click the Run Macro button, select RemoveGrid, and then click Edit to look at the resulting code. Ignoring the comment lines, here's what it looks like:

```
Sub RemoveGrid()
    ActiveWindow.DisplayGridlines = False
End Sub
```

In Part 2 you will learn more about objects.

This macro is very similar to the FormatCurrency macro. You can read it as "Let 'False' be the DisplayGridlines property of the active window." This time you're not changing the selection, but rather the active window. In both cases you are changing an *object*, an Excel element that you can control with macros. However, this time the object is not a range of cells, but a window.

Run the macro from the Visual Basic Editor

You can easily change the macro to make it restore the gridlines.

1 In the RemoveGrid macro, replace *False* with **True**.

You can't use a shortcut key from the Visual Basic Editor, but you don't actually need it, because Visual Basic has its own shortcut for running whatever macro you are currently editing.

2 Press F5 to run the macro.

The gridlines reappear in the current Excel worksheet. Pressing F5 from Visual Basic is a fast way to run a macro while you are testing it.

TIP If you are in Visual Basic and want to display the Macro dialog box so that you can select a macro, click outside of any macro before you press F5.

Toggle the value of a property with a macro

You could create one macro to turn the gridlines off and a second macro to turn them back on, but somehow, letting a single macro toggle the value of the property seems more natural. In order to toggle the value of a property, you first have to ask Excel for the current value. You do that by storing the property value in a special container called a *variable*. You assign the current value of the property to a variable, and then change the value as you assign the variable back to the property. Here's how:

1 Insert a new blank line after the comments.

2 Select *ActiveWindow.DisplayGridlines* and hold down the CTRL key as you drag it up to the blank line.

This makes a copy of the statement.

17

3 At the beginning of the new line, type **myGrid** = ; the resulting statement is *myGrid = ActiveWindow.DisplayGridlines*. This stores the current value of DisplayGridlines, whether True or False, in the variable myGrid.

> **NOTE** You can use any name you want as a variable name, but you should avoid names already used by Excel or Visual Basic. If you add a prefix such as *my* to the variable name, you will most likely avoid any potential conflict.

4 Double-click *True* in the original statement, and replace it with **Not myGrid**. The Visual Basic keyword Not turns the value True into False and False into True.

5 Change the name RemoveGrid to **ToggleGrid**, to better reflect the macro's new capabilities.

This is what the macro should look like now:

```
Sub ToggleGrid()
    myGrid = ActiveWindow.DisplayGridlines
    ActiveWindow.DisplayGridlines = Not myGrid
End Sub
```

> **TIP** If *Option Explicit* appears at the top of the module, delete it before running this macro.

6 Save the Lesson1 workbook, and then press F5 several times to test the macro.

The macro reads the old value of the property, changes it to the opposite with the keyword Not, and assigns the newly inverted value back to the property.

Recording Actions in a Macro

By now you should see a pattern to creating a simple convenience macro: Try out an action interactively. Once you know how to do the task, start the recorder. Do the task with the recorder on. Stop the recorder.

So far, all the macros you have recorded have changed the value of one or more properties of an object. Some actions that you can record do not change the value of a property. Let's see what a macro looks like when it doesn't change a property.

Suppose you want to freeze the formulas of some cells in the Budget97 worksheet at their current values. First change the formulas to values using menu commands, and then create a macro that can change any formula to a value.

Convert a formula to a value using menu commands

1 Activate the Budget97 window, and select cell D4.

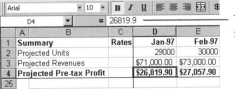

The formula bar shows a formula.

Notice the formula in the formula bar: =D3-D68.

2 On the Edit menu, click the Copy command.

3 Don't change the selection. On the Edit menu, click the Paste Special command.

The Paste Special dialog box appears.

4 Select the Values option from the Paste group and click OK.

Excel pastes the value from the cell over the top of the existing cell, eliminating the formula that was in it. The moving border is still visible around the cell, indicating that you could paste the value again somewhere else if you wanted.

5 Press ESC to get out of copy mode and clear the moving border.

The formula bar now shows a value.

Look at the formula bar: cell D4 now contains the value 26819.9.

As you carry out the copy and paste actions with the menus, notice that the Copy command does not bring up a dialog box. You see a moving border around the cells and a message in the status bar, but you don't need to tell Excel how to do the copying. The Paste Special command, on the other hand, does require additional information from you in order to carry out its job, so it displays a dialog box. Some actions in Excel require additional information about how to carry out the action, and some don't.

Convert a formula to a value with a macro

Watch how the macro recorder handles actions that display a dialog box, compared with how it handles actions that don't.

1 On the Budget97 worksheet, select cell E4.

Notice the formula in the formula bar: =E3-E68.

2 On the Tools menu, point to Macro, and then click Record New Macro.

3 Replace the default name with **ConvertToValues**.

4 Set the shortcut key to CTRL+SHIFT+V, and click OK.

5 On the Edit menu, click Copy.

6 On the Edit menu, click Paste Special, click the Values option, and click OK.

7 Press ESC to get rid of the moving border.

8 Click the Stop Recording button, and save the Lesson1 workbook.

Look at the formula bar. Cell E4 now contains the value 27057.9.

Stop Recording button

9 Switch to Visual Basic to look at the recorded macro.

```
Sub ConvertToValues()
    Selection.Copy
     Selection.PasteSpecial Paste:=xlValues, Operation:=xlNone, _
        SkipBlanks:=False, Transpose:=False
    Application.CutCopyMode = False
End Sub
```

The basic structure of this macro is the same as that of the other macros you have seen in this lesson. The last line, for example, sets the value of the CutCopyMode property in much the same way that the ToggleGrid macro changed the DisplayGridlines property setting of the active window. The two lines that begin with *Selection*, however, are something new. Neither has a simple equal sign in it.

Selection.Copy looks similar to *Selection.NumberFormat* from the FormatCurrency macro. In that macro, NumberFormat was a property of the selection and you were assigning a new value to the NumberFormat property. Copy, however, is not a property. That is why it doesn't have an equal sign after it. You don't assign anything to Copy; you just do it. Actions that don't use an equal sign to set the value of a property—that is, actions like Copy—are called *methods*. Like the names of properties, the names of methods are recorded by Excel and displayed at the end of the object's name.

When you use the Copy command from the menu, Excel does not ask you for any extra information. In the same way, when you use the Copy method in a macro, you don't give any extra information to the method.

PasteSpecial is also a method in Excel. PasteSpecial does not have an equal sign after it; it is not a property that you assign a value to. The Paste Special command on the Edit menu displays a dialog box, but the dialog box does not show you properties to change; it just asks how to carry out the paste special action. When you execute the PasteSpecial method in a macro, you give the extra information to the method. The extra pieces of information you give to a method are called *arguments*.

Using a method with an object is like giving instructions to your nine-year-old. With some instructions—like, "Come eat"—you don't have to give any extra information. With other instructions—like, "Go to the store for me"—you have to tell what to buy (milk), how to get there (on your bike), and when to come home (immediately). Giving these extra pieces of information to your child is like giving arguments to an Excel method. (You call them arguments because whenever you tell your child how to do something, you end up with one.)

The four arguments you give to PasteSpecial correspond exactly to the four option groups in the Paste Special dialog box. Each argument consists of a name for the argument (for example, Paste) joined to the argument value (for example, xlValues) by a colon and an equal sign (:=).

Do not confuse an argument with a property. When you assign a new value to a property, you separate the value from the property with an equal sign, as in this statement:

```
ActiveWindow.DisplayWorkbookTabs = False
```

You read this statement as "Let 'False' be the DisplayWorkbookTabs property of the active window."

Assigning a value to a property can appear superficially similar to using a named argument with a method. When you use a named argument with a method, you separate the method name from the argument name with a space, and you separate the argument name from the argument value with a colon and an equal sign. You must never confuse an equal sign with a colon and equal sign, any more than you would confuse beer with root beer.

When you have more than one argument, separate each one from the next with a comma and a space, as in this statement:

```
Selection.PasteSpecial Paste:=xlValues, Operation:=xlNone
```

An argument looks a lot like a property, but an argument always follows a method name, whereas a property follows an object. Also, a property is followed by an equal sign, but an argument is followed by a colon and equal sign.

Make a long statement more readable

When one of the statements in a macro gets to be longer than about 70 characters, the macro recorder puts a space and an underscore (_) after a convenient word and continues the statement on the next line. The underscore tells the macro that it should treat the second line as part of the same statement. You can manually break long statements into several lines, as long as you break the line after a space. You can also indent related lines with tabs, to make the macro easier to read.

1 In the ConvertToValues macro, put each argument of the PasteSpecial statement on a separate line, using a space and an underscore character at the end of each line except the last.

```
Sub ConvertToValues()
    Selection.Copy
    Selection.PasteSpecial _
        Paste:=xlValues, _
        Operation:=xlNone, _
        SkipBlanks:=False, _
        Transpose:=False
    Application.CutCopyMode = False
End Sub
```

Splitting a statement into several lines does not change the way the macro runs; it just makes it easier to read.

2 In Excel, select cell F4 and press CTRL+SHIFT+V to run the macro. Look at the formula bar to make sure the formula changed to a value.

3 Save the Lesson1 workbook and quit Excel.

Most of the macros in this chapter change the settings of object properties, but this macro executes object methods. Properties and methods look very similar: both are separated from objects by periods. However, you assign new values to properties, whereas you execute methods, sometimes giving the method arguments along the way.

Excel's Virus Warning Notice

When you open a workbook that contains a macro, Excel displays a message warning you that macros can contain viruses that can harm your computer.

Clear this checkbox if you create your own macros.

Ideally, Excel should be able to tell the difference between a workbook you create yourself and a workbook you download from the Web, but that technology is not yet available. In the meantime, this dialog box was created to warn a person who downloads a workbook from the Internet, but doesn't realize that the workbook can contain macros.

Once you start creating your own macros, you should clear the check box that offers to "always ask before opening workbooks with macros." Otherwise you will go crazy opening your own workbooks. You know that workbooks can contain macros and that you must be careful when you get a workbook from an unknown source.

If you download a workbook from an unknown source and want to check to see if it has any macros in it, you can turn the warning back on. For instructions, ask the Assistant for help, using the words "macro warning."

Lesson Summary

To	Do this	Button
Show the Visual Basic toolbar	Right-click any toolbar, and click Visual Basic from the menu.	
Turn on the recorder	On the Visual Basic toolbar, click the Record Macro button.	
Turn off the recorder	Click the Stop Recording button.	
Run a macro	Click the Run Macro button, select the name of the macro, and click Run.	
Look at a macro	Click the Run Macro button, select the name of the macro, and click Edit.	
Add a shortcut key	Click the Run Macro button, select the name of the macro, and click Options.	
Save the value of a property	Make up a variable name and assign the property value to it.	
Change the value of a property	Change the value that the recorded macro assigns to the property.	
Split a long statement into multiple lines	Break lines after convenient words and put a space and an underscore (_) at the end of each line except the last.	

For online information about	Ask the Assistant for help using the words
Recording macros	"Recording Macros"

Preview of the Next Lesson

In the next lesson you will learn how to combine small macros to automate whole tasks. You will also learn how to find and fix problems when your macros don't work quite the way you want.

Make a Macro
Do Complex Tasks

In this lesson you will learn how to:

Estimated time
45 min.

- Break a complex project into manageable pieces.
- Watch a macro run one statement at a time.
- Enter values into a macro while it is running.
- Record movements relative to the active cell.
- Create a macro that runs other macros.

Rube Goldberg was famous for intricate contraptions in which a ball drops into a bucket, and the weight of the bucket lifts a lever that releases a spring that wakes up a cat, and so forth. Rube Goldberg contraptions are fun to look at. Milton Bradley has been successful for years with the Mousetrap game based on a Rube Goldberg concept. Boston's Logan International Airport has two massive, perpetually working Rube Goldberg contraptions in the lobby that entertain irritated travelers for hours.

Entertainment is one thing. Getting your job done is another. Sometimes the list of steps you have to go through to get out a monthly report can seem like a Rube Goldberg contraption. First you import the monthly order file and add some new columns to it. Then you sort it and print it and sort it a different way and print it again. Then you paste it onto the end of the cumulative order history file, and so forth. Each step has to be completed just right before the next one is started, and you start making sure you don't schedule your vacation during the wrong time of the month because you would never want to have to explain to someone else how to get it all done right. Right?

One good use for macros is putting together all the steps to turn a cumbersome Rube Goldberg monthly report into a breeze. This lesson will help you learn how to do it.

Start the lesson

Save button

1   Start Microsoft Excel, and save the blank default workbook as Lesson2 in the folder that contains the practice files for this book. (On the toolbar, click the Save button, then click the Look In Favorites button, double-click the Excel VBA Practice folder, type **Lesson2** as the filename, and click Save.)

Look In Favorites button

2   Display the Visual Basic toolbar.

Divide and Conquer

The secret to creating a macro capable of handling a long, intricate project is to break the project into small pieces, create a macro for each separate piece, and then glue the pieces together. If you just turn on the recorder, carry out four hundred steps, and cross your fingers hoping for the best, you have about a 1-in-400 chance of having your macro work properly. Let's look at a hypothetical example.

As the bookkeeper at Miller Textiles' Screen Printing division, you have an elaborate month-end project you would like to automate so that you can delegate it to subordinates when you go on vacation. Currently, you get a monthly summary report of orders for the previous month from the order processing system.

```
                          Miller Textiles
                   Order Summary for November 1997

State     Channel     Price   Category        Qty   Dollars    List     Gross
========  ==========  ======  ==============  ====  =========  =======  =========
WA        Retail      Mid     Kids               9      40.50     4.50      40.50
                      Low                       143     434.06     3.50     500.50
                      High    Art                17      93.50     5.50      93.50
                      Mid                        23     103.50     4.50     103.50
                      High    Sports             26     143.00     5.50     143.00
                      Mid                         6      27.00     4.50      27.00
                      Low                         4      14.00     3.50      14.00
                      High    Seattle            13      71.50     5.50      71.50
                      Mid                         7      31.50     4.50      31.50
                      Low                        25      87.50     3.50      87.50
                      Mid     Dinosaurs          22      99.00     4.50      99.00
                      Low                        22      77.00     3.50      77.00
                      Mid     Humorous          143     554.32     4.50     643.50
                      Low                        13      45.50     3.50      45.50
                      Mid     Environment        35     157.50     4.50     157.50
                      Low                        40     140.00     3.50     140.00
          Wholesale   Mid     Kids               30      67.50     2.25      67.50
                      Low                        10      17.50     1.75      17.50
                      High    Art               410   1,062.13     2.75   1,127.50
                      Mid                       900   1,848.48     2.25   2,025.00
                      High    Sports             25      68.75     2.75      68.75
                      Mid                        30      67.50     2.25      67.50
                      Low                         5       8.75     1.75       8.75
                      High    Seattle           910   2,134.83     2.75   2,502.50
                      Mid                        60     135.00     2.25     135.00
                      Low                       405     687.60     1.75     708.75
```

The report shows sales information for each state, channel, category, and price combination. The order processing system exports the report as a text file. You prepare the file and add the new month's orders to a cumulative order history database.

This lesson will show you how to record the tasks that make up this large, complex project and then combine these small macros into one comprehensive macro. Along the way, you may learn some useful techniques for completing everyday tasks as well.

Task One: Opening the Report File

The orders for the most recent month, November 1997, are in the text file Ord9711.txt. The first task is to open the file, splitting it into columns as you do, and move the file into the workbook with the macro.

Open the report file

NOTE You may want to do steps 3 through 6 as a dry run before recording the macro.

Restore Window button

1 If the Lesson2 workbook window is maximized, click the Restore Window button.

Record Macro button

2 On the Visual Basic toolbar, click the Record Macro button, type **ImportFile** as the macro name, and click OK.

Open button

3 Click the Open button, type **Ord9711.txt** in the File Name box, and click Open.

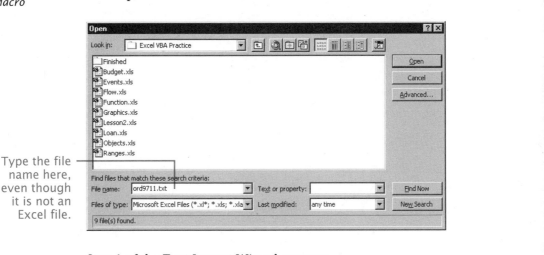

Type the file name here, even though it is not an Excel file.

Step 1 of the Text Import Wizard appears.

4 The first three rows of the file contain the report title and a blank line, so change the Start Import At Row value to **4**. The other default options in the Text Import Wizard are suitable for this file, so click Finish.

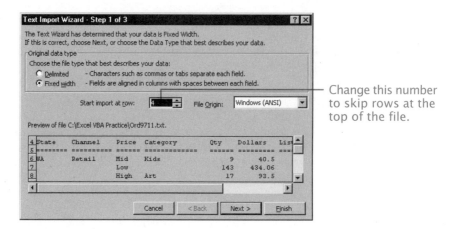

Change this number to skip rows at the top of the file.

The text file opens, with the columns split into Excel columns.

5 Drag up the bottom of the new window, so that you can see the tabs at the bottom of the Lesson2 workbook. Then drag the tab for the Ord9711 worksheet down in front of the Sheet1 tab of the Lesson2 workbook.

Drag the Ord9711 tab from here...

...to here to move the sheet to the Lesson2 Workbook.

The Ord9711 worksheet moves to the Lesson2 workbook, and the Ord9711.txt workbook disappears (because it lost its only worksheet, and a workbook cannot exist without at least one sheet).

> **NOTE** You will have several copies of the Ord9711 worksheet after you test this macro several times. Multiple copies will be useful as you develop the macros for the later project tasks. Because you already have a worksheet named Ord9711 in the workbook, new copies are automatically named Ord9711 (2), Ord9711 (3), and so forth.

6 Row 2 contains equal signs that you do not need. Select cell A2, choose the Edit menu and click the Delete command, select the Entire Row option in the Delete dialog box, and click OK.

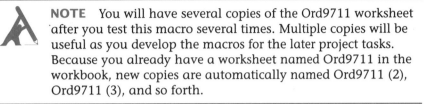

Select this option to delete the row containing the selected cell.

7 Select cell A1 and click the Stop Recording button to stop the recorder.

Stop Recording button

You should now have the imported file split into columns and stripped of extraneous rows.

Watch the ImportFile macro run

Rather than merely read the macro, you can both read it and test it as you watch it work. As you step through the macro, make notes of minor changes you may want to make to the macro.

Whenever you step through a macro, the Visual Basic Editor window appears over the top of the workbook. The Visual Basic window displays the selected macro and allows you to see which statement will execute next.

Run Macro button

1 Click the Run Macro button, select ImportFile from the Macro Name list, and click Step Into.

29

The Visual Basic window appears on top of the workbook, with your recorded macro visible in the module. The statement that is ready to execute is highlighted in yellow, with a yellow arrow in the left margin.

The arrow shows which statement will execute next.

The highlighted statement is the first statement in the macro, the statement that contains the macro name:

```
Sub ImportFile()
```

2   Press F8 to highlight the first statement in the body of the macro:

In your recorded macro, the line divisions will differ from those in this example.

```
Workbooks.OpenText _
    FileName:="C:\Excel VBA Practice\Ord9711.txt", _
    Origin:= xlWindows, _
    StartRow:=4, _
    DataType:=xlFixedWidth, _
    FieldInfo:=Array(Array(0, 1), Array(8, 1), _
        Array(20, 1), Array(26, 1), Array(41, 1), _
        Array(49, 1), Array(59, 1), Array (67, 1))
```

This long statement opens the text file. You can probably identify the argument that specifies the filename. The Origin and DataType arguments were default values in the first step of the Text Import Wizard. The StartRow argument is where you specified the number of rows to skip. The FieldInfo argument tells how to split the text file into columns. Be grateful that the macro recorder can create this statement so that you don't have to!

The macro recorder divides this long statement into several lines by putting a space and an underscore at the end of each partial line. However, it does not divide the statement at the most logical places. When you edit the macro, you should redivide the statement into meaningful lines (dividing before each new argument usually clarifies a statement). You can use the way the statement is divided above as a model.

This month, you opened the Ord9711.txt file. Next month, however, you will open the Ord9712.txt file. Make a note to change the macro statement to let you select the file you want to open. You will learn how to generalize your macro in the next section.

See Appendix A for alternatives to using F8 to step through the macro.

3 Press F8 to open the file and highlight the next statement, which is the first line of this With structure:

```
With ActiveWindow
    .Width = 452.25
    .Height = 254.25
End With
```

These four statements were added when you moved the window out of the way. (Your Width and Height properties may have different values.) When you edit the macro, you will be able to delete these statements without harming the macro.

4 Press F8 to step through the statements that moved the window. You may have more than four statements that change the size of the window. Make a note to delete all of them.

The next statement is now highlighted:

```
Sheets("Ord9711").Select
```

This statement makes the Ord9711 sheet into the active sheet, even though it was already the active sheet. (Macro recorders can't be too cautious, now.) You will be able to delete this statement later also.

 NOTE You can edit many statements while stepping through the macro. For example, you could delete the Select statement. Some changes, however, would force you to restart the macro. For example, you can't delete a With structure without restarting the macro (although you can delete individual statements inside a With structure). Visual Basic will warn you if you try to make a change that would require you to restart the macro.

---

5 Press F8 to highlight the next statement:

```
Sheets("Ord9711").Move _
    Before:=Workbooks("Lesson2.xls").Sheets(1)
```

This statement moves the new sheet into the Lesson2 workbook. But when you run this macro next month, the sheet will not be named Ord9711. It will be Ord9712. If you change *Sheets("Ord9711")* to *ActiveSheet* in the macro, however, it will work every month.

31

6 Press F8 to move the worksheet and highlight the next statement:

```
Range("A2").Select
```

This statement selects cell A2 of the worksheet.

7 Press F8 to select cell A2 and highlight the next statement:

```
Selection.EntireRow.Delete
```

Because the selected cell is A2, and this statement deletes the entire row of the selected cell, this statement deletes row 2.

8 Press F8 to delete the row and highlight the next statement:

```
Range("A1").Select
```

This statement selects cell A1.

9 Press F8 to select cell A1 and highlight the final statement of the macro:

```
End Sub
```

10 Press F8 to end the macro.

In summary, this is how you want to modify the macro:

- Allow the user to decide which file to open.
- Delete unnecessary statements.
- Make the macro work with any month's file.

The next section will show you how to make these changes.

Generalize the macro

Excel provides a method that prompts the user to open a file, but doesn't actually open the file. Instead it returns the name of the file, which you can turn over to the OpenText method.

1 Make the statement that begins with *Workbooks.Open* easier to read by dividing it into meaningful lines. Put a space and an underscore at the end of each partial line. Follow the example on page 30 in the preceding section.

2 Insert a new line immediately before the Workbooks.OpenText statement, and enter this statement:

```
myFile = Application.GetOpenFilename("Text Files,*.txt")
```

As soon as you type the period after Application, Visual Basic displays a list of all the methods and properties that can be used with an Application object. This feature is called *Auto List Members*. (The word *Members* refers to both methods and properties.) When you type the letter G, the list scrolls to show methods and properties that begin with that letter. At that point, you can press the DOWN ARROW key to select GetOpenFilename and press the TAB key to enter the method name into the macro.

When you type the opening parentheses, Visual Basic displays the possible arguments for the GetOpenFilename method. This feature is called *Auto Quick Info*. You can ignore it for now. Just type the words in parentheses as they appear above.

The Application.GetOpenFilename method displays the Open dialog box, just as if you had clicked the Open toolbar button. The words in parentheses tell the method to display only text files—files ending with the *.txt* extension. (Be careful to type the quotation marks just as they appear above.) The word *myFile* at the beginning of the statement is a variable for storing the selected filename.

If Option Explicit *appears at the top of your module sheet, delete it before continuing.*

3 In the Workbooks.OpenText statement, select the entire filename, including the quotation marks, and delete it. In its place, type **myFile**.

The first part of the statement should look like this when you finish:

```
Workbooks.OpenText _
    Filename:=myFile, _
    Origin:=xlWindows, _
    StartRow:=4, _
```

By the time this statement executes, the variable myFile will contain the name of the file.

4 Delete the statements that resize the window, and also the statement that selects the Ord9711 sheet.

5 Change the words *Sheets("Ord9711").Move* to **ActiveSheet.Move**.

When you're finished, the macro should look like this:

```
Sub ImportFile()
    myFile = Application.GetOpenFilename("Text Files,*.txt")
    Workbooks.OpenText _
        FileName:=myFile, _
        Origin:=xlWindows, _
        StartRow:=4, _
        DataType:=xlFixedWidth, _
        FieldInfo:=Array(Array(0, 1), Array(8, 1), _
            Array(20, 1), Array(26, 1), Array(41, 1), _
            Array(49, 1), Array(59, 1), Array(67, 1))
    ActiveSheet.Move Before:=Workbooks("Lesson2.xls").Sheets(1)
    Range("A2").Select
    Selection.EntireRow.Delete
    Range("A1").Select
End Sub
```

6 Press F5 to run the macro and make sure it works. It should display the Open dialog box (displaying only text files), and then it should open the file that you select and move the worksheet to the Lesson2 workbook.

7 Save the Lesson2 workbook.

That concludes the macro for the first task of your month-end processing project. By now you should have several copies of the Ord9711 worksheet in the Lesson2 workbook. You are ready to move on to the next task.

Task Two: Filling in Missing Labels

When the order processing system produces a summary report, it only enters a label in a column the first time that label appears. Leaving out duplicate labels is one way to make a report easier for a human being to read, but for the computer to sort and summarize the data properly, you need to fill in the missing labels.

Fill the blank cells with the label from the cell above.

	A	B	C	D	E	F	G	H
1	State	Channel	Price	Category	Qty	Dollars	List	Gross
2	WA	Retail	Mid	Kids	9	40.5	4.5	40.5
3			Low		143	434.06	3.5	500.5
4			High	Art	17	93.5	5.5	93.5
5			Mid		23	103.5	4.5	103.5
6			High	Sports	26	143	5.5	143
7			Mid		6	27	4.5	27

You might assume that you need to write a complex macro to examine each cell and determine whether it is empty, and if so, what value it needs. In fact, you can use Excel's built-in capabilities to do most of the work for you. Because this part of the project introduces some powerful worksheet features, you will go through the steps before recording the macro.

Select only the blank cells

Look at the places where you want to fill in missing labels. What value do you want in each empty cell? You want each empty cell to contain the value from the first nonempty cell above it. In fact, if you were to select each empty cell in turn and put into it a formula pointing at the cell immediately above it, you would have the result you want. The range of empty cells is an irregular shape, however, which makes the prospect of filling all the cells with a formula daunting. Fortunately, Excel has a built-in tool for selecting an irregular range of blank cells.

1 In the Lesson2 workbook, select cell A1.

2 Choose the Edit menu and click the Go To command.

See Appendix B for alternative ways to display the Go To dialog box.

The Go To dialog box appears.

3 In the Go To dialog box, click the Special button.

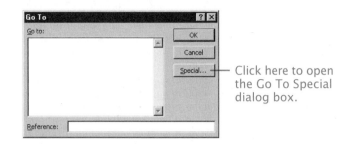

Click here to open the Go To Special dialog box.

You can also press CTRL+SHIFT+ to select the current region. Hold down the CTRL key while pressing * on the numeric keypad or SHIFT+8 on the regular keyboard.*

4 In the Go To Special dialog box, click the Current Region option and click OK.

Click here to select the current region.

Excel selects the *current region*—the rectangle of cells including the active cell that is surrounded by blank cells or worksheet borders.

5 Choose the Edit menu, click Go To, and click the Special button.

6 In the Go To Special dialog box, click the Blanks option and click OK.

Excel subselects only the blank cells from the selection. These are the cells that need new values.

Go To Special, Blanks selects just the cells you need to fill.

	A	B	C	D	E	F
1	State	Channel	Price	Category	Qty	Dollars
2	WA	Retail	Mid	Kids	9	40.5
3			Low		143	434.06
4			High	Art	17	93.5
5			Mid		23	103.5
6			High	Sports	26	143
7			Mid		6	27

Excel's built-in Go To Special feature can save you—and your macro—a lot of work.

Fill the selection with values

You now want to fill each of the selected cells with a formula that points at the cell above. Normally when you enter a formula, Excel puts the formula into only the active cell. You can, however, if you ask politely, have Excel put a formula into all the selected cells at once.

1 With the blank cells selected and D3 as the active cell, type an equal sign (=) and press the UP ARROW key to point at cell D2.

The cell reference D2—when found in cell D3—actually means "one cell above me in the same column."

2 Press CTRL+ENTER to fill the formula into all the currently selected cells.

Use CTRL+ENTER to fill all the selected cells.

	A	B	C	D	E	F
1	State	Channel	Price	Category	Qty	Dollars
2	WA	Retail	Mid	Kids	9	40.5
3	WA	Retail	Low	Kids	143	434.06
4	WA	Retail	High	Art	17	93.5
5	WA	Retail	Mid	Art	23	103.5
6	WA	Retail	High	Sports	26	143
7	WA	Retail	Mid	Sports	6	27

When more than one cell is selected, if you type a formula and press CTRL+ENTER, the formula is copied into all the cells of the selection. If you press ENTER without holding down the CTRL key, the formula goes into only the one active cell.

Each cell with the new formula points to the cell above it.

3 Press CTRL+SHIFT+* to select the current region.

4 Choose the Edit menu and click Copy. Then choose the Edit menu, click Paste Special, click the Values option, and click OK.

5 Press ESC to get out of copy mode, and then select cell A1.

Now the block of cells contains all the missing label cells as values, so the contents won't change if you happen to re-sort the summary data. Select a different copy of the imported worksheet, and follow the same steps, but with the macro recorder turned on.

Record filling the missing values

1 Select a copy of the Ord9711 worksheet (one that does not have the labels filled in), or run the ImportFile macro again.

Record Macro button

2 Click the Record Macro button, type **FillLabels** as the name of the macro, and click OK.

3 Select cell A1 (even if it's already selected), press CTRL+SHIFT+*, choose the Edit menu, click Go To, click the Special button, click the Blanks option, and then click OK.

4 Type =, press the UP ARROW key, and press CTRL+ENTER.

5 Press CTRL+SHIFT+*.

6 Choose the Edit menu and click Copy. Next choose the Edit menu, click Paste Special, click the Values option, and then click OK.

7 Press ESC to get out of copy mode, and then select cell A1.

8 Click the Stop Recording button.

Stop Recording button

You've finished creating the FillLabels macro. Read it while you step through the macro.

Watch the FillLabels macro run

1 Select another copy of the imported worksheet, or run the ImportFile macro again.

Run Macro button

2 Click the Run Macro button, select the FillLabels macro, and click Step Into.

The Debug window appears, with the header statement of the macro highlighted.

3 Press F8 to move to the first statement in the body of the macro:

```
Range("A1").Select
```

This statement selects cell A1. It doesn't matter how you got to cell A1—whether you clicked the cell, pressed CTRL+HOME, or pressed various arrow keys—because the macro recorder always records just the result of the selection process.

4 Press F8 to select cell A1 and highlight the next statement:

```
Selection.CurrentRegion.Select
```

This statement selects the current region of the original selection.

5 Press F8 to select the current region and move to the next statement:

```
Selection.SpecialCells(xlCellTypeBlanks).Select
```

This statement selects the blank special cells of the original selection. (The word *SpecialCells* refers to cells you selected using the Go To Special dialog box.)

6 Press F8 to select just the blank cells and move to the next statement:

For more information about R1C1 notation, ask the Assistant for help using the words "R1C1 references" (with the Excel window active).

```
Selection.FormulaR1C1 = "=R[-1]C"
```

This statement assigns =*R[-1]C* as the formula for the entire selection. When you entered the formula, the formula you saw was =C2, not =R[-1]C. The formula =C2 really means "get the value from the cell just above me"—only as long as the active cell happens to be cell C3. The formula =R[-1]C also means "get the value from the cell just above me," but without regard for which cell is active.

37

You could change this statement to *Selection.Formula = "=C2"* and the macro would work exactly the same—provided that the order file you use when you run the macro is identical to the order file you used when you recorded the macro, and the active cell happens to be cell C3 when the macro runs. If the command that selects blanks produces a different active cell, however, the revised macro will fail. The macro recorder uses R1C1 notation so that your macro will always work correctly.

7   Press F5 to execute the remaining statements in the macro:

```
Selection.CurrentRegion.Select
Selection.Copy
Selection.PasteSpecial Paste:=xlValues, Operation:=xlNone, _
    SkipBlanks:=False, Transpose:=False
Application.CutCopyMode = False
Range("A1").Select
```

These statements select the current region, convert the formulas to values, cancel copy mode, and select cell A1.

8   Save the Lesson2 workbook.

You have completed the macro for the second task of your month-end project. Now you can start a new macro to carry out the next task—adding dates.

Task Three: Adding a Column of Dates

The order summary report you are working with does not include the date in each row, since the text file includes numbers for only a single month. Before you can append these new records to the order history database, you will need to add the current month to each record.

Add a constant date

First you will create a macro that fills the range with the date *Nov-97*, by inserting a new column A and putting the date into each row that contains data.

Record Macro button

1   Select a worksheet that has the labels filled in, click the Record Macro button, type **AddDates** as the name of the macro, and click OK.

2   Select cell A1, and then choose the Insert menu and click Columns.

Excel inserts a new column A, shifting the other columns over to the right.

3   Type **Date** in cell A1, and press ENTER.

4   Press CTRL+SHIFT+* to select the current region.

5   Choose the Edit menu, click Go To, and click the Special button. Click the Blanks option, and click OK to select only the blank cells. These are the cells where the dates should go.

6   Type **Nov-97** and press CTRL+ENTER to fill the date into all the cells.

Excel fills the date into all the rows.

7   Select cell A1, and click the Stop Recording button to stop the recorder.

Stop Recording button

Step through the macro

1   With cell A1 selected, choose the Edit menu, click Delete, click the Entire Column option, and click OK.

2   Click the Run Macro button, select the AddDates macro, and click Step Into.

Run Macro button

This is what the macro should look like:

```
Sub AddDates()
    Range("A1").Select
    Selection.EntireColumn.Insert
    ActiveCell.FormulaR1C1 = "Date"
    Range("A2").Select
    Selection.CurrentRegion.Select
    Selection.SpecialCells(xlCellTypeBlanks).Select
    Selection.FormulaR1C1 = "Nov-97"
    Range("A1").Select
End Sub
```

3   Press F8 repeatedly to step through the macro.

This macro is pretty straightforward. Notice that the statement that enters the word *Date* changes the "formula" of only the active cell, whereas the statement that enters the actual date changes the "formula" of the entire selection. When you enter a formula using the ENTER key alone, the macro uses the word *ActiveCell*. When you enter a formula using CTRL+ENTER, the macro uses the word *Selection*. (If the selection is only a single cell, then *ActiveCell* and *Selection* are equivalent.)

The recorder always records putting a value into a cell by using the Formula R1C1 property—even if you enter a label—just in case you might have entered a formula.

Prompt for the date

Your recorded macro should work just fine if you always run it using the same month's data file. But the next time you actually use this macro, you will be working with December orders, not November orders. You need to change the macro so that it asks you for the date when you run it.

1   Insert a new line after the comments in the AddDates macro, and enter this new statement:

```
myDate = InputBox("Enter the date in MMM-YY format")
```

InputBox is a Visual Basic function that prompts for information while a macro runs. The words in parentheses are the message it displays. The variable myDate stores the date until the macro is ready to use it.

   TIP   The InputBox function is a useful tool for making a macro work in slightly changing circumstances.

2   Select and delete the text "*Nov-97*" in the macro. Be sure to delete the quotation marks.

3   Type **myDate** where the old date used to be.

The revised statement should look like this:

```
Selection.FormulaR1C1 = myDate
```

4   Activate a worksheet that needs the date column added. (Delete the old date column, or run the FillLabels macro, as needed.)

5   Click the Run Macro button, select the AddDates macro, and click Run.

Run Macro button

The macro prompts for the date and then inserts the date into the appropriate cells in column A.

NOTE   If you click the Cancel button, the macro leaves the date cells empty. In Lesson 7, you will learn how to program the macro to determine whether the user clicked the Cancel button.

6   Type **Nov-97** and click OK.

Microsoft Excel	✕
Enter the date in MMM-YY format	OK
	Cancel
Nov-97	

Type a date here and the macro will fill it into the worksheet.

7   Save the Lesson2 workbook.

This completes your third task. Now you're ready to append the new data to the database.

Task Four: Appending to the Database

Now that you have added monthly dates to the imported Ord9711 worksheet, it has the same columns as the order history database, so you can just copy the worksheet and append it to the first blank row below the database. Of course, you don't want to include the column headings.

Append a worksheet to a database

You may want to do steps 2 through 10 as a dry run before recording the macro.

Record Macro button

First you will copy the data (without the headings) from the Ord9711 worksheet. Then you will open the database, select the first blank cell below the database, rename the database range to include the new rows, and close the database file.

1 Select one of the Ord9711 worksheets that has the labels filled and the dates added, click the Record Macro button, type **AppendDatabase** as the macro name, and click OK.

2 Select cell A1. Choose the Edit menu, click Delete, click the Entire Row option, and click OK.

This deletes the heading row so you won't include it in the range you copy to the database.

3 Press CTRL+SHIFT+* to select the current region, and click Copy on the Edit menu.

Open button

4 Click the Open toolbar button, type **Orders.dbf** in the File Name box, and click Open.

The Orders.dbf database file opens with cell A1 selected. (The dates in the database look different from those in Ord9711 due to formatting differences.)

5 Press CTRL+DOWN ARROW to go to the last row of the database.

6 Press the DOWN ARROW key to select the first cell below the database. (It should be cell A3301.)

You want to paste into the first cells under the database.

	A	B	C	D	E	F
3299	10/1/97	WA	Retail	Mid	Seattle	6
3300	10/1/97	WA	Retail	Mid	Sports	5
3301						
3302						
3303						
3304						

7 Choose the Edit menu, click Paste to append the rows you previously copied, and then press ESC to remove the copy message from the status bar. (The newly appended rows contain two additional columns.)

	A	B	C	D	E	F
3299	10/1/97	WA	Retail	Mid	Seattle	6
3300	10/1/97	WA	Retail	Mid	Sports	5
3301	Nov-97	WA	Retail	Mid	Kids	9
3302	Nov-97	WA	Retail	Low	Kids	143
3303	Nov-97	WA	Retail	High	Art	17
3304	Nov-97	WA	Retail	Mid	Art	23

8 Press CTRL+SHIFT+* to select the entire new database range, including the newly appended rows.

> **NOTE** When you open a dBase file in Excel, the range containing the actual database records is automatically named Database. When you save the updated Orders.dbf file as a dBase file, only the values within the range named Database are saved. Any other cell values in the file are discarded. In order to have the new rows saved with the file, you must enlarge the Database range definition to include them.

9 Choose the Insert menu, choose the Name submenu, and click the Define command. Type **Database** in the Names In Workbook box, and click OK.

> **IMPORTANT** Do *not* select Database from the list of names. If you do, the range name will keep its current definition.

Type the name here to redefine the database. Do not select it from the list.

Now the entire database, including the new rows, is included in the Database range name and will be saved with the file.

10 Choose the File menu, click Close, and then click No when asked if you want to save changes.

For now, you don't actually want to save the database with the new records back to the Orders.dbf file, because you will want to test the macro.

Stop Recording button

11 Select cell A1, and click the Stop Recording button to turn off the recorder.

Step through the AppendDatabase macro

Step through the macro to see it work, and make notes of any changes you should make.

1 Activate a worksheet with the labels filled in and the dates added. (Run the ImportFile, FillLabels, and AddDates macros if necessary.)

2 Click the Run Macro button, select the AppendDatabase macro, and click the Step Into button. Look at the first five lines of the macro:

Run Macro button

```
Sub AppendDatabase()
    Range("A1").Select
    Selection.EntireRow.Delete
    Selection.CurrentRegion.Select
    Selection.Copy
```

These statements are similar to statements you have seen in earlier macros.

3 Press F8 five times to execute the first five statements in the macro.

In the Debug window, the Open statement should be highlighted:

```
Workbooks.Open Filename:="C:\Excel VBA Practice\Orders.dbf"
```

This statement opens the database.

> **TIP** If you remove everything except Orders.dbf from the filename, the macro will look for the file in the current folder. That would be useful if you move the project to a new folder.

4 Press F8 to execute the statement containing the Open method and move to the next statement:

```
Selection.End(xlDown).Select
```

This statement is equivalent to pressing CTRL+DOWN ARROW. It starts with the active cell, searches down to the last non-blank cell, and selects that cell.

5 Press F8 to select the last cell in the database and move to the next statement:

```
Range("A3301").Select
```

43

This statement selects cell A3301. That is the first cell below the database this month, but next month it will be wrong. This is the statement the recorder created when you pressed the DOWN ARROW key. What you wanted was a statement that moves one cell down from the active cell. You will need to fix this statement. Make a note to do so.

6   Press F8 to select cell A3301 and move to the next statement. The next two statements work together:

```
ActiveSheet.Paste
Application.CutCopyMode = False
```

These statements paste the new rows into the database and remove the status bar message.

7   Press F8 twice. The next two statements redefine the Database range:

```
Selection.CurrentRegion.Select
ActiveWorkbook.Names.Add Name:="Database", RefersToR1C1:= _
        "=Orders!R1C1:R3478C9"
```

The first statement selects the current region, which is the correct range for the new database range. The second statement gives the name Database to the specific range R1C1:R3478C9 (A1:I3478). This is not what you want. You want the name Database to be assigned to what-ever selection is current at the time the statement executes. You will also need to fix this statement. Make a note to do so.

8   Press F8 twice to move to the statement that closes the workbook file:

```
ActiveWorkbook.Close
```

This statement closes the active workbook. If you have made changes to the workbook, it also prompts for whether to save the changes. You can change this so that it always saves changes or (while testing) never saves changes.

9   Press F8 to close the database workbook. Click No when asked if you want to save changes. Only two statements remain in the macro:

```
    Range("A1").Select
End Sub
```

10   Press F8 twice to end the macro.

The macro works now only because you are running it under circumstances identical to those when you recorded it, with the same current month file and the same database file. Here is a recap of the changes you will need to make:

■ Select the first row under the database.

■ Give the name Database to the current selection.

■ Don't prompt when closing the database.

The next few sections will show you how to make these changes.

Record a relative movement

Take a closer look at the two AppendDatabase statements that find the first blank cell under the database. Imagine what will happen when you run this next month, when the database will have more rows. The statement

```
Selection.End(xlDown).Select
```

will select the bottom row, but then the statement

```
Range("A3301").Select
```

will always select the absolute cell A3301 anyway.

When you select a cell, the macro recorder does not know whether you want the absolute cell you selected or a cell relative to where you started. For example, when you select a cell in row 1 to change the label of a column title, you always want the same absolute cell, without regard to where you started. But when you select the first blank cell at the bottom of a database, you want the macro to select a cell relative to where you started.

The macro recorder cannot automatically know whether you want to record absolute cell addresses or relative movements, but you can tell the recorder which kind of selection you want. Use the recorder to record a new statement that you can use to replace the offending statement. You will record the new statement in a new, temporary macro, and then copy the statement and delete the temporary macro.

Record Macro button

Relative Reference button

Stop Recording button

1 Click the Record Macro button, type **DeleteMe** as the macro name and click OK.

2 On the Stop Recording toolbar, click the Relative Reference button.

When this button is activated, the recorder makes all new cell selections *relative* to the original selection. Now you need to replace the statement that selects cell A3301 with one that makes a relative movement.

You want to record the action of moving down one cell, so you can record the macro from any cell, on any worksheet.

3 Press the DOWN ARROW key once to record a relative movement.

4 Click the Relative Reference button to deselect it, and then click the Stop Recording button.

5 Edit the DeleteMe macro and look at the change.

The new statement you recorded should look like this:

```
ActiveCell.Offset(1,0).Range("A1").Select
```

This statement means, "Select the cell below the active cell." It really does. At this point, you don't need to understand everything about how this statement works. Just trust the recorder. But you may wonder why the statement includes the words *Range("A1")* when it has nothing to do with cell A1. This statement calculates a new single-cell range shifted down one cell from the original active cell. The macro treats that new range as if it were the top left corner of an entire "virtual" worksheet and selects cell A1 of that imaginary worksheet!

6 Select the new statement and copy it. Select *Range("A3301").Select*, delete it, and paste the new statement in its place.

7 Delete the DeleteMe macro by selecting all the statements from *Sub DeleteMe* to *End Sub*, and then pressing the DELETE key.

Lesson 4 discusses the Offset method in more detail.

With the Relative Reference button, you can control whether selections are absolute or relative to the current active cell. You can turn the Relative Reference button on and off as many times as you need while you are recording a macro.

Name the current selection

The statement in the macro that defines the Database range name contains a potentially serious problem:

```
ActiveWorkbook.Names.Add Name:="Database", RefersToR1C1:= _
    "=Orders!R1C1:R3478C9"
```

This statement sets the name Database to the range that the database occupies at the end of this month. If you don't change this statement before next month, December orders will be discarded from the database when you save it. This is a case where the macro recorder generates a complicated statement when a very simple one would work better.

  Replace the entire recorded statement with this one:

```
Selection.Name = "Database"
```

Name is a property of a range. By simply assigning a word in quotation marks as the value of the Name property you can name the range.

Save changes while closing a file

The statement that closes the database file looks like this:

```
ActiveWorkbook.Close
```

It triggers a prompt that asks you if you want to save changes to the file, because you have made changes to it since you opened it. Sometimes when you automate a process, you know that you always will (or won't) want to save changes. The Close method has an optional argument that allows you to specify whether to save changes. For now, while you are testing the macro, set the statement to *not* save the changes.

1   Change the statement that closes the workbook to this:

```
ActiveWorkbook.Close SaveChanges:=False
```

The SaveChanges argument answers the dialog box's question before it even gets asked.

2   Now run and test the macro yourself.

3   Once you have finished testing the macro and are ready to use it regularly, change the word *False* to **True**.

4   Save the Lesson2 workbook.

NOTE   Technically, since the active workbook happens to be a dBase file, setting the SaveChanges argument to True prevents Excel from asking if you want to save the changes, but it still displays a dialog box to ensure that you want to save the file as a dBase file. If the active workbook is a native Excel workbook, however, the SaveChanges argument causes Excel to save it quietly.

Here's the final version of the AppendDatabase macro:

```
Sub AppendDatabase()
    Range("A1").Select
    Selection.EntireRow.Delete
    Selection.CurrentRegion.Select
    Selection.Copy
    Workbooks.Open Filename:="C:\Excel VBA Practice\Orders.dbf"
    Selection.End(xlDown).Select
    ActiveCell.Offset(1, 0).Range("A1").Select
    ActiveSheet.Paste
    Application.CutCopyMode = False
    Selection.CurrentRegion.Select
    Selection.Name = "Database"
    ActiveWorkbook.Close SaveChanges:=False
    Range("A1").Select
End Sub
```

If you want, you can run the macro again now. It will work the same as it did before, but it is also ready for next month, when the database will have more records.

You're almost finished. The only task left is to get rid of the imported worksheet.

Task Five: Deleting the Worksheet

You imported the text file worksheet so that you could fill in the labels and add a column of dates before appending the data to the database. Once the data is safely appended, you don't need the imported worksheet any more.

Create a macro to delete the active sheet

Record Macro button

1 Activate an expendable worksheet, click the Record Macro button, type **DeleteSheet** as the macro name, and click OK.

2 Choose the Edit menu, click Delete Sheet, and then click OK when asked to confirm.

3 Click the Stop Recording button to turn off the recorder.

Stop Recording button

4 Select another expendable worksheet, and step through the DeleteSheet macro:

```
Sub DeleteSheet()
    ActiveWindow.SelectedSheets.Delete
End Sub
```

The recorded statement refers to the "selected sheets of the active window" because it is possible to select and delete multiple sheets at the same time. (Hold down the CTRL key as you click several sheet tabs to see how you can select multiple sheets. Then click an unselected sheet without using the CTRL key to deselect the sheets.) Because you're deleting only one sheet, you could change the statement to *ActiveSheet.Delete* if you wanted, but that is not necessary.

The only problem with this macro is that it asks for confirmation each time you run it. When the macro deletes the imported sheet as part of the larger project, you would prefer not to be prompted.

Make the macro operate quietly

The Delete method doesn't have an optional argument that eliminates the confirmation prompt. You must add a new statement to turn off the warning.

Run Macro button

1 Click the Run Macro button, select the DeleteSheet macro, and click Edit.

2 Insert a new line after the statement *Sub DeleteSheet()* and enter this statement:

```
Application.DisplayAlerts = False
```

DisplayAlerts is a property of the Excel application. When you set the value of DisplayAlerts to False, any confirmation prompts that you would normally see are treated as if you had selected the default answer. The DisplayAlerts setting lasts only until the macro finishes running; you do not need to set it back to True. However, you do need to be careful not to run this macro when the active sheet is something you care about. You should also, naturally, save your work often.

TIP The Auto List Members feature will help you type the words *DisplayAlerts* and *False*. When you select a word in the list, press the TAB key to finish entering the word into the statement.

---

3 Save the Lesson2 workbook.

4 Select an expendable worksheet and run the DeleteSheet macro.

Assembling the Pieces

You have all the subordinate task macros ready for carrying out your complex monthly project:

- ImportFile opens and parses the text file.
- FillLabels makes the file look like a database.
- AddDates distinguishes one month from another in the database.
- AppendDatabase adds the new rows to the bottom of the saved database.
- DeleteSheet cleans up the temporary worksheet.

Each piece is prepared and tested. Now you get to put them all together.

Record a macro that runs other macros

The easiest way to glue macros together is to record a macro that runs other macros.

Record Macro button

1 Click the Record Macro button, type **MonthlyProject** as the macro name, and click OK.

*Run Macro
button*

2 Click the Run Macro button, click ImportFile, and click Run.

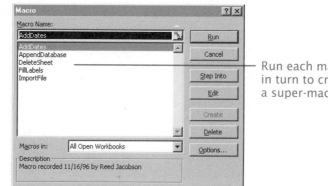

Run each macro
in turn to create
a super-macro.

3 Select the text file you want to import and click Open.

4 Click the Run Macro button, click FillLabels, and click Run.

5 Click the Run Macro button, click AddDates, and click Run.

6 Type an appropriate date and click OK.

7 Click the Run Macro button, click AppendDatabase, and click Run.

8 Click the Run Macro button, click DeleteSheet, and click Run.

9 Click the Stop Recording button.

*Stop Recording
button*

Now you can look at what you created.

> Click the Run Macro button, select the MonthlyProject macro, and click
> Edit. Here's what the macro to run other macros looks like:

```
Sub MonthlyProject()
'
' MonthlyProject Macro
' Macro recorded 10/31/96 by Reed Jacobson
'


'
    Application.Run "Lesson2.xls!ImportFile"
    Application.Run "Lesson2.xls!FillLabels"
    Application.Run "Lesson2.xls!AddDates"
    Application.Run "Lesson2.xls!AppendDatabase"
    Application.Run "Lesson2.xls!DeleteSheet"
End Sub
```

The MonthlyProject macro will run each of the subordinate macros in turn. The subordinate macros are known as *subroutines.* (By the way, this is the reason you start macros with the word *Sub,* so that you can turn them into subroutines simply by running them from another macro.)

Simplify the subroutine statements

The statement that the macro recorder creates for running a subroutine is somewhat unwieldy. You can simplify the statement, making it easier to read and faster to run.

1   Delete everything from each recorded subroutine statement except the name of the macro itself.

Here's what the macro should look like when you're done:

```
Sub MonthlyProject()
    ImportFile
    FillLabels
    AddDates
    AppendDatabase
    DeleteSheet
End Sub
```

2   Save the Lesson2 workbook.

3   Press F5 to test the MonthlyProject macro. (You might also want to try pressing F8 to step through the main macro and each of the subroutines.)

You've worked hard and deserve a rest. Take the rest of the day off.

Lesson Summary

To	Do this	Button
Select the current region	Press CTRL+SHIFT+*.	
Select blank cells in the current selection	Choose the Edit menu, click Go To, click the Special button, and then click the Blanks option.	
Fill all the selected cells at one time	Press CTRL+ENTER instead of just ENTER.	
Watch a macro execute one statement at a time	Select the macro name in the Macro dialog box and click Step Into. Press F8 to execute the next statement.	

Lesson Summary, *continued*

To	Do this	Button
Have your macro give the name TestRange, for example, to the selected range	Use the statement *Selection.Name = "TestRange"*.	
Allow the user to select a file name from a dialog box	Use the Application.GetOpenFilename method.	
Prompt for a value while the macro runs	Use the InputBox function.	
Record movements relative to the active cell	On the Stop Recording toolbar, click the Relative Reference button.	
Create a macro to run other macros	Type the names of the other macros into one main macro shell.	

For online information about	Ask the Assistant for help using the words
Editing Visual Basic macros	"Edit Macros" (with Excel window active)
Stepping through a macro	"Step Into" (with Visual Basic window active)

Preview of the Next Lesson

In this lesson, you learned how to break a complex project into pieces, record and test each piece, and then pull all the pieces together into a single macro. You ended up with a macro that does a lot of work, and you used the macro recorder to create most of the macro. In the next lesson, you will learn how to manipulate objects without relying on the macro recorder.

Exploring
Objects

Lesson 3

Lesson 4

Lesson 5

Lesson 6

Explore Microsoft Excel's Object Library

Estimated time
45 min.

In this lesson you will learn how to:

- Store values and objects in variables.
- Change object property values.
- Navigate to new objects.
- Use different resources in Microsoft Excel to learn about objects.

Last year, on a certain spring holiday known for having children search for candy, my wife and I put together a special hunt for our children. For example, I gave my youngest son a note that said, "Look under the armchair in the living room." When he got there he found another note that said, "Look in the oven." When he got there he found a note that said, "Look in your toy cupboard." When he got there, he found a basket of candy. Wasn't that fun!

One of the notes—not coincidentally the last one—pointed to a basket of candy. Each of the other notes merely pointed to the location of another note. What my son cared about was the basket of candy, but he couldn't get there without following a chain of pointers.

In a macro, some methods and properties carry out actions and some point— or *refer*—to objects. Once you start modifying recorded statements, or especially when you start writing statements from scratch, you need to understand methods and properties that refer to objects. In this lesson you will learn how methods and properties refer to objects, and how you can use Visual Basic's tools for learning more about objects.

Start the lesson

 Start Excel. In the folder containing the practice files for this book, open the Objects workbook, and save a copy as **Lesson3**.

Using the Locals Window to Learn About Objects

Methods and properties fall into two groups. Those in one group—for example, Copy, PasteSpecial, NumberFormat, and FormulaR1C1—come at the end of a statement and actually carry out an action. I call these *action words*. Those from the other group—for example, Application, ActiveWindow, and Range("A1")—refer to objects.

> **NOTE** Technically, a word such as *ActiveCell* means "a property that returns a reference to an Active Cell object." Informally, you can just call it an object, because that is what it refers to.

You can store an object—or, rather, a reference to an object—in a variable in much the same way that you store a value in a variable. Visual Basic has a powerful tool for letting you see what a variable contains: the Locals window.

Store values in variables

First, let's watch the Locals window as a macro stores some simple values in a variable. This is a very simple macro that assigns several different values to a variable.

Run Macro button

1   In the Lesson3 workbook, click the Run Macro button, select StoreValue, and click Edit.

```
Sub StoreValue()
    myValue = 500
    myValue = "Dog"
    myValue = True
    myValue = #5/1/95#
    myValue = 125.3
End Sub
```

2   From the View menu, select the Locals Window command.

The Locals window appears, but it is empty. The Locals window shows variables only while you are stepping through a macro.

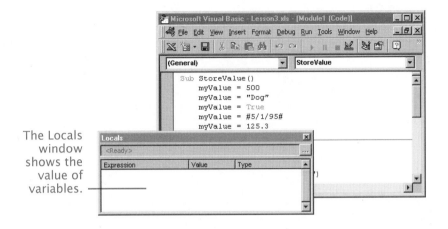

The Locals window shows the value of variables.

TIP If the Locals window is squeezed into the same area as the Module1 code window (that is, if it is *docked*), then hold down the CTRL key as you drag the Locals title bar away from the code window. Holding down the CTRL key prevents a Visual Basic window from docking with another window.

---

3 Click the Module window and press F8 to start stepping into the macro.

The Locals window now shows Module1 (which you can ignore), and it also shows the variable myValue. In the Value column, it shows that myValue is *Empty* (which means that you haven't assigned anything to it.) In the Type column, it shows that myValue is *Variant* (which means that you can assign anything to it), and that it does not yet have anything assigned to it.

A variant is Empty until you assign something to it.

4   Press F8 twice to assign the value 500 to the variable.

Now the Locals window shows that the value is 500. The Type column shows that the type is *Integer*. An Integer is a whole number, one that doesn't have any decimal places.

Executing this statement...

...changes the variant to an Integer.

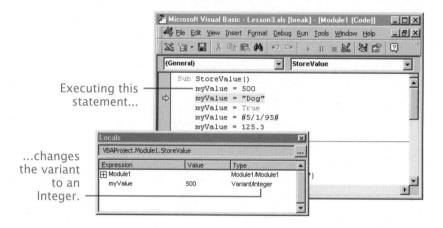

5   Press F8 again to assign the value "Dog" to the variable.

The Locals window shows the new value and indicates that the type is *String*. A string is any text. If you don't put quotation marks around a string, Visual Basic tries to interpret it as a variable.

6   Press F8 again to assign the value True to the variable. The Locals window shows that the type is now *Boolean*. Boolean is simply a fancy word for a value that can be only True or False.

7   Press F8 again to assign the value #5/1/95# to the variable. The Locals window shows the type as *Date*. The number signs indicate that this is a date and not the numeral 5 divided by 1 divided by 95. Number signs indicate dates in the same way that quotation marks indicate strings.

8   Press F8 to assign the value 125.3 to the variable. The type is now *Double*. A Double is a number with a decimal portion. In general, small numbers used for counting things are Integers, and large numbers used for serious calculations are Doubles.

9   Press F8 to end the subroutine.

You usually don't need to worry about what data type a value has. As you can see, Visual Basic automatically changed myValue to hold whatever type of value you wanted to assign to it. Numbers, strings, dates, and Booleans are all different kinds of simple values. In the Locals window, you see the value in the Value column. Now let's see what a variable looks like when you assign an object reference to it.

Store objects in variables

When you assign a value to a variable, you just use an equal sign to assign the value. When you assign an object reference to a variable, however, you still use an equal sign, but you also must put the keyword Set at the beginning of the statement.

1 Click on the StoreObject procedure. It is a simple test procedure to let you see the difference between assigning a value and assigning an object reference.

```
Sub StoreObject()
    myObject = Range("A1")
    Set myObject = Range("A1")
End Sub
```

2 Press F8 to start stepping through the macro. Once again, you see Module1 and an empty variable.

3 Press F8 twice to assign Range("A1") to the variable. The value in cell A1 is the string "Test Cell." The Locals window shows that the variable now contains the string value "Test Cell." This statement did not use the keyword Set to assign the range, so Visual Basic retrieved the value from the cell and assigned that value to the variable.

Executing this statement...

...assigns the contents of the range to the variable.

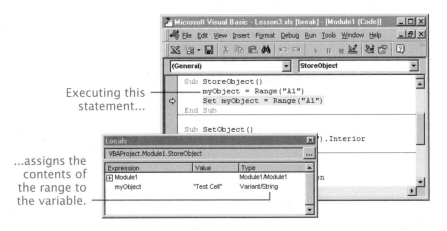

4 Press F8 again to assign Range("A1") to the variable using the Set keyword. The Locals window doesn't show anything as the value of myObject. Rather, myObject now has a plus sign next to it, and says

59

Variant/Object/Range under Type. The variable now contains a reference to an object—specifically, to a Range object.

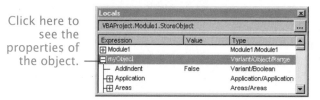

Executing this statement...

...assigns a reference to the Range object to the variable.

5 In the Locals window, click the plus sign next to the myObject variable. A list with all the properties of the cell A1 Range object appears. This list includes only properties, not methods. Each property either shows a value or has a plus sign next to it. A property that has a plus sign is really a reference to another object. A property that does not have a plus sign is a value.

Click here to see the properties of the object.

6 Scroll down until you see the Value property. The value of the cell is the string "Test Cell." This is the property Visual Basic used when the macro assigned Range("A1") to the variable without using the Set keyword.

To assign a value to a variable, use an equal sign. To assign an object reference to a variable, use an equal sign and also put the word Set at the front of the statement.

Change object property values

You can actually change the value of a property right in the Locals window. Some properties are *read-only* so you can't change them, but other properties are available to change. Changing the property in the Locals window has the exact same effect as changing the property in a Visual Basic statement, so you can try out properties interactively as you're trying to find the property you want.

1   In the Locals window, scroll from the Value property you were just looking at up to the ColumnWidth property. (Rearrange windows as necessary so that you can see cell A1 in Excel.)

The width of column A...

...appears as the ColumnWidth property.

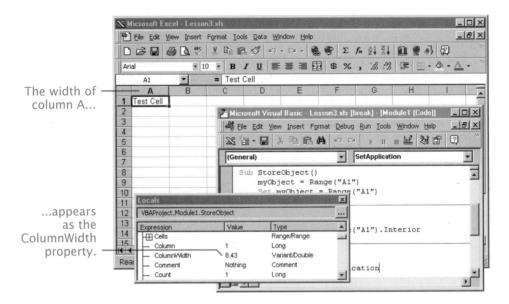

2   Click ColumnWidth to select the entire row. Then click 8.43 in the Value column to select just the number. This is the default width of a column.

3   Type 25 and press ENTER. The width of the column changes. Changing the value of the property tells Excel to change the object on the screen.

Type a value here to change the column width in Excel.

4 In the Visual Basic module window, insert a new line above the End Sub statement and type **myObject.ColumnWidth = 5**. This is the Visual Basic code equivalent of changing the value of the property in the Locals window.

5 Click Column to select the row with the Column property. Then click the 1 in the Value column.

Nothing happens. Sorry, you just can't change which column cell A1 is in by assigning a new value to the Column property. Column is a read-only property.

6 Drag the yellow arrow that points at the End Sub statement up to point at the new ColumnWidth statement that you just typed.

Drag the arrow to change which statement will execute next.

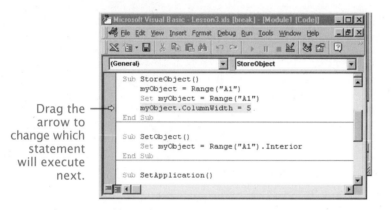

Dragging the arrow changes which statement will execute next.

7 Press F8 to execute the new statement. The column width shrinks.

The Locals window gives you a very quick view of all the properties that belong to a particular object. The Locals window also makes it clear which properties contain values—the ones that have a value in the Value column—and which contain a reference to an object—the ones that have a plus sign next to them. It also makes it easy to find out whether a value-holding property is read-only: just click the value and see if you can change it.

Next, let's look at what happens when you delve into one of those properties that contains a reference to an object.

Navigate to new objects

1 With the StoreObject macro still stopped on the End Sub statement, click the plus sign next to the Interior property of myObject.

The Interior property is a whole new object, with its own properties.

The Interior property of a Range object returns a reference to a new object, an *Interior* object. The Interior object controls the color and pattern of the interior of the cell. The reason Interior is a separate object is that many different objects can have interiors—most notably many of the components of a chart.

2 Click the Color property, then click the number 16777215 in the Value column.

Theoretically, a cell can have any of 16,777,215 possible values ranging from 0 (Black) to 16,777,215 (White). In practice, Excel picks out 56 of those colors into a palette. When you assign a number between 0 and 16,777,215 to the Color property, Excel "rounds" the number to the closest color in the palette. Fortunately, Visual Basic has some pre-defined names for common colors.

3 Type **vbRed** as the value of Color and press ENTER.

The interior of cell A1 changes to red, the Color property value changes to 255 (which happens to be the color number for red), and the ColorIndex number changes to 3.

Type **vbRed** to change the color of the cell interior.

NOTE The ColorIndex property is a value between 0 and 56, corresponding to the colors in Excel's palette. The numbers used to match up to the boxes in the Fill Color toolbar palette on Excel's Formatting toolbar, but then the colors were arranged into a more logical order, while keeping the color index numbers the same as they were for backwards compatibility. So there is no longer any apparent order to the numbers.

4   Click the ColorIndex property and then click the number 3. Type **34** and press ENTER.

Locals			
VBAProject.Module1.StoreObject			...
Expression	Value	Type	
⊟ Interior		Interior/Interior	
⊞ Application		Application/Application	
— Color	16777164	Variant/Double	
— ColorIndex	34	Variant/Long	
— Creator	xlCreatorCode	XlCreator	

Changing the ColorIndex property changes the Color property, too.

The cell changes to a nice pale blue.

5   In the Code window, just above the End Sub statement, type **myObject.Interior.ColorIndex = 45**.

6   Drag the yellow pointer up to the new statement and press F8.

The interior of the cell changes to orange.

7   Press F5 to finish executing the macro.

The purpose of this section was not to teach you about cell colors, but rather to show you how you can link from one object to another using properties. You can try out the properties—whether properties that refer to other objects, or properties that contain values—in the Locals window as you explore ways to bend Excel to your unbridled will.

Using the Immediate Window to Learn About Objects

Each object in Excel has methods and properties that allow you to navigate to other objects. One common way to navigate between objects is to move up and down Excel's hierarchy of objects. In this hierarchy each object in Excel has a parent object. You can move up the hierarchy by using the Parent property. In this section, you will navigate up and down the Excel hierarchy using a powerful Visual Basic feature: the Immediate window.

Navigate up by using parent

1 Click on the SetObject macro. It looks like this:

```
Sub SetObject()
    Set myObject = Range("A1").Interior
End Sub
```

This is a trivial macro. It simply assigns the interior of cell A1 to a variable.

2 Press F8 three times to assign the object.

Look at the Locals window. The object type is listed as Variant/Object/Interior.

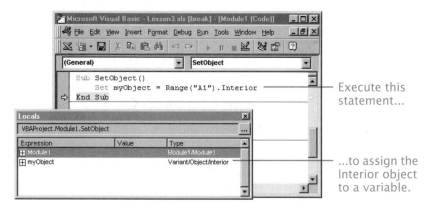

Execute this statement...

...to assign the Interior object to a variable.

3 From the View menu click the Immediate Window command. (If the window docks with one of the other windows, hold down the CTRL key and drag it away.)

In the Immediate window you can enter any statement you want and execute it immediately, without modifying the macro in the module.

4 In the Immediate window, type **Set myObject = myObject.Parent** and press ENTER.

The description in the Type column of the Locals window shows that the object is a range, because the parent of this particular interior object is a range.

The parent of the Interior object...

...is a Range object.

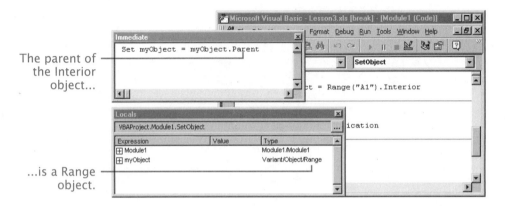

5 Move the cursor back to the same statement in the Immediate window (it doesn't have to be at the end), and press ENTER again.

The variable type changes to Worksheet, because the parent of a cell is a worksheet.

6 Execute the statement again.

This time the type changes to ThisWorkbook.

7 Execute it once again.

The type changes to Application.

8 Just for good measure, execute the statement one more time.

The type doesn't change. It is still Application.

9 Press F5 to end the macro.

Each object has a parent. (Because the top object is the Application object, the Application object is also its own parent. Wouldn't Freud have had fun with that one?) This particular chain went from Interior to Range to Worksheet to ThisWorkbook to Application.

Navigate down by using collections

When you look at an open workbook, you usually see multiple sheet tabs at the bottom. It is easy when moving up Excel's object hierarchy to tell which workbook is the parent of any of the worksheets, but when moving down the hierarchy, you have to get more specific.

The way the object library deals with this clustering of objects as you go down is to group related items in a *collection*. When you navigate down the object hierarchy, you need to select single items from each collection. To select an item from a collection, you specify either the item number or the item name.

1 Click on the SetApplication macro. It looks like this:

```
Sub SetApplication()
    Set myObject = Application
End Sub
```

This trivial macro starts at the top of the hierarchy. It assigns the Application object to myObject.

2 Press F8 three times to assign the Application object.

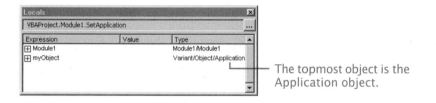

The topmost object is the Application object.

The Locals window shows that the variable contains a reference to the Application object. One of the properties of the Application object is the Workbooks property. The Workbooks property returns a reference to an object that is a collection of Workbook objects. You can specify a single item from the collection.

3 In the Immediate window, type **Set myObject = myObject.Workbooks(1)** and press ENTER.

To move down the hierarchy, specify an item from a collection.

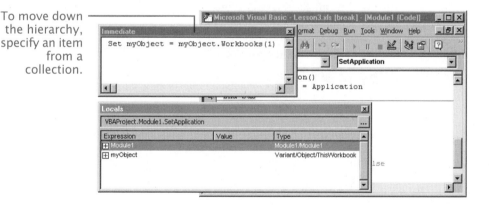

The Locals window shows that the variable now contains a reference to a ThisWorkbook object, which is really a Workbook object. Putting parentheses after the collection allows you to single out one item from the collection. A workbook in the collection is numbered based on the order in which the workbooks were opened. Close a workbook, and the number for each subsequent workbook changes.

One of the properties of a Workbook object is the Worksheets property. The Worksheets property returns a reference to an object that contains a collection of Worksheet objects. Once again, you can specify a single item from the collection.

4   In the Immediate window, type **Set myObject = myObject.Worksheets("Sheet2")** and press ENTER.

Specify an item by number or by name.

```
Set myObject = myObject.Workbooks(1)
Set myObject = myObject.Worksheets("Sheet2")
```

```
Locals
VBAProject.Module1.SetApplication
Expression          Value       Type
⊞ Module1                        Module1/Module1
⊞ myObject                       Variant/Object/Sheet2
```

The Locals window shows that the variable now contains a reference to a Sheet2 object, which is really a Worksheet object. Once again, Worksheets is a property that returns a collection, and the parentheses allow you to specify a single item. You can specify an item either by name (in quotation marks) or by number. The number is sometimes called an *Index*. A Worksheet in the collection is numbered based on the current position of its sheet tab. Move a worksheet, and its number in the collection changes. Press F5 to end the macro.

When you specify an item from a collection, you can use either a number or a name and get a reference to the same object. Choose the method of specifying that is most convenient in a given situation.

 TIP   You can execute statements in the Immediate window even when you are not stepping through a macro, but you can't see variables in the Locals window unless you are stepping.

Navigate from object to object

All objects in Excel fit somewhere in the object library hierarchy—you can tell where an object is in the hierarchy by finding the object referred to by its Parent property—but that doesn't mean that you are limited to navigating up and down the hierarchy.

1   Select the SetApplication macro and press F8 three times to assign the application object to the variable.

2 Click the plus sign next to myObject, which contains the Application object.

ActiveCell is a property of the Application object.

The list shows the properties that belong to an Application object. The first property in the list is ActiveCell, which returns a reference to a Range object. You can navigate directly from the Application object to the active cell, even though the Application object is not the parent of a Range object. (The worksheet is the parent of a range.)

3 Click the plus sign next to ActiveCell.

Application is a property of a Range object.

This list shows the properties of a Range object. The second property in the list is Application. It has a plus sign and returns a reference to the Application object. Every object has an Application property that returns a reference directly to the top of the hierarchy.

4 Click the plus sign next to the Application property.

The list shows another ActiveCell property.

5 Click the plus sign next to ActiveCell. Then click the plus sign next to the subsequent Application. (How many of these are there?)

You can continue the chain indefinitely.

69

6 When you're bored, click the minus sign next to myObject to collapse everything back. (I drilled down 88 times, which is the most I could fit on the screen at 1280x1024 resolution.) Press F5 to end the macro.

When you get a reference to an object, regardless of how you get that reference, it is exactly the same as if you had gotten the reference by any other means. Assuming cell A1 is the active cell, ActiveCell, Application.ActiveCell, ActiveSheet.ActiveCell, Range("A1"), ActiveSheet.Range("A1"), and Application.ActiveWorkbook.ActiveSheet.Range("A1"), along with about 6,273 other expressions, all give you a reference to the same exact object.

You can navigate by moving up and down the object hierarchy, or you can follow shortcut methods and properties that refer directly to an object in a different part of the family tree. Once you get an object reference, there is no way to tell how you got it. Navigating objects is like a very efficient money-laundering scheme.

Using Help to Learn About Objects

You could learn about all of Excel's objects by navigating up and down the hierarchy using the Locals window and the Immediate window, but it still might be difficult to see the big picture. Fortunately, the Excel Visual Basic Reference Help file contains an overview diagram that you will find very useful for putting all the objects into perspective.

Find the object hierarchy in help

1 Click on the word *Application* in the SetApplication macro, and press F1.

A description of the Application property appears. This topic indicates that the Application property returns a reference to the Application object.

The Property help topic...

...links to the Object topic.

Application Property

See Also   Example   Applies To

Used *without* an object qualifier, this property returns an **Application** object that represents the Microsoft Excel application. Used *with* an object qualifier, this property returns an **Application** object that represents the creator of the specified object (you can use this property with an OLE Automation object to return that object's application). Read-only.

2 Click on the word *Application* in the first sentence.

A description of the Application object appears. At the top of the topic is a diagram showing the Application object in a box.

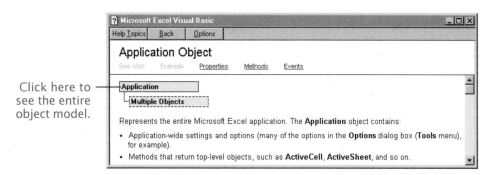

Click here to see the entire object model.

3 Click the Application box.

The Excel Objects topic appears.

Click here to see the Worksheet part of the model.

This diagram shows about one third of the Excel Object Model. You can see the Application object at the top. It is the parent of a Workbook object. (The Workbook's object appears blue but should be yellow because it comes in a collection.) A workbook is the parent of a Worksheet object (which is yellow because it comes in a collection).

4 Click the red arrow next to the Worksheet object.

This diagram shows more of the object model, starting from the Worksheet object.

Click here to get back to the top half of the model.

A Worksheet object is the parent of a Range object. The Range object is blue because it is not really a collection. A Range object is just weird. A Range object is the parent of an Interior object. So the parent chain goes from Interior to Range to Worksheet to Workbook to Application, as you saw in an earlier section.

You will learn more about Range objects and collections in Lesson 4.

5 Click the red triangle at the right of the Worksheet object to get back to the top part of the object model.

On the right side of the main part of the model, you can see other objects that have the application as a parent. Most of them are objects that you will only need in very advanced situations.

Find new methods in help

You can jump directly to the description for any object by clicking the object's box. Once you go to the topic for an object, you can learn about that object's methods and properties.

1   Click the Workbooks object box.

The topic for the Workbooks collection object appears. At the top are options to show the properties and methods for the Workbooks object.

A Workbook object comes in a Workbooks collection.

2   Click Properties.

The dialog box shows all the properties that apply to the Workbooks collection.

Every object has a Parent property, an Application property, and a Creator property. You learned about the Parent and Application properties earlier in this lesson. The Creator property is useful only on a Macintosh computer. All collection objects have the Count and Item properties. Count tells you how many items are in the collection. The Item property is another way of retrieving a single item from a collection.

3 Click the Cancel button, and then click the Methods option.

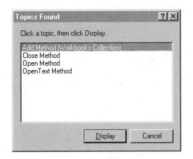

These are the methods that apply to the Workbooks collection. You can Add a new workbook to the collection, Close all the workbooks together, Open an existing workbook, or OpenText to open a text file and divide the contents into columns. (In Lesson 2, the macro recorder created a statement using the OpenText method. To find out what that statement means, look there.)

4 Double-click the Add Method topic.

The first paragraph describes how the Add method creates a new work-book (optionally using a template file), and then says that the Add method "returns a Workbook object." What that means is that when you create a new workbook using the Add method, you get back a reference that you can assign to a variable using Set. In the next section, you'll see how to do that.

5   The word *Workbook* is highlighted. You can jump directly to the Workbook Object Topic. Click the Workbook link.

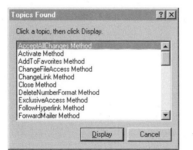

As you can see, a Workbook object is different from the Workbooks collection object. The Workbooks Object topic has its own lists of properties and methods. (You will learn about Events in Lesson 9.)

6   Click the Methods link.

A Workbook object has many more methods available than a Workbooks collection object.

7   Double-click the Close Method topic.

When you record closing a file, you will never see arguments used with the Close method. As you can see from the Help topic, however, the Close method can take optional arguments. The most useful is the SaveChanges argument, which allows you to close a workbook without prompting for whether to save changes or not.

8 Close Help to return to Excel Visual Basic.

Help is a very useful tool for learning about objects and their associated methods and properties. Help is particularly useful for finding out methods or properties that you know nothing about. If you have even a vague recollection of the method or property you want, Visual Basic provides some very convenient tools for discovering the exact spelling of a method, or the precise name of an argument.

Using Auto Lists to Learn About Objects

One very convenient tool for discovering or remembering methods and properties is the automatic list that Visual Basic can pop up while you are typing. See how the Auto List features can make writing macros easier.

Add and close a workbook

Create a new macro from scratch using the methods you saw in Help.

1 At the bottom of the module, type **Sub MakeBook** and press ENTER to create a new macro.

You don't need to type the parentheses at the end; Visual Basic will add the parentheses and the End Sub statement for you.

2 Press the TAB key to indent the body of the macro, and then type **Workbooks.** (Be sure to type the period.)

As soon as you type the period, Visual Basic displays a list of all the methods and properties available for the Workbooks collection.

When you type a period after an object Visual Basic recognizes...

...it displays a list of methods and properties for the object.

This list is like a combination of the two lists you saw in Help. The icon next to the name distinguishes methods and properties. The icon for a property looks like a finger pointing at a box. The icon for a method looks like a green clam hurtling through space.

3 The word *Add* is already highlighted at the top of the list. Press the TAB key to enter it into the statement, and then press ENTER to go to the next line.

Entering the name of the Add method was pretty slick, right? You didn't have to type anything. You did have to type the word *Workbooks*, though. Perhaps you are too lazy to do even that much.

4 Press CTRL+SPACEBAR, press the DOWN ARROW key until you highlight ActiveWorkbook, and then press TAB. Was that easy enough for you?

Press CTRL+SPACEBAR to see a list of global methods and properties.

5 Type a period.

Once again, as soon as you type the period, Visual Basic displays the list of methods and properties available for a Workbook object.

6 Type **C** to jump quickly down the list, select Close from the list, and press the TAB key. (Don't press ENTER yet.)

Type a letter...

...and then press the DOWN ARROW key to select the member you want.

77

You saw in Help that the Close method has optional arguments. See what happens when you get ready to type one of them.

7 Type a space.

Visual Basic displays a Quick Info box showing the possible arguments for the Close method. You want to tell Close not to prompt to save changes. Since the SaveChanges argument is the first one in the list, you don't need to type the name of the argument, but you do want to specify a value.

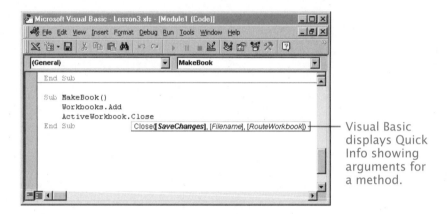

Visual Basic displays Quick Info showing arguments for a method.

8 Type **False**.

9 Test the macro by pressing F8 five times.

You should see the new workbook appear and then disappear quietly.

Auto Lists not only let you know what methods and properties are available in the current context, they also let you be lazy. What a deal!

Use Auto Lists to learn constant values

Many properties and arguments allow only a limited number of values. A limited set of values is called an *enumerated list*, because you can number them. Visual Basic has Auto Lists that help you select a value from an enumerated list.

1 In the MakeBook macro, insert a new line after the Workbooks.Add statement, type (or press CTRL+SPACEBAR and select) **ActiveWindow**, type a period, type (or select) **WindowState**, and then type an equal sign (=). Or, simply type **ActiveWindow.WindowState=**.

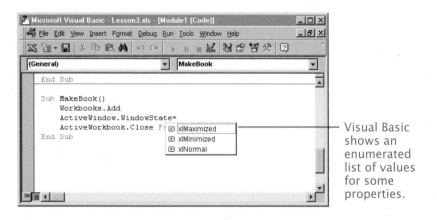

Visual Basic shows an enumerated list of values for some properties.

The WindowState property controls whether the window is minimized, maximized, or sizable. As soon as you finish typing the equal sign, Visual Basic displays a list enumerating the three possible values: xlMaximized, xlMinimized, and xlNormal.

2 Select xlMinimized from the list, and press ENTER.

3 Type **Windows.Arrange** (or construct it using the Auto Lists), and then press the SPACEBAR.

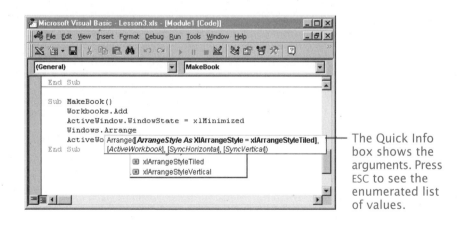

The Quick Info box shows the arguments. Press ESC to see the enumerated list of values.

Visual Basic displays the Quick Info box, showing you what the possible arguments are for the Arrange method. The first argument is ArrangeStyle. This argument controls how the windows will be arranged. After the argument name are the words *As XlArrangeStyle = xlArrangeStyleTiled*. What these mean is that Excel's object library contains a list named XlArrangeStyle that enumerates all the possible values for this argument. The expression *= xlArrangeStyleTiled* means that if you don't tell Arrange otherwise, it will tile the windows.

4   Press ESC to remove the Quick Info box, leaving behind the list of possible values.

5   Select xlArrangeStyleCascade, and press the TAB key to enter it into the statement.

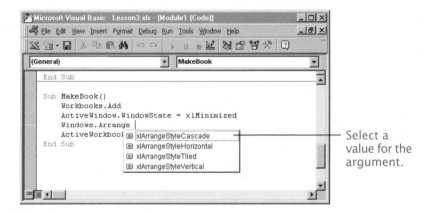

Select a value for the argument.

Save button

6   Click the Save button on the Visual Basic Standard toolbar to save the workbook, and then press F8 five times to step through part of the macro. Do not step through the statement that closes the workbook! (If you do, you better hope that you saved the workbook when I told you to.)

The macro creates a new workbook, minimizes it, and arranges the other workbook. If you execute the last statement now, you will close the Lesson3 workbook, rather than the workbook you just created.

7   Click the Reset button to stop the macro without closing the workbook.

Reset button

Declare variables to enable Auto Lists

When you create a new workbook, you can use ActiveWorkbook to refer to it, unless, of course, you activate a different workbook first. You need some way of storing a reference to the original workbook so that you can get back to it when you are ready. Store a reference? Hmm, store a reference? Wasn't there something we learned about how to store a reference? Remember, the description of the Add method in Help said that the Add method returns a reference to the new workbook. You can use Set to store that reference in a variable.

1 Delete the ActiveWorkbook.Close statement from the end of the macro.

2 Insert the words **Set myBook** = at the beginning of the Workbooks.Add statement. The resulting statement is *Set myBook = Workbooks.Add.*

   In the "Add and close a workbook" section, an automatic list appeared as soon as you typed a period after the word *ActiveWorkbook.* You have now told the macro to assign a reference to a workbook in myBook. Will the list automatically appear when you type a period after myBook?

3 Insert a new line before the End Sub statement and type **myBook.** (Be sure to type the period). Nothing happened. The list did not appear. Why not?

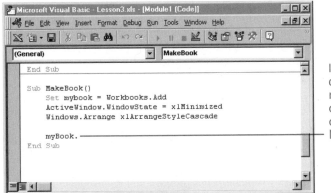

If Visual Basic does not recognize the object type, it can't show the list of members.

The word myBook acts as a variable. When you create a new word and use it as a variable, Visual Basic makes it *Variant.* Variant means that you can assign anything you want to the variable and it will change from Integer to String to Workbook to Range as fast as you can assign different values or objects to it. Visual Basic can't display the Auto List, because it really doesn't know what type of value or object will be assigned to the variable at any given moment. You can, however, promise Visual Basic that you will never, ever assign anything other than a Workbook to the myBook variable.

4 Delete the period you just typed.

   At the top of the macro, just below the Sub MakeBook statement, enter this statement: **Dim myBook As Workbook**

   This statement *declares* the variable to Visual Basic. That is, you declare to Visual Basic that myBook is a variable and that the only thing you will ever assign to it is a reference to a Workbook object.

   (*Dim* is an archaic term. It is short for *Dimension*, and has to do with telling the computer how much space you will need for the variable.)

5   Scroll back down to the statement beginning with *myBook*—wait for the drum roll—and type a period. Cymbals crash, and the Auto List appears. Select Close, and then type **False** as an argument.

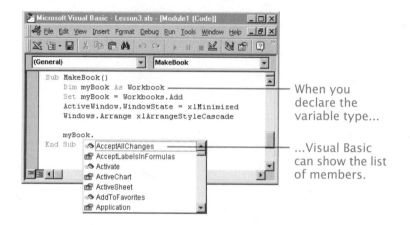

When you declare the variable type...

...Visual Basic can show the list of members.

6   Save the workbook, and press F8 repeatedly to step through the macro.

You can create a variable "on the fly" by simply assigning a value or an object to it, or you can use Dim to declare proudly to Visual Basic that you intend to use a variable of an unchanging type.

Using the Object Browser to Learn About Objects

Visual Basic has yet another tool to help you explore Excel's object library. In fact, this last tool may be the most powerful of all: the Object Browser.

Find a new argument for a familiar method

The CopyRange macro in the Lesson3 workbook is what the macro recorder created when I copied cell A1 and pasted it into the D1:D6 range:

```
Sub CopyRange()
    Range("A1").Select
    Selection.Copy
    Range("D1:D6")
    ActiveSheet.Paste
    Application.CutCopyMode = False
End Sub
```

This macro first selects the source range, then copies it, then selects the target range, pastes the cells, and turns off the copy buffer. The macro recorder doesn't give you any clues about how you could make this macro simpler, but the Object Browser can.

Object Browser button

1 Click the Object Browser button in the Visual Basic toolbar.

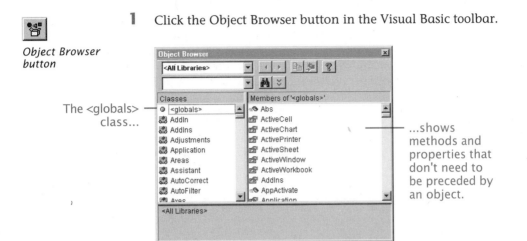

The <globals> class... — ...shows methods and properties that don't need to be preceded by an object.

The Object Browser consists primarily of two lists. The one on the left is labeled *Classes*, which is a fancy name for object types, and the one on the right is labeled *Members*, which is a fancy name for methods and properties.

NOTE If you want to make the Object Browser float like the Locals window and the Immediate window, right-click in the middle of the Object Browser window and click the Dockable command. If it still doesn't float, hold down the CTRL key as you drag the caption bar off to the side.

The <globals> list of methods and properties are the ones you can use without an object in front of them.

2 In the list on the left, <globals> should be selected. If not, select it. It's at the top of the list. In the list on the right, click ActiveCell.

The box at the bottom of the Object Browser changes to display information about ActiveCell.

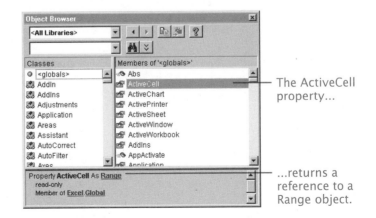

The ActiveCell property...

...returns a reference to a Range object.

The description, *Property ActiveCell As Range*, tells you that ActiveCell is a property, and that it returns a reference to a Range object. In other words, the object that ActiveCell returns belongs to the Range class. When the word following a member name is green and underlined, it means that the member returns a reference to that kind of object. You can jump quickly to the object class.

3   Click Range.

The list of classes on the left scrolls to show you the Range class. The list of members on the right now shows you all the methods and properties available for any Range object.

The Range class... 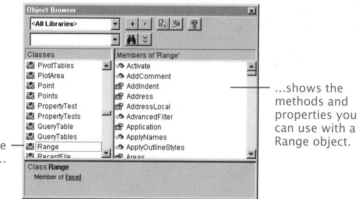 ...shows the methods and properties you can use with a Range object.

TIP   If all you see are properties, right-click the list and deselect the Group Members command.

The list of members on the right is exactly the same as what you would see pop up if you typed **ActiveCell** and then a period. Notice the icons showing which members are methods and which are properties. These methods and properties apply to any object that belongs to the Range class.

4   Scroll down the list of members and click the Copy method.

The box at the bottom of the dialog box shows a description of the Copy method.

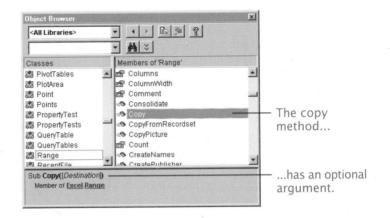

The copy method...

...has an optional argument.

The macro recorder always uses the Copy method without arguments (which copies the cell to the clipboard), but the description at the bottom of the Object Browser shows you that you can give the Copy method a Destination. The Destination argument is in square brackets, indicating that it is optional.

5 Click the Close Window button to close the Object Browser.

6 In the module window, delete all the statements that form the body of the CopyRange macro (everything between the Sub and End Sub statements), and leave a blank line for the replacement statement.

7 Type **Range("A1").Copy** and press the SPACEBAR. The Quick Info box shows the optional Destination argument. Type **Range("D1:D6")** as the argument.

Close Window button

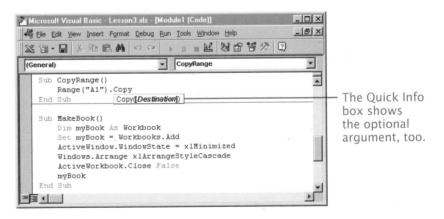

The Quick Info box shows the optional argument, too.

8 Press F5 to test the macro. The finished macro looks like this:

```
Sub CopyRange()
    Range("A1").Copy Range("D1:D6")
End Sub
```

The revised macro does not change the selection, and it is easier to read than the recorded macro. The macro recorder shows you that there is a Copy method, but it doesn't show you that the Copy method can use an argument. The Auto List displays the Copy method, but in order to see the arguments, you must actually enter the method into a statement. In the Object Browser, you can quickly see the arguments for all the methods simply by scrolling up and down through the list of members.

9 Save the Lesson3 workbook and quit Excel.

The Object Browser can be an extremely powerful tool for exploring the wealth of Excel objects.

Dockable Views

The windows in the Visual Basic Editor can be very confusing. You may find it easier to understand how they work if you compare them to windows in the Excel environment.

In Excel, each workbook you open has its own window. A workbook window can be either maximized to fill Excel's entire work area, or it can be sizable so that you can have more than one window visible at a time. A worksheet window can never move outside the boundary of the Excel application. It is completely owned by the main Excel window. This kind of window is a *child* window.

A toolbar, on the other hand, can be either docked or floating. A toolbar can be docked to the top, left, bottom, or right side of Excel's main window. To undock a toolbar, you drag the toolbar away from the docking position. A floating toolbar can be placed anywhere; it does not have to remain inside Excel's main window. A toolbar is actually a kind of window—a *dockable* window.

The Visual Basic Environment has both dockable and child windows. A module window is a child window. It can be minimized, restored, or maximized, but it can never move outside the boundaries of the Visual Basic Environment window.

The Locals window is by default a dockable window, just like toolbars in Excel. You can dock the Locals window to the top, left, bottom, or right sides of the Visual Basic window, or you can make it float by dragging it away from a docking position. You can also prevent the window from docking by holding down the CTRL key as you move the window.

Dockable Views, *continued*

> Visual Basic has six dockable windows: the Locals window, the Immediate window, the Watch window, the Project Explorer window, the Properties window, and the Object Browser window. You can display any of these windows by choosing the appropriate command from the View menu.
>
> To change a Visual Basic dockable window into a child window, right-click the window and then click the Dockable command to turn off the check mark. With the dockable setting turned off, the window behaves just like any child window; you can minimize, maximize, restore, cascade, or tile it, but you can't move it outside the main window, and it can't float above another active window.
>
> I usually make all windows dockable but undocked. I move, hide, and unhide windows as necessary. I also maximize the module window and keep it relatively small so that I can see the Excel window in the background.

Lesson Summary

To	Do this	Button
Watch the value of variables as you step through a macro	Click the View menu and then the Locals Window command.	
Undock a dockable window	Hold down the CTRL key as you drag the window's caption bar.	
Store a reference to an object in a variable	Put the keyword Set at the beginning of the assignment statement.	
Execute a statement without running a macro	From the View menu, click the Immediate Window command, then type the statement in the Immediate window and press ENTER.	
Retrieve a reference to the parent of an object	Use the Parent property.	
Select an item from a collection	Put the name in quotes or the number of the item in parentheses after the collection.	
Show the list of global methods and properties	In a module, press CTRL+SPACEBAR.	

Lesson Summary, *continued*

To	Do this	Button
Make Auto Lists appear after a variable that contains an object reference	Declare the variable as an object using Dim. For example, type *Dim myObject As Worksheet.*	
Display the Object Browser	Click the Object Browser button.	
Find a word in the Object Browser	Type the word in the search box and click the Find button.	

For online information about	Ask the Assistant for help using the words
Using objects	"Understanding Objects"
Using the Immediate window	"Immediate Window"
Using the Object Browser	"Object Browser"
Using dockable windows	"Docking"

Preview of the Next Lesson

One of the most important objects in Excel is the Range object. Because Range objects are so important, there are many different ways of working with them. The next lesson will help you see how to put Range objects to work for you.

Explore Range Objects

In this lesson you will learn how to:

- Simplify macros that record selections.
- Manipulate Range objects from Visual Basic statements.
- Put formulas into cells.
- Create references dynamically as the macro runs.

The world would be much simpler if everybody were the same size. Cars would not need adjustable seats; heads would never get bumped on door frames; feet would never dangle from a chair. Of course, some new complexities would probably arise. When exchanging that ghastly outfit you received for your birthday, you would not be able to claim it was the wrong size.

In Microsoft Excel, if your worksheets and data files are all the same size, you don't need to worry about Range objects. If you never insert new lines into a budget, if you always put yearly totals in column M, if every month's transaction file has 5 columns and 120 rows, the macro recorder can take care of dealing with ranges for you.

In the real world of humans, however, people are different sizes, and clothes and cars have to adjust to fit them. And in the real world of worksheets, models and data files are also different sizes, and you want your macros to fit them. Excel provides many properties for working with Range objects. In this lesson you will explore Range objects, and you will find out several exciting ways of working with them.

Start the lesson

➤ Start Excel, switch to the folder containing the practice files for this book, and open the Ranges workbook. Save a copy of the workbook as **Lesson4**.

Enhancing Recorded Selections

When you carry out actions in Excel, you first select something—say, a cell—and then you do something to it—say, enter a value. The macro recorder always dutifully records both the "select" and the "do" of all your actions. When the macro finishes, the selection is often in a different place from when it started. Often, however, when you run a recorded macro, you don't need the macro to change the selection.

A powerful technique for simplifying macros begins with watching for a statement ending in *Select* followed by one or more statements beginning with *Selection* or *ActiveCell*. What you do depends on whether *Select* and *Selection* form a pair or a group.

Simplify Select... Selection pairs

When a Select statement and a Selection statement form a pair, you can collapse the two statements into one. Let's record and simplify a macro that puts the names of the months across the top of a worksheet.

1 Insert a blank worksheet, and start recording a macro named **LabelMonths**.

2 Type the labels **January**, **February**, and **March** in the cells B1, C1, and D1. Turn off the recorder, and then edit the macro.

The macro should look similar to this:

```
Sub LabelMonths()
    Range("B1").Select
    ActiveCell.FormulaR1C1 = "January"
    Range("C1").Select
    ActiveCell.FormulaR1C1 = "February"
    Range("D1").Select
```

```
        ActiveCell.FormulaR1C1 = "March"
        Range("D2").Select
    End Sub
```

Each time you see *Select* at the end of one line followed by either *Selection* or *ActiveCell* at the beginning of the next, you can delete them both, leaving only a single period, without changing the behavior of the macro. If a Select statement is the last one in a macro, you can delete it entirely.

3 Delete the unnecessary selections from the LabelMonths macro, as described in the preceding paragraph.

The final macro should look like this:

```
Sub LabelMonths()
    Range("B1").FormulaR1C1 = "January"
    Range("C1").FormulaR1C1 = "February"
    Range("D1").FormulaR1C1 = "March"
End Sub
```

4 Insert a new blank worksheet, and test the macro.

The labels appear in the cells, but the original selection doesn't change.

5 Save the Lesson4 workbook.

Why should you get rid of Select... Selection pairs? One reason is that doing so makes the macro run faster. Another reason is that running a macro can seem less disruptive if it doesn't change the current selection. But the most important reason must undoubtedly be that Select...Selection pairs in a macro are one of the surest signs of a neophyte macro writer.

Simplify Select groups

When you eliminate Select... Selection pairs using the preceding approach, be sure that they do come in pairs. If you have a single Select statement followed by two or more statements that use the selection, you can still avoid changing the selection, but you must do it in a different way.

1 In Excel, select a sheet with labels in the first row and start recording a macro named **MakeBoldItalic**.

2 Click cell B1, click the Bold button, click the Italic button, and then click the Stop Recording button.

Stop Recording button

	A	B	C	D	E
1		*January*	February	March	
2					
3					

3   Edit the macro. It will look like this:

```
Sub MakeBoldItalic()
    Range("B1").Select
    Selection.Font.Bold = True
    Selection.Font.Italic = True
End Sub
```

Obviously, if you delete the first Select… Selection pair, you will not be able to predict what cells will become italicized.

4   Edit the macro to assign the range to a variable named myRange. Then replace the Selection object with the myRange object.

The finished macro should look like this:

```
Sub MakeBoldItalic()
    Dim myRange as Range
    Set myRange = Range("B1")
    myRange.Font.Bold = True
    myRange.Font.Italic = True
End Sub
```

5   Change *"B1"* to *"C1"* in the macro, and then press F8 repeatedly to step through the macro. Watch how the format of the cell changes without changing which cell is originally selected.

6   Save the Lesson4 workbook.

 NOTE   You could also replace the Select group with a With structure, like this:

```
With Range("B1")
    .Font.Bold = True
    .Font.Italic = True
End With
```

Here's what the With structure does secretly in the background: it creates a hidden variable, takes the object from the With statement and assigns that object to the hidden variable, and then puts the hidden variable in front of each "dangling" period. The End With statement discards the hidden variable.

Eliminating the selection when there is a group may not seem like much of a simplification. With only two statements, it probably isn't. When you have several statements that use the same selection, however, converting the selection to an object variable can make the macro much easier to read.

Exploring Ranges

Range objects are probably the most important object class in Excel. You put values into ranges. You put formulas into ranges. You format ranges into reports. You base charts on the numbers in ranges. You put drawing objects on top of ranges. You manipulate PivotTables in ranges. You therefore need to move beyond the kind of references to ranges that the macro recorder can create.

Explore the Range property

Probably the most important property that returns a Range object is the Range property. The Range property can be used in either of two ways. You can use it with two arguments that give the two end points of a range, or you can use it with a single argument that gives anything that Excel can interpret as a range address.

The WatchRange macro demonstrates several uses of the Range property. Here is the macro in its entirety. We will look at each statement in turn as you step through the macro.

```
Sub WatchRange()
    Range("A1", "D2").Select
    Range(ActiveCell, "B6").Select
    Range("B3:C8").Select
    Range("B2:E4").Name = "TestRange"
    Range("TestRange").Select
    Range("B2").Select
    ActiveCell.Range("B2").Select
    Range("TestRange").Range("A1").Select
End Sub
```

1   Edit the WatchRange macro and press F8 three times to execute the *Range("A1","D2").Select* statement.

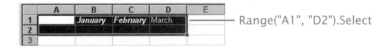

Range("A1", "D2").Select

Excel selects the range A1:D2. With this form of the Range property, you use two arguments. Each argument can be a cell address, in A1 notation, in quotation marks. The Range object that the property returns is the rectangle formed by the two end points.

2 Press F8 to execute the *Range(ActiveCell, "B6").Select* statement.

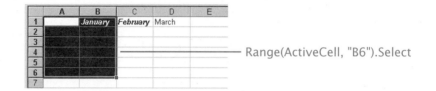

Range(ActiveCell, "B6").Select

Excel selects the range A1:B6. Each of the two arguments you give the Range property can be either a simple cell address or a Range object. If you assign a Range object to a variable, you can use that variable as an argument to the Range property.

3 Press F8 to execute the *Range("B3:C8").Select* statement.

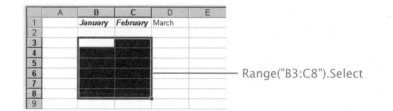

Range("B3:C8").Select

Excel selects the range B3:C8. The Range property can also be used with a single argument. When you use a single argument, you can put anything inside the quotation marks that Excel can interpret as a cell reference.

4 Press F8 to execute the *Range("B2:E4").Name = "TestRange"* statement. This assigns a name to the specified range.

5 Press F8 to execute the *Range("TestRange").Select* statement.

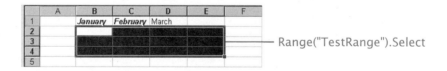

Range("TestRange").Select

Excel selects the range B2:E4. You should see the word *TestRange*, the name of the selected range, in the Reference area to the left of the formula bar. You can use a defined Excel range name as the argument to the Range property.

6 Press F8 to execute the *Range("B2").Select* statement.

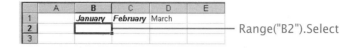

As you might have guessed, Excel selects cell B2. The Range property in this example is the global Range property. The reference B2 means "second row, second column." In this case, Excel uses cell A1 of the worksheet as the starting point.

7 Press F8 to execute the *ActiveCell.Range("B2").Select* statement.

As you might *not* have guessed, Excel selects cell C3. Excel uses cell B2, the Range object returned by the ActiveCell property, as the starting point because the Range property in this example belongs to the Range object. The address B2 still means "second row, second column."

8 Press F8 to execute the *Range("TestRange").Range("A1").Select* statement.

Excel selects cell B2, because that's the top left cell of TestRange (B2:E4).

9 Press F8 to finish the macro.

The Range property is a flexible way of establishing a link to an arbitrary Range object. You can either use a single text string that contains any valid reference as an argument to the Range property, or you can use two arguments that define a rectangular range. If you use the global Range property, or if you use the Range property with the Application object or with a Worksheet object, the addresses are relative to the top left cell of the worksheet. If you use the Range property with a Range object, the addresses are relative to the top left cell of that range.

Explore a range as a collection

A workbook can contain multiple worksheets, so in the Excel Object Library, Worksheets is defined as an object class. A Worksheets object has a separate list of methods and properties from a Worksheet object.

Similarly, a range can contain multiple cells. You might expect that Excel would have a Cells collection object. But a collection of cells is a little more complicated than a collection of worksheets, because cells come in two dimensions—rows as well as columns. You can think of the range A1:B3 as a collection of six cells, but you can also think of it as a collection of three rows, or as a collection of two columns.

Excel therefore has three properties that look at a range as a collection: the Cells property returns a collection of cells, the Rows property returns a collection of rows, and the Columns property returns a collection of columns. These are not separate classes, however. The result of any of these properties is still a Range object, and it can use any of the methods or properties of any other Range object.

The WatchCollections macro demonstrates how to use a range as a collection. Here is the macro in its entirety:

```
Sub WatchCollection()
    Dim myRange As Range
    Set myRange = Range("B2:E4")
    myRange.Interior.Color = vbYellow
    myRange.Cells(1, 4).Select
    myRange.Cells(6).Select
    myRange.Cells(myRange.Cells.Count).Select
    Cells(Cells.Count).Select
    myRange.Rows(2).Select
    myRange.Columns(myRange.Columns.Count).Select
    Columns(2).Select
End Sub
```

1   Click in the WatchCollections macro and press F8 four times to assign the range B2:E4 to the variable myRange and to color the range to make it easier to see.

2   Press F8 to execute the *myRange.Cells(1,4).Select* statement.

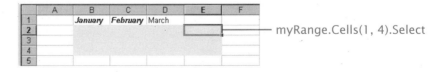

Excel selects cell E2, the fourth cell in the first row of the range. The Cells property treats the range as a collection of cells. You typically use two numbers with the Cells property, the first for the row and the second for the column.

 NOTE For Excel developers familiar with the R1C1 notation used by Excel version 4 macros, the Cells property with two arguments provides the same benefits as R1C1 notation, without requiring you to combine the row and column numbers into a single text string.

3 Press F8 to execute the *myRange.Cells(6).Select* statement.

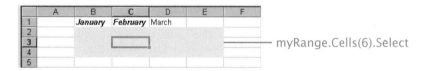

Excel selects cell C3, the sixth item in the collection. You can also use a single argument with the Cells property. If you do, the number specifies a cell in the first row. If the number is greater than the number of columns in the range, it wraps to the next row. Since myRange contains only four columns, the sixth item is really the second cell in the second row.

4 Press F8 to execute the *myRange.Cells(myRange.Cells.Count).Select* statement.

myRange.Cells(myRange.Cells.Count).Select

This one is a little bit tricky, but very useful. This statement uses the Cells property twice: first to find out the number of cells in the range, and a second time to select the last cell. Since there are twelve cells in the range, the twelfth item in the collection is the fourth cell on the third row.

TIP Hold the mouse pointer over the expression *myRange.Cells.Count* and Visual Basic will display a box showing the value.

5 Press F8 to execute the *Cells(Cells.Count).Select* statement.

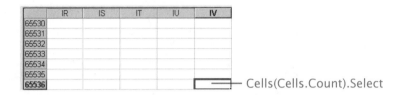 — Cells(Cells.Count).Select

Excel selects the very last cell in the worksheet. If you use the Cells property without a Range object in front of it (that is, if you use the global Cells property), then it returns the collection of all the cells on the active worksheet. This statement selects the 16,777,216th cell on the worksheet.

 NOTE   *Range* is both the name of the property that returns a Range object and the name of the Range object class itself. In the Object Browser, you will find the word *Range* as a class name (on the left) and also as a property (on the right) under the <globals>, Application, Worksheet, and Range classes.

The word *Cells*, however, is only the name of a property. The Cells property returns a Range object. In the Object Browser, you will not find the word *Cells* in the list of object names, but you will find it as a property under the <globals>, Application, Worksheet, and Range classes.

6 Press F8 to execute the *myRange.Rows(2).Select* statement.

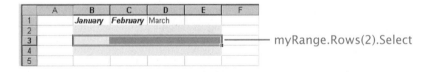 — myRange.Rows(2).Select

Excel selects the range B3:E3, which is the second row of myRange. The Rows property of a range treats the range as a collection of rows. You can refer to any item you want from the collection.

The expression *myRange.Rows* refers to the exact same range as *myRange.Cells*, which is also the exact same range as the variable myRange. Using Rows or Cells only makes a difference when you select a single item from the collection, or when you look at the Count property of the collection.

7 Press F8 to execute the *myRange.Columns(myRange.Columns.Count).Select* statement.

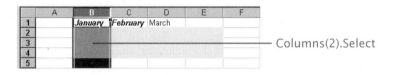

myRange.Columns(myRange.Columns.Count).Select

Excel selects the range E2:E4, which happens to be the last column of the range.

8 Press F8 to execute the *Columns(2).Select* statement.

Columns(2).Select

The global Columns property uses the entire worksheet as a range.

 TIP Since columns have letter labels that can act as names, you can specify an item from the Columns collection using either a number—for example, *Columns(3)*—or a name in quotation marks—for example, *Columns("D")*.

9 Press F8 to end the macro.

A Range object is extremely important in Excel. Excel has properties that allow you to look at a range as a collection of cells, as a collection of rows, or as a collection of columns. In any case, you can use standard Range object methods and properties on the resulting object.

Explore calculated ranges

Excel has other properties that can calculate a new range based on an existing range. The Offset property references a range shifted down, up, left, or right from a starting range. The Resize property adjusts the number of rows or columns in a range. The EntireColumn and EntireRow properties extend a range to the edges of the worksheet. In this section, you will see each of these properties in action.

The WatchCalculated macro demonstrates how to manipulate a range. Here is the macro in its entirety:

```
Sub WatchCalculated()
    Dim myRange As Range
    Sheets("Prices").Select
    Set myRange = Range("C4:E5")
    myRange.Interior.Color = vbYellow
    myRange.Offset(1, 0).Select
    myRange.Offset(0, myRange.Columns.Count).Select
    myRange.Resize(, 4).Select
    myRange.Offset(-1, -1).Resize(myRange.Rows.Count + 2, _
        myRange.Columns.Count + 2).Select
    myRange.Cells(1).EntireRow.Select
    myRange.EntireColumn.Select
    myRange.CurrentRegion.Select
End Sub
```

1　Click on the WatchCalculated macro, and press F8 five times to select the Prices sheet, assign a range to a variable, and color the range.

	A	B	C	D	E	F
1		Retail	Wholesale	Margin		
2	High	5.50	2.75	2.75		
3	Mid	4.50	2.25	2.25		
4	Low	3.50	1.75	1.75		
5						
6						

myRange.Interior.Color=vbYellow

2　Press F8 to execute the *myRange.Offset(1,0).Select* statement.

	A	B	C	D	E	F
1		Retail	Wholesale	Margin		
2	High	5.50	2.75	2.75		
3	Mid	4.50	2.25	2.25		
4	Low	3.50	1.75	1.75		
5						
6						
7						

myRange.Offset(1,0).Select

Excel selects the range C5:E6, one cell down from the yellow range. The Offset property takes two arguments. The first is the number of rows down to shift the reference. The second is the number of columns to the right to shift it. I always think of myself as standing on the top left cell of the starting range. For the first argument, I face the bottom of the worksheet and determine the number of steps forward (or backward, if the offset is negative) I want to take. For the second argument, I face the right side of the worksheet and do the same. Zero steps means no movement. The new range is the same size as the original range.

3 Press F8 to execute the *myRange.Offset(0,myRange.Columns.Count).Select* statement.

	A	B	C	D	E	F	G	H	I
1		Retail	Wholesale	Margin					
2	High	5.50	2.75	2.75					
3	Mid	4.50	2.25	2.25					
4	Low	3.50	1.75	1.75					
5									
6									

myRange.Offset(0,myRange.Columns.Count).Select

Excel selects the range F4:H5, the same size as myRange and adjacent to myRange. Imagine yourself standing in the top left cell of myRange. There are three columns in myRange, so take three steps forward. That's the starting cell for the new reference.

4 Press F8 to execute the *myRange.Resize(,4).Select* statement.

	A	B	C	D	E	F	G
1		Retail	Wholesale	Margin			
2	High	5.50	2.75	2.75			
3	Mid	4.50	2.25	2.25			
4	Low	3.50	1.75	1.75			
5							
6							

myRange.Resize(,4).Select

Excel selects the range C4:F5, one column wider than myRange. The Resize property returns a range that has been, well, resized. The first argument is the number of rows in the new reference. The second argument is the number of columns. To leave the rows or columns the same as the original range, omit the corresponding argument altogether (but leave a comma if you omit the first argument).

5 Press F8 to execute the *myRange.Offset(-1,-1).Resize(myRange.Rows.Count+2, myRange.Columns.Count+2).Select* statement.

	A	B	C	D	E	F	G
1		Retail	Wholesale	Margin			
2	High	5.50	2.75	2.75			
3	Mid	4.50	2.25	2.25			
4	Low	3.50	1.75	1.75			
5							
6							
7							

myRange.Offset(-1,-1).Resize
(myRange.Rows.Count+2,
myRange.Columns.Count+2).Select

Excel selects a rectangle one cell larger in all directions than the original range. The Offset property shifts the starting point up one cell and left one cell. The Resize property makes the new range two cells taller and two cells wider than it originally was. Pretty cool, huh?

 NOTE The combined functionality of the Offset and Resize properties is equivalent to that of the OFFSET function available on worksheets.

6 Press F8 to execute the *myRange.Cells(1).EntireRow.Select* statement.

myRange.Cells(1).EntireRow.Select

Excel selects all of row 4. The variable myRange returns a reference to the range C4:E5. The Cells property returns the first (that is, top left) cell of that range: C4. The EntireRow property extends that reference to all of row 4. Each property in the chain returns a reference to another object until you get to the final Select method, which does the real work.

7 Press F8 to execute the *myRange.EntireColumn.Select* statement.

myRange.EntireColumn.Select

Excel selects all of columns C:E. You can select the EntireRow or EntireColumn of more than a single cell. Excel simply extends whatever range you give it to the limits of the worksheet.

8 Press F8 to execute the *myRange.CurrentRegion.Select* statement.

myRange.CurrentRegion.Select

Excel selects the range A1:D4. The CurrentRegion property extends the selection to form a rectangle bounded by either blank cells or the edge of the worksheet. It always includes the top left cell of the starting range, but may not include the other cells.

The Offset and Resize properties, along with the EntireRow, EntireColumn, and CurrentRegion properties, provide you with flexible tools for calculating new Range objects based on an original starting range.

Exploring Formulas

Selecting ranges helps you understand how to manipulate Range objects, but to get real work done, you must format cells, put values and formulas into cells, retrieve values from cells, retrieve formulas from cells, and retrieve formatted values from cells. First, you should understand how references work in formulas in Excel, and then you can see how to create formulas in a macro.

Relative References

Most formulas perform arithmetic operations on values retrieved from other cells. Excel formulas use cell references to retrieve values from cells. Take, for example, the list of prices on the Prices worksheet, but without the margin formulas.

	A	B	C	D
1		Retail	Wholesale	
2	High	5.50	2.75	
3	Mid	4.50	2.25	
4	Low	3.50	1.75	
5				

Suppose you want to add a column to the list that calculates the *gross margin*— the difference between the price and the cost—for each item. You would put the label **Margin** in cell D1, and then enter the first formula into cell D2. The formula subtracts the first wholesale cost (cell C2) from the first retail price (cell B2). So you would enter **=B2-C2** into cell D2. (The formula has already been entered for you in the practice file.)

	A	B	C	D	E
1		Retail	Wholesale	Margin	
2	High	5.50	2.75	2.75	— =B2-C2
3	Mid	4.50	2.25		
4	Low	3.50	1.75		
5					

You make $2.75 on the margin. Now you need to copy the formula to the other rows. The formula you typed into cell D2 refers explicitly to cells C2 and B2. When you copy the formula to cell D3, you want the formula to automatically adjust to refer to C3 and B3. Fortunately, when you copy the formulas, Excel automatically adjusts the references because, by default, references are relative to the cell that contains the formula.

	A	B	C	D	E
1		Retail	Wholesale	Margin	
2	High	5.50	2.75	2.75	=B2-C2
3	Mid	4.50	2.25	2.25	=B3-C3
4	Low	3.50	1.75	1.75	=B4-C4
5					
6					

If the reference =C2 is found in cell D2, it really means "one cell to my left." When you copy the formula to cell D3, it still means "one cell to my left," but now that meaning is represented by the reference =C3.

Absolute References

Sometimes you do not want relative references. Look, for example, at the prices and quantities on the Revenue sheet. Now you will add formulas yourself.

	A	B	C	D	E	F	G
1		Price				Discount	
2	Quantity	$5	$10	$15		10%	
3	10						
4	20						
5	30						
6	40						
7	50						
8							

You want to add formulas to calculate the revenue for each combination. To calculate the first revenue value (cell B3), you need to multiply the first price (cell B2) by the first quantity (cell A3). When you type **=B2*A3** into cell B3, you get the correct answer, $50.

	A	B	C	D	E	F	G
1		Price				Discount	
2	Quantity	$5	$10	$15		10%	
3	10	$50					=B2*A3
4	20						
5	30						
6	40						
7	50						
8							

But if you copy that formula to cell B4, you get the ridiculous answer of $1000. That's because the cell references are relative. You are not really referring to cells B2 and A3; you are referring to "one cell above me" and "one cell to my left." When you put the formula into cell B4, "one cell above me" now refers to cell B3, not cell B2.

You want the prices to adjust from column to column, and you want the quantities to adjust from row to row, but you always want the price to be from row 2, and the quantity to be from column A. The solution is to put a dollar sign ($) in front of the *2* in the first price reference (C$2) and in front of the *A* in the first quantity reference ($A3). The formula that should go into cell B3 is **=B$2*$A3**. The dollar sign "anchors" that part of the formula, making it absolute. When you copy the formula to the rest of B3:D7, you get correct answers.

	A	B	C	D	E	F	G
1		Price				Discount	
2	Quantity	$5	$10	$15		10%	
3	10	$50	$100	$150			
4	20	$100	$200	$300			
5	30	$150	$300	$450			
6	40	$200	$400	$600			
7	50	$250	$500	$750			
8							

=B$2*$A3

=D$2*$A7

The relative portion of the formula changes with the row or column of the cell that contains the formula. The absolute portion remains fixed.

If you want to modify the formula so that it also takes into account the discount value from cell F2, you must make both the row and the column of the discount reference absolute. The correct formula would be **=B$2*$A3*(1-$F$2)**.

R1C1 Notation

The reference =B3, when found in cell D3, does not really say what it means. What it says is "cell B3," but what it means is "two cells to my left." Notice that you don't know what the reference really means until you know which cell contains the reference.

Excel has an alternative notation for references that really does say what it means. It is called R1C1 notation.

To turn on R1C1 notation, choose the Tools menu, click Options, and then click the General tab. Select the R1C1 Reference Style check box, and click OK. (To turn off R1C1 notation, clear the check box.)

Use this option to switch between R1C1 and A1 notation.

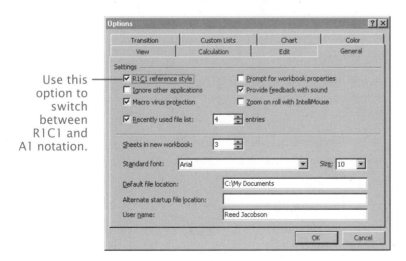

In R1C1 notation, you specify an absolute row with the letter *R* plus the row number and you specify an absolute column with *C* plus the column number. The reference =R1C1 refers to what is usually known as cell A1. The notation that Excel displays by default is called A1 notation.

To specify a relative reference on the same row or column as the cell with the formula, you simply use an *R* or a *C*. For example, the reference =RC3 means "the cell in column 3 of the same row as me," and the reference =R2C means "the cell in row 2 of the same column as me."

To specify a relative reference in a different row or column, you specify the amount of the difference, in square brackets, after the *R* or the *C*. For example, the reference =R[-1]C means "one cell above me," and the reference =R5C[2] means "two columns to my right in row 5."

The formula to calculate the gross margin was =B2-C2 (but only while entered into cell D2). In R1C1 notation, the same formula is =RC[-2]-RC[-1]. The formula to calculate the discounted price was =B$2*$A3*(1-$F$2). In R1C1 notation, the same formula is R2C*RC1*(1-R2C6).

NOTE When you use A1 notation, the formula changes depending on what you copy the formula into. When you use R1C1 notation, the formula is the same, regardless of which cell it goes into.

Put values and formulas into a range

References are not much use until you do something with them. Typically in a spreadsheet, you put values or formulas into cells. The WatchFormulas macro demonstrates several aspects of putting values and formulas into a range. As you step through the macro and watch it work, you can learn how to use Excel formulas. Here is the macro in its entirety:

```
Sub WatchFormulas()
    Worksheets.Add
    Range("B2:B6").Select
    Selection.Formula = 100
    ActiveCell.Formula = 0
    ActiveCell.Offset(-1, 0).Formula = 1
    Selection.Formula = "=B1*5"
    MsgBox ActiveCell.Value
    MsgBox ActiveCell.Formula
    MsgBox ActiveCell.FormulaR1C1
End Sub
```

1. Click on the WatchFormulas macro and press F8 three times to execute the *Worksheets.Add* statement, which creates a fresh worksheet.

2. Press F8 to execute the *Range("B2:B6").Select* statement. This selects a sample starting range of cells.

Range("B2:B6").Select

3. Press F8 to execute the *Selection.Formula = 100* statement.

Selection.Formula = 100

The number 100 fills all the cells of the selection. Formula is a property of the range. When you set the Formula property for the selection, you change the formula for all the cells in the selection.

The number 100 is not actually a formula; it is a constant. In fact, you could just as well have used *Selection.Value = 100* to assign the constant to the cell. But the Formula property is equivalent to whatever you see in the formula bar when the cell is selected. The formula bar can contain constants as well as formulas, and so can the Formula property. When you assign a value to a cell, the Formula property and the Value property have the same effect.

4. Press F8 to execute the *ActiveCell.Formula = 0* statement.

ActiveCell.Formula = 0

Only cell B2 changes to zero, because you changed the formula of only the active cell.

Suppose you want to enter a value in the first cell above the active cell, and you don't want to assume that the active cell is cell B2.

5   Press F8 to execute the *ActiveCell.Offset(-1, 0).Formula = 1* statement.

The cell A1 changes to 1.

This statement starts with the active cell, uses the Offset property to calculate a new cell one up from that starting cell, and then sets the Formula property for the resulting cell.

This formula is very similar to the one you created with the macro recorder in Lesson 2, except that it uses the Formula property instead of the FormulaR1C1 property.

6   Press F8 to execute the *Selection.Formula = "=B1*5"* statement.

Now the selected cells each contain a real formula, not a constant. When you entered the formula, the active cell was B2. From the point of view of cell B2, the reference B1 means "one cell above." As Excel enters the formula into all the cells of the range, it adjusts the reference as needed to always mean "one cell above."

You could have used the statement *Selection.Value = "=B1*5"* to assign a formula to the range. When you assign a value or a formula to the cell, the Value and Formula properties have the same effect.

7   Press F8 to execute the *MsgBox ActiveCell.Value* statement.

An alert box displaying the value 5 appears. The Value property retrieves the result of any formula in a cell. When you retrieve the contents of the cell, the Value property gives you the result of any formula in the cell.

8   Click OK, and press F8 to execute the *MsgBox ActiveCell.Formula* statement.

 ActiveCell.Formula

An alert box displaying the formula =B1*5 appears. The Formula property retrieves the actual formula in a cell. If the cell contains a constant, the Formula property retrieves it as text, even if it is a number. The Formula property always retrieves the formula using A1 notation references.

9   Click OK, and press F8 to execute the *MsgBox ActiveCell.FormulaR1C1* statement.

 ActiveCell.FormulaR1C1

An alert box displaying the formula =R[-1]C*5 appears. This is the same formula as =B1*5, except that it is displayed using R1C1 notation.

10   Click OK, and press F8 to complete the macro.

All cells have Formula, FormulaR1C1, and Value properties. The Value property and the Formula property are the same when you are writing to the cell. When you read the value of a cell, the Value property gives you the value, and the Formula property gives you the formula using A1 notation references. The FormulaR1C1 property is the same as the Formula property, except that it uses all references in R1C1 notation, whether assigning a formula to the cell, or reading the formula from a cell.

TIP   The Value property always gives you the unformatted value of the number in a cell. A cell also has a *Text* property, which returns the formatted value of the cell. The Text property is read-only, because it is a combination of the Value property and the NumberFormat property.

Use the address of a range to build formulas

Sometimes you need a macro to create formulas that contain references. For example, suppose you have a range of cells like the one on the Totals sheet, and you want to put a row of totals across the bottom. If the size of the range can change, you don't know until the macro runs which cells should be included in the SUM formula.

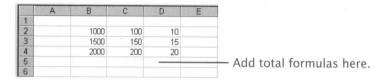

	A	B	C	D	E
1					
2		1000	100	10	
3		1500	150	15	
4		2000	200	20	
5					
6					

———— Add total formulas here.

Sometimes the range of cells will extend from B2:D4, in which case the formula in cell B5 should be =SUM(B2:B4). Another time, the range of cells will extend from B2:D10, in which case the formula should be =SUM(B2:B10), this time in cell B11. Interactively, you would use the AutoSum button to create the formulas, but if you ever try clicking the AutoSum button while you are recording a macro, you will see that the macro the AutoSum button creates is not usually very useful. (That was a carefully restrained understatement.)

What you need to do is create a macro that behaves like a simplified version of the AutoSum button. The MakeTotals macro shows you how to do that. Some of the statements in the macro are not necessary, but are there to help you understand how the macro works. We will then step through the macro, looking at each statement. Here is the macro in its entirety.

```
Sub MakeTotals()
    Dim myRange as Range
    Dim myTotal as Range
    Set myRange = ActiveCell.CurrentRegion
    Set myTotal = myRange.Offset(myRange.Rows.Count).Rows(1)
    myTotal.Cells(1) = myRange.Columns(1).Address
    myTotal.Cells(1) = myRange.Columns(1).Address(False,False)
    myTotal.Formula = "=SUM(" & myRange.Columns(1).Address(False,False) & ")"
End Sub
```

1   In Excel, select the Totals sheet, and select cell B2.

2   In Visual Basic, click on the MakeTotals macro and press F8 three times to execute the *Set myRange = ActiveCell.CurrentRegion* statement.

    This assigns the block of cells surrounding the active cell to the myRange variable.

3   Press F8 to execute the *Set myTotal = myRange.Offset(myRange.Rows.Count).Rows(1)* statement.

    This creates a new reference shifted down however many rows are in the original range, but only one row tall, and then assigns that reference to the myTotal variable. (You could use Resize(1) instead of Rows(1) and get the same effect.) This is the range where the totals will go.

4 Press F8 to execute the *myTotal.Cells(1) = myRange.Columns(1).Address* statement.

	A	B	C	D	E
1					
2		1000	100	10	
3		1500	150	15	
4		2000	200	20	
5		$B$2:$B$4			
6					

myRange.Columns(1).Address

This is one of the statements that doesn't need to be in the final macro. It retrieves the address of the first column of the original rectangle, and puts that address into the first cell of the totals row. If you put this address inside a SUM function, the total would be correct for the first cell, but the dollar signs mean that the reference is absolute. You need to make the reference relative so that it will adjust as you put it into all the columns of the totals row.

5 Press F8 to execute the *myTotal.Cells(1) = myRange.Columns(1).Address(False,False)* statement.

	A	B	C	D	E
1					
2		1000	100	10	
3		1500	150	15	
4		2000	200	20	
5		B2:B4			
6					

myRange.Columns(1).Address(False, False)

This is another statement that doesn't need to be in the final macro. The Address property has optional arguments that control the way the address is returned. The first two arguments determine whether the row and column parts of the reference are absolute. The default is that both parts are absolute. This statement tells the Address property to make both parts relative. You can now put this reference into the SUM function and fill it across the totals row.

6 Press F8 to execute the *myTotal.Formula = "=SUM(" & myRange.Columns(1).Address(False,False) & ")"* statement.

	A	B	C	D	E
1					
2		1000	100	10	
3		1500	150	15	
4		2000	200	20	
5		4500	450	45	
6					

"=SUM(" & myRange.Columns(1).
Address(False,False) & ")"

=SUM(B2:B4)

This statement constructs the final formula by joining the first part of the SUM function with the relative reference returned by the Address property, and then adds the closing parenthesis. If the current region containing the active cell were B2:E5, the resulting formula would be =SUM(B2:B5).

The totals appear in the row at the bottom, appropriately different for each column.

7 Press F8 to finish the macro, and then press F5 to run it again, adding a second row of totals.

This is a little silly, but it shows how the macro automatically adjusts as new rows are added to the data. The CurrentRegion property includes any new rows. The Address property calculates the appropriate reference for the SUM function.

8 Save the Lesson4 workbook if you have made any changes to the macros or added any notes.

Ranges are a powerful tool in Excel. You can select ranges, assign them to variables, add formulas to them, name them, and retrieve their addresses. By manipulating ranges you can build powerful, dynamic worksheet models.

Lesson Summary

To	Do this
Simplify a Select...Selection pair in a recorded macro	Delete from *Select* through *Selection*, leaving only a single period.
Select the range B2:C5 on the active worksheet	Use the statement *Range("B2:C5").Select.*
Select the fifth cell in the third row of the active worksheet	Use the statement *Cells(3,5).Select.*
Count the columns in the current selection	Use the expression *Selection.Columns.Count.*
Select a new range one row down from the selection	Use the statement *Selection.Offset(1,0).Select.*
Fill the cells in the selection with the value 100	Use the statement *Selection.Formula = 100.*
Enter into the active cell a formula that calculates the value of the cell above	Use the statement *ActiveCell.FormulaR1C1="=R[-1]C".*
Retrieve a value from the active cell	Use the expression *ActiveCell.Value.*

To	Do this
Retrieve a formula from the active cell	Use the expression *ActiveCell.Formula* or the expression *ActiveCell.FormulaR1C1*.
Retrieve the address of a range	Use the Address property, with arguments to control whether the address is relative or absolute.

For online information about	Ask the Assistant for help using the words
Referencing ranges	"References," then select "How to reference cells and ranges." (A highly recommended list of topics.)
The Selection property	"Selection"
The Range property	"Range Property"
The Address property	"Address"

Preview of the Next Lesson

Excel is well-known for its exceptional graphic output. In the next lesson you will explore graphic objects. Graphic objects include not only circles and rectangles on the worksheet, but also text boxes and charts. Graphics can give your applications tremendous impact, and you can write macros that can simplify your work with them.

Explore Graphical Objects

Estimated time

35 min.

In this lesson you will learn how to:

- Manipulate drawing objects on a worksheet.
- Manipulate chart objects.
- Use the macro recorder as a reference tool.

On a warm summer day, nothing is grander than to lie on your back in a grassy field and watch clouds float across the sky. Trees and mountains and buildings just sit there; they are attached firmly to the ground. But clouds move. Clouds change shape. They change color. Clouds can come in layers, too, with closer clouds drifting in front of the clouds in back.

On a worksheet, ranges with their formulas and formats are attached firmly to the worksheet just as buildings are attached to the ground. Cell A1 will always be in the top left corner of the worksheet. Drawing objects, however, are like clouds. They float freely above the worksheet. They can disappear and reappear. They can change color and shape.

Drawing objects—including not only shapes such as rectangles, ovals, and lines, but also charts, and even list box controls and spinner controls—add interest, information, and functionality to a worksheet. In this lesson, you will learn how to work with drawing objects from within a Visual Basic macro, and along the way you will find out more about how to use Microsoft Excel 97's reference tools to learn more about objects, properties, and methods.

Start the lesson

> Start Excel. Change to the folder containing the practice files for this book. Open the Graphics workbook, and save it as **Lesson5**.

Exploring Graphical Objects

The Object Browser and the Help system are like a spelling dictionary. In the same way that you practically have to know how to spell a word before you can find it in the dictionary, you practically have to know the property or method before you can find it in the Object Browser or in Help. In this regard one of the most useful reference tools for learning how to use Excel objects may not seem to be a reference tool at all: the macro recorder.

Some people think of the macro recorder as a tool for beginners—and it is. In Part 1 of this book, you used the macro recorder to build finished macros without having to understand very much about how Excel objects really work. But the macro recorder is also a powerful reference tool for advanced developers. In this lesson you will see how you can use the macro recorder as a reference tool for learning how to work with Excel objects.

Record a macro to create a rectangle

Graphical objects—such as rectangles, ovals, text boxes, and charts—can make your worksheets appealing and understandable. One of the exciting new features in Microsoft Office 97 is the greatly expanded collection of graphical objects. The macro recorder is a very good tool for learning how to work with these graphical objects. Record creating a rectangle, and see how much you can learn from a simple recorded macro.

Drawing button

1 Select the Shapes worksheet in the Lesson 5 workbook, and click the Drawing button on the Standard toolbar to display the Drawing toolbar.

> The Drawing Toolbar

Record Macro button

2 Click the Record Macro button on the Visual Basic toolbar, replace the default macro name with **MakeRectangle**, and click OK.

Rectangle button

3 Click the Rectangle button on the Drawing toolbar, and then click the top left corner of cell B2 and drag to the bottom right corner of cell B3.

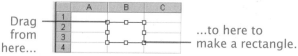

Drag from here... ...to here to make a rectangle.

*Fill Color
button*

4 Click the arrow next to the Fill Color button on the Drawing toolbar, and then click the third box down in the first column.

Click this box
to change the
interior of
the rectangle
to red.

No Fill
More Fill Colors...
Fill Effects...

The rectangle changes to red.

*Stop Recording
button*

5 Click the Stop Recording button and edit the macro. Your macro's line continuation may occur in a different place from the code sample below.

```
Sub MakeRectangle()
    ActiveSheet.Shapes.AddShape(msoShapeRectangle, _
        48, 13, 48, 25.5).Select
    Selection.ShapeRange.Fill.ForeColor.SchemeColor = 10
    Selection.ShapeRange.Fill.Visible = msoTrue
    Selection.ShapeRange.Fill.Solid
End Sub
```

This macro is very short, but it does a lot. Look at the second statement:

```
ActiveSheet.Shapes.AddShape(msoShapeRectangle, _
    48, 13, 48, 25.5).Select
```

The statement starts by pointing at the active sheet and ends by selecting something. *Shapes* is a plural noun, so it might be a collection. To add a new item to most collections, you use the Add method, but *Shapes* is followed by the word *AddShape*. *AddShape* is followed by a list of arguments in parentheses. (The numbers in your list may differ somewhat.) The first argument seems to tell what kind of shape you created, and the numbers seem to have something to do with the location and size of the rectangle, since nothing else in the macro sets the location.

These recorded statements give you several clues about how to create a new rectangle. Now you can build a macro on your own, using information from the recorder, coupled with the Auto Lists that Visual Basic displays.

Write a macro to create a rectangle

1 Under the recorded macro, type **Sub MakeNewRectangle** and press ENTER. Visual Basic automatically adds the closing parentheses and the End Sub statement.

In order for Visual Basic to display an Auto List of methods and properties for an object, it must know for sure which object's list to use. The properties ActiveSheet and Selection are too general: either one can refer to any of several different types of objects. The best way to let Visual Basic know what kind of object you are using is to assign the object to a variable and declare its type.

2 Type the following three statements to declare the variables and assign the active sheet to a variable.

```
Dim mySheet As Worksheet
Dim myShape As Shape
Set mySheet = ActiveSheet
```

All drawing objects belong to the Shape class. By declaring the variables, you give Visual Basic the information it needs to help you as you enter statements.

3 Type **Set myShape = mySheet.Shapes.** (including the period).

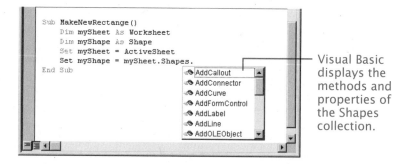

Visual Basic displays the methods and properties of the Shapes collection.

As soon as you type the period, Visual Basic shows the list of methods and properties for the Shapes collection. Apparently, you can add a lot more than just a Shape. You can add Callouts and Curves and Connectors and others. That's why the Shapes collection doesn't just use a simple Add method. You know from the recorded macro that you want to use the AddShape method to add a rectangle.

4 Type (or select) **AddShape(** and then press the DOWN ARROW key.

You can create over 100 different types of shapes.

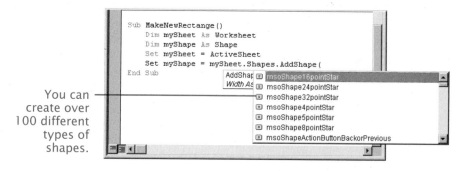

As soon as you type the opening parenthesis, Visual Basic shows you the list of possible values for the first argument. There are well over 100 different types of shapes you can add. You know from the recorded macro that you want the msoShapeRectangle option. (You can experiment with others later.)

5 Type (or select) **msoShapeRectangle,**

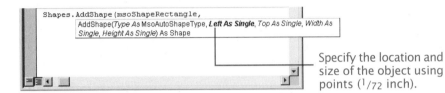

Specify the location and size of the object using points ($1/72$ inch).

A point is a unit of measurement traditionally used to lay out text for publishing.

When you type the comma, you see that the remaining arguments are Left, Top, Width, and Height. You specify each of these values in *points*. A point is 1/72 inch.

6 For the remaining arguments, type **72** for Left, **36** for Top, **72** for Width, and **36** for Height. Then type a closing parenthesis and press ENTER.

The statement in the recorded macro ended with the Select method. When you assign an object to a variable, you do not put a Select method at the end of the statement.

7 Type **myShape.Fill.ForeColor.SchemeColor = 10** and press ENTER.

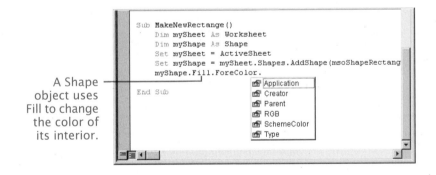

A Shape object uses Fill to change the color of its interior.

Each time you type a period, Visual Basic helps with a list of possible methods and properties. If you had not assigned the rectangle to a variable—if instead you had used Select and Selection the way the recorded macro does—Visual Basic would not be able to display the Auto Lists.

119

NOTE A shape object uses many sub-objects to group formatting options. The Fill property returns a FillFormat object. (The object class name is different from the property name because for chart objects, the Fill property returns a ChartFillFormat object.) A FillFormat object controls the formatting of the interior of the object. The ForeColor property returns a ColorFormat object. (The object class name is different from the property name because a ColorFormat object can be returned by either the ForeColor property or the BackColor property.) Click any property name and press F1 to see the Help topic for the property and, if applicable, its related object.

8 Press F8 repeatedly to step through the macro.

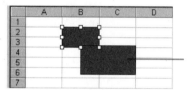

You create a new rectangle without selecting it.

Depending on your screen size and resolution, a new rectangle appears on the worksheet, about one half inch from the top and 1 inch from the left. The rectangle is about one-half inch high and 1 inch wide. The rectangle never has selection handles around its border, because you never select it. You just assign a reference to a variable.

In this example, you were able to create a rectangle by following the pattern given by the recorder, but you also saw how Visual Basic's Auto Lists can help you create variations of the recorded macro.

Modify an existing shape

Sometimes you will want to modify one or more shapes that already exist on the worksheet. The macro recorder can help you see how to select a shape, and then you can use what you know about objects to convert the selection into an object variable.

1 Select the Shapes sheet in the Lesson 5 workbook. Show the Drawing toolbar, and start recording a macro named **SelectShapes**.

2 Click the first square box you created earlier, then hold down the SHIFT key and click the Sun object off to the right, and then turn off the recorder.

Hold down the SHIFT key to select multiple objects.

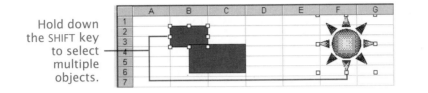

3 Edit the macro. It should look something like this:

The names in quotation marks may be different in your macro, depending on how many rectangles you created.

```
Sub SelectShapes()
    ActiveSheet.Shapes("Rectangle 2").Select
    ActiveSheet.Shapes.Range(Array("Rectangle 2", _
        "Shape3")).Select
End Sub
```

The Shapes property returns a collection of all the Shape objects on a worksheet. You must specify the sheet that contains the shapes. To select a single shape, you simply index into the Shapes collection, using the name or the number of the item, the same as selecting an item from any other collection. This returns a Shape (singular) object, which you can select or assign to a variable.

When you need to refer to more than one shape object, Excel has a different collection, called the ShapeRange collection. A ShapeRange is just like a Shape, except that a ShapeRange can include more than one object. To create a ShapeRange object from a Shapes collection, you use the Range property along with Visual Basic's Array function. The Array function allows you to group a list of items together.

4 At the top of the macro, insert these two declaration statements:

```
Dim myShape as Shape
Dim myShapeRange as ShapeRange
```

5 Convert the first selection to assign the object to the myShape variable, rather than select it. Do not change the name inside the quotation marks. The resulting statement should look something like this:

```
Set myShape = ActiveSheet.Shapes("Rectangle 2")
```

6 Insert a second statement to change the RGB value of the foreground color of the fill of the shape to yellow. The final statement should look like this:

```
MyShape.Fill.ForeColor.RGB = vbYellow
```

121

7 Convert the second selection to assign the ShapeRange object to the myShape variable, rather than select it. The resulting statement should look like this, with the possible exception of the names inside quotation marks:

```
Set myShapeRange = ActiveSheet.Shapes.Range(Array("Rectangle 2",
    "Shape 3"))
```

8 Insert another statement to change the RGB value of the foreground color of the fill of the shape range to blue. The final statement should look like this:

```
MyShapeRange.Fill.ForeColor.RGB = vbBlue
```

9 Step through the macro, watching the objects change color.

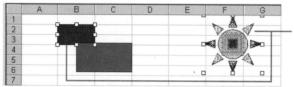

A ShapeRange object lets you change the color of multiple shapes at one time.

Shapes allow you to create extremely powerful graphical effects. But keeping the different types of objects straight can be a little bit confusing at first.

Shapes collection   Use the Shapes collection object for selecting shapes and for adding new shapes. You can't use the Shapes object to do any formatting.

Shape object   Use the Shape object for formatting a single shape.

ShapeRange collection   Use the ShapeRange collection for formatting multiple objects at the same time.

Rename shapes

When you create a new shape on the worksheet, Excel gives it a default name, usually something like Rectangle 2 or Oval 5. When you record a macro that refers to the shape, the recorder puts that same name into the macro. You will make your macros easier to read and less likely to have errors if you change the name of shapes to something meaningful.

1   On the Excel worksheet, click the first rectangle you created. It has a name like Rectangle 2. You can see the name in the Name Box to the left of the formula bar.

This box shows the name of...  ...the selected object.

2   Click in the Name Box and type **Box** as a new name for the rectangle. Press ENTER or else Excel will not recognize that you changed the name.

Type the new name here and press ENTER.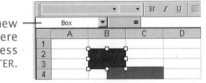

3   Click the second, larger rectangle you created and give it the name **BigBox**. Then give the sun shape the name **Sun**. Be sure to press ENTER after typing each name in the Name Box.

4   In the SelectShapes macro, change *Rectangle 2* to **Box** (both times it appears) and *Shape 3* to **Sun**.

5   Change the colors in the macro from *vbYellow* to **vbRed** and from *vbBlue* to **vbMagenta**, then run the macro to test it. Here's what the final macro should look like:

```
Sub SelectShapes()
    Dim myShape as Shape
    Dim myShapeRange as ShapeRange
    Set myShape = ActiveSheet.Shapes("Box")
    MyShape.Fill.ForeColor.RGB = vbRed
    Set myShapeRange = ActiveSheet.Shapes.Range(Array("Box", _
        "Sun"))
    MyShapeRange.Fill.ForeColor.RGB = vbMagenta
End Sub
```

In the same way that you can give worksheets meaningful names, rather than keeping the default Sheet1, Sheet2, and so forth, you can give meaningful names to shapes on the worksheet, even though these names are less noticeable. Your macros will thank you for it.

Excel 97 can now create hundreds of different types of shapes. All these shapes work in much the same way that rectangles do. Embedded charts are also shapes in Excel. You add, manipulate, and delete Chart objects in the much the same way you do rectangles. Chart objects, of course, have additional properties that are unique to charts; the macro recorder is an effective tool for finding out what they are.

Shapes and DrawingObjects

Shapes are an entirely new feature for Excel. Shapes are shared by all Microsoft Office applications and replace the earlier graphical objects that Excel used. Earlier graphical objects belonged to an object class called *DrawingObjects*, and you can still see some relics of DrawingObjects in Excel today.

For example, Shape objects format the interior of an object using the Fill property. DrawingObjects referred to the interior of an object using the Interior property. Shapes refer to colors that represent the red, green, and blue components of the color using the RGB property. DrawingObjects referred to the same type of color using the Color property. Shapes refer to colors from a palette using the SchemeColor property, while DrawingObjects used the ColorIndex property. As you may recognize, the Range object still uses all the formatting properties that were used by the old DrawingObjects: Interior, Color, and ColorIndex.

In order to maintain backward compatibility, Excel did not remove the old DrawingObjects. They are still there, but they are hidden. Occasionally, you may see some relics of these old graphical objects.

Exploring Chart Objects

Chart objects have hundreds of properties and methods. Many of the attributes of a chart are themselves separate objects. Learning how to create and manipulate charts by reading a reference manual is very difficult because charts have so many objects and properties. But creating and manipulating a chart is easy to record, and even though you may see many new methods, properties, and objects, the new objects work according to the same principles as do other objects in Excel.

Record a macro that creates a chart

1 Activate the ChartData sheet in the Lesson 5 workbook, and select cell A1.

	A	B	C	D
1	Price	Units	Net	
2	High	6,443	22,600	
3	Mid	12,599	22,800	
4	Low	8,670	19,401	
5				

Record Macro button

2 Click the Record Macro button on the Visual Basic toolbar, type **MakeChart** as the name for the macro, and click OK.

Chart Wizard button

3 Click the ChartWizard button on the Standard toolbar, and then click the Finish button to create the default chart.

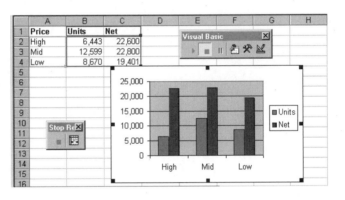

Stop Recording button

4 Click the Stop Recording button, delete the chart, and then edit the recorded macro. Here's what it looks like:

```
Sub MakeChart()
    Charts.Add
    ActiveChart.ChartType = xlColumnClustered
    ActiveChart.SetSourceData _
        Source:=Sheets("ChartData").Range("A1:C4")
    ActiveChart.Location Where:=xlLocationAsObject, _
        Name:="ChartData"
End Sub
```

The macro creates an embedded chart in four steps. First, it uses the Add method to create a new, blank chart (as a stand-alone sheet). Second, it uses the ChartType property to set the type of the chart. Third, it uses the SetSourceData method to assign a data range to the chart. And finally, it uses the Location method to move the chart onto the worksheet.

Modify the macro that creates a chart

Once you have recorded the macro to create a chart, you can make modifications to it to instantly create exactly the type of chart you want.

1   Click the word *xlColumnClustered* in the macro. This is one of an enumerated list of values that can be assigned to the ChartType property.

2   Choose the Edit menu and the List Constants command.

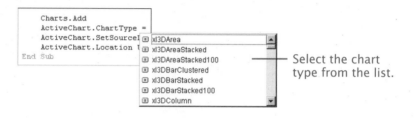

Select the chart type from the list.

Excel displays the entire list of possible chart types.

  TIP   Visual Basic is able to display the list of possible values because it knows that ActiveChart can return only a chart variable. If you try to display a list of values, and nothing happens, it might be because the statement uses ActiveSheet or Selection as the object, and Visual Basic is not sure what kind of object will be currently selected. In that case, try declaring an object variable and assigning the object to the variable. Then Visual Basic will be able to display the helpful lists.

3   Select xlConeBarStacked from the list, and double-click it to insert it into the code. Here's what the revised macro looks like:

```
Sub MakeChart()
    Charts.Add
    ActiveChart.ChartType = xlConeBarStacked
    ActiveChart.SetSourceData _
        Source:=Sheets("ChartData").Range("A1:C4")
    ActiveChart.Location Where:=xlLocationAsObject, _
        Name:="ChartData"
End Sub
```

4 Press F8 repeatedly to step through the modified macro. Watch how Excel creates the chart as a separate sheet first, then adds the data, and finally moves it onto the worksheet.

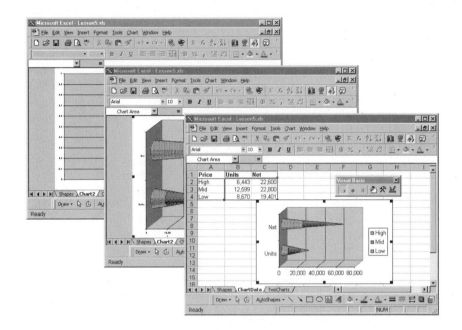

An Excel chart can exist in either of two locations. It can exist as a separate sheet in the workbook, or it can be embedded in a worksheet. Regardless of where a chart is located, it behaves the same way. There are some differences, however, in how you refer to each type of chart.

Refer to an existing embedded chart

When you create a new chart, Excel automatically selects the chart, so you can use ActiveChart to refer to it. If a chart already exists, you have to refer to it differently. A chart that is on a separate sheet is easy to refer to: simply index into the Charts collection. Referring to a chart that is embedded on a worksheet, however, can be confusing. Fortunately for you, this section will make it all clear.

1 In Visual Basic, at the bottom of the open module, type **Sub SelectChart** and press ENTER. Add these three declaration statements to the top of the macro:

```
Dim myShape As Shape
Dim myObject As ChartObject
Dim myChart As Chart
```

You will assign objects to these variables to see how Excel handles charts embedded on a worksheet.

2   Press F8 twice to step down to the End Sub statement in the new macro. From the View menu, click the Immediate Window command to display the Immediate window.

3   In the Immediate window, type **Set myShape = ActiveSheet.Shapes(1)** to assign a reference to the chart's container to the myShape variable.

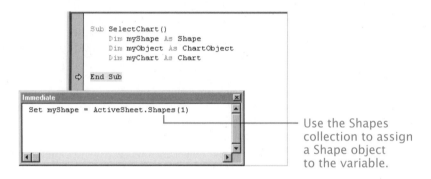

```
Sub SelectChart()
    Dim myShape As Shape
    Dim myObject As ChartObject
    Dim myChart As Chart

⇨  End Sub
```

```
Immediate
Set myShape = ActiveSheet.Shapes(1)
```

Use the Shapes collection to assign a Shape object to the variable.

4   In the Immediate window, type **Set myObject = ActiveSheet.ChartObjects(1)** to assign a reference to the chart's container to the myObject variable.

Both myShape and myObject refer to the same actual chart container object, but myShape refers to the chart as a Shape object, and myObject refers to the chart as a ChartObject object.

5   In the Immediate window, type **?myObject.Name** and press ENTER. The name of the chart appears.

 NOTE   In the Immediate window, if you type a question mark in front of an expression that returns a value, and then press ENTER, you will see the value displayed immediately.

Use a question mark in the Immediate window to show a value.

```
Immediate
Set myShape = ActiveSheet.Shapes(1)
Set myObject = ActiveSheet.ChartObjects(1)
?myObject.Name
Chart 2
```

6 In the Immediate window, type **?myShape.Name** and press ENTER. The same name appears again. Both myObject and myShape refer to the same object.

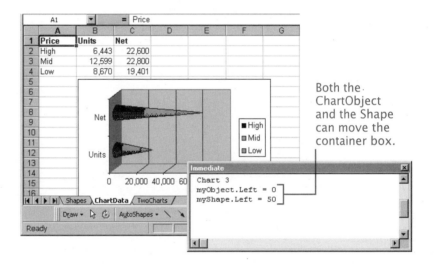

Both the ChartObject object and the Shape object refer to the same chart container.

7 In the Immediate window, type **myObject.Left = 0** and press ENTER, and then type **myShape.Left = 50** and press ENTER. In each case, the chart shifts. You can use either container object to move and resize the chart.

Both the ChartObject and the Shape can move the container box.

8 In the Immediate window, type **myObject.Select** and press ENTER, and then type **myShape.Select** and press ENTER. In both cases, the statement works and you see white boxes at the corner of the chart. These statements select the container object, and not the chart inside.

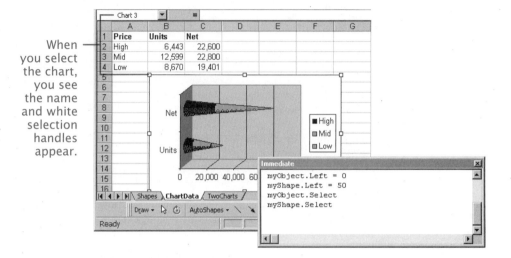

When you select the chart, you see the name and white selection handles appear.

9 In the Immediate window, type **myObject.Activate** and press ENTER. Then type **myShape.Activate** and press ENTER. (Click OK to close the error message.)

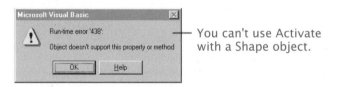

You can't use Activate with a Shape object.

When you try to activate the ChartObject, you see the boxes at the corners of the chart turn black, indicating that you are now inside the chart. When you try to activate the Shape object, you get an error, because the Shape object does not have an Activate method.

NOTE The ChartObjects collection is left over from the old-style Excel drawing objects. It could not be hidden like the other old graphical object collections because the "new" Shape object does not have an Activate method that can work with charts.

10 In the Immediate window, type **Set myChart = myObject.Chart** and press ENTER. In this statement, the Chart property assigns to the variable myChart a reference to the chart that is contained in the ChartObject object. In the same way that a Shape object does not have an Activate method, it does not have a Chart property either.

11   In the Immediate window, type **myChart.ChartArea.Interior.Color = vbRed** and press ENTER.

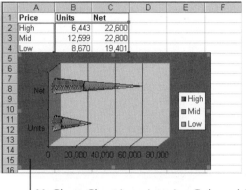

MyChart.ChartArea.Interior.Color=vbRed

The interior of the chart changes to red. Once you have a reference to the chart, you can manipulate the objects inside it.

12   Close the Immediate window, and press F8 to finish the macro.

A chart that is embedded in a worksheet consists of two parts: the container box (a ChartObject object) and the chart inside (a Chart object). You can refer to the container box using either the Shapes collection (which returns a Shape object) or the ChartObjects collection (which returns a ChartObject object), but to get to the chart inside, you must use the ChartObjects collection, not the Shapes collection. For example, you can move and resize the container using either the Shapes collection or the ChartObjects collection, but to change the color of the chart area, you must get to the chart inside using the ChartObjects collection.

Record a macro that modifies chart attributes

Now that you understand how Excel refers to the chart container and the chart inside, you can record a macro that changes a chart and learn what methods and properties you use to control a chart.

1   On the ChartData worksheet, select cell A1. Start recording a macro named **ChangeChart**.

2   Click the chart you created in the section "Modify the macro that creates a chart." This activates the chart.

131

3   Double-click one of the numbers along the bottom of the chart. Doing this selects the value axis and displays the Format Axis dialog box. Select the Scale tab.

Format Axis dialog box — Scale tab showing:

- Patterns, Scale, Font, Number, Alignment tabs
- Value (Z) axis scale
- Auto
  - ☑ Minimum: -1000
  - ☐ Maximum: 50000 — Type a value here to change the maximum value for the axis.
  - ☑ Major unit: 2000
  - ☑ Minor unit: 400
  - ☑ Floor (XY plane)
  - Crosses at: 0
  - ☐ Logarithmic scale
  - ☐ Values in reverse order
  - ☐ Floor (XY plane) crosses at minimum value
- OK   Cancel

4   Change the Maximum value to **50,000**. (Entering a value clears the Auto check box.) Click OK.

5   Turn off the recorder and edit the macro. It looks similar to this:

The chart name inside quotation marks will probably be different in your macro.

```
Sub ChangeChart()
    ActiveSheet.ChartObjects("Chart 15").Activate
    ActiveChart.ChartArea.Select
    ActiveChart.Axes(xlValue).Select
    With ActiveChart.Axes(xlValue)
        .MinimumScaleIsAuto = True
        .MaximumScale = 50000
        .MinorUnitIsAuto = True
        .MajorUnitIsAuto = True
        .Crosses = xlAutomatic
        .ReversePlotOrder = False
        .ScaleType = xlLinear
    End With
End Sub
```

The macro first activates the chart, using the ChartObjects collection. (If you want to refer to the chart inside the embedded container without activating it, you must use the Chart property of the ChartObject object.) The macro then selects the ChartArea. This statement is superfluous because the statement after it selects the Value Axis. The macro then changes several properties of the Value Axis, even though you only changed one in the dialog box.

You could simplify this entire macro to a single statement:

```
ActiveSheet.ChartObjects("Chart 15").Chart.Axes(xlValue) _
    .MaximumScale = 50000
```

You can be grateful, however, that the recorder included everything it did, because you can learn the names of a lot of properties very quickly. In the next section, we will put some of those properties to work in a very useful macro.

Write a macro that modifies a chart

On the TwoCharts sheet are two charts that show total orders for two different regions.

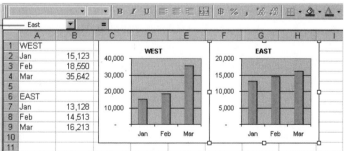

East seems to be doing as well as West. But it's not.

Based on a quick glance at the charts, you might conclude that the performance of the two regions was roughly equal. But that would be wrong. The East region is substantially lower than the West, but Excel automatically scales the axes to fit the data. Let's create a macro that will change the value axis on the East chart to match the axis on the West chart.

Select Objects button

1 Name the charts so that you can refer to them by descriptive names: on the Drawing toolbar, click the Select Objects button, click the West chart, and then enter **West** in the Name Box. Follow the same steps to give the name **East** to the East chart. Then turn off the Select Objects button.

Select a chart and type a new name here.

133

2 In Visual Basic, at the bottom of the module, type **Sub SynchronizeCharts** and press ENTER. Then enter the following two variable declarations:

```
Dim myWest As Chart
Dim myEast As Chart
```

You will store a reference to a chart in each of these variables.

3 Next, enter the following two statements to assign the charts to the variables:

```
Set myWest = ActiveSheet.ChartObjects("West").Chart
Set myEast = ActiveSheet.ChartObjects("East").Chart
```

You must include the Chart property to move from the container to the chart inside. If you had not renamed the charts, you would have to either use the default Chart 1 and Chart 2, or the numbers 1 and 2 (and determine which was which by trial and error). Giving the charts explicit, meaningful names makes your code easier to read and less likely to contain errors.

4 Add the following statement to make sure that the value axis on the West chart is automatic:

```
myWest.Axes(xlValue).MaximumScaleIsAuto = True
```

The expression Axes(xlValue) was in the recorded macro. That's how you know how to refer to the value axis. The MaximumScaleIsAuto property did not appear in the recorded macro, but the MinimumScaleIsAuto property did, and you can guess the rest.

5 Add the following statement to make the axes have the same maximum scale:

```
myEast.Axes(xlValue).MaximumScale = _
    myWest.Axes(xlValue).MaximumScale
```

Even though the maximum scale of the West chart is set to automatic, you can still read the current value from it.

6 Press F8 repeatedly to step through the macro.

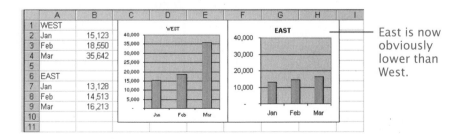

East is now obviously lower than West.

The difference between the two regions is much more obvious now.

7   On the worksheet, change the March value for the West region to **15,000**. Then run the SynchronizeCharts macro again.

You could add additional synchronization tasks to this macro as well. For example, you could make the minimum value for each axis the same. You could make it so that if you interactively change the color of the background on the West chart, running the macro would make the East chart the same color. For each enhancement, you simply record a macro to learn what you need to change, and then add it to your macro.

Formatting Charts

Charts are an interesting hybrid of Excel's older DrawingObjects and Microsoft Office's new Shapes. Charts have been around since the first version of Excel, so all of the features that can be controlled with old properties, such as Interior, still use those properties. For example, to set the color of the ChartArea of a chart assigned to the myChart variable to red, you could use the statement *myChart.Interior.Color = vbRed*.

Charts also, however, take advantage of the fancy new formatting that is a part of a Shape object. To get to those new features, you must use the Fill property. For example, to create a gradient background for the ChartArea, you could use the statement *myChart.Fill.TwoColorGradient msoGradientHorizontal, 1*.

The formatting properties that can be set using the Interior property cannot be set using the Fill property. For example, you can set the fill color of a shape using the statement *myShape.Fill.ForeColor.RGB = vbRed*, but with a chart, the RGB property is read-only. You can find out the color using the new property, but you have to change it using the old one. Because the properties and methods of the fill for a chart are somewhat different from those of a shape, the Fill property for a chart object returns a ChartFillFormat object, whereas the Fill property for a shape returns a FillFormat object.

Lesson Summary

To	Do this
Create an approximately 1-inch rectangle in the top left corner of the active sheet	Use the statement *ActiveSheet.Shapes .AddShape(msoShapeRectangle, 0,0,72,72).Select*.
Change the color of the selected shape to red	Use the statement *Selection.ShapeRange.Fill.ForeColor.RGB = vbRed*.
Select a shape named *Square*	Use the statement *ActiveSheet.Shapes("Square").Select*.
Select two shapes named *Square* and *Sun*	Use the statement *ActiveSheet.Shapes.Range (Array("Square","Sun")).Select*.
Create a chart	Use the statement *Charts.Add*.
Assign a data range to a chart	Use the chart's SetSourceData method.
Specify a chart's location	Use the chart's Location method.
Assign an embedded chart named *West* to a variable myChart	Use the statement *Set myChart = ActiveSheet.ChartObjects("West").Chart*.
Rename a shape or a chart	Click the Select Objects button on the Drawing toolbar (to select a chart), and then click the object and enter a new name in the Name Box.

For online information about	Ask the Assistant for help using the words
Using shapes	"Working with Shapes"
Using charts	"Charts"
Visual Basic colors	"Colors" (or click a sample color constant, such as vbRed, and press F1)

Preview of the Next Lesson

Charts and other graphical shapes can add clarity and impact to information that you have to present. Excel has another powerful tool for analyzing information: the PivotTable. In the next lesson, you will learn how to manipulate PivotTables using Visual Basic.

Explore
PivotTable Objects

Estimated time
30 min.

In this lesson you will learn how to:

- Build a PivotTable.
- Manipulate fields and items in a PivotTable.

Since the turn of the century, one of the mainstays of medical technology has been x-ray photography. One of the problems with an x-ray photograph, however, is that it shows you only the angle at which it was taken. If the bones or organs are badly aligned, the photographs may not properly reveal the problem. In 1974, the British company EMI Ltd. made use of the money they had made selling Beatles records to develop computerized axial tomography (CAT) scan technology, which does not suffer from the blind spots of conventional x-rays.

A database report is like an x-ray photograph. It is an image, but it is a static image. If the rows and columns are not defined properly, the person reviewing the report may miss important relationships. A PivotTable, in contrast, is like a CAT scan. It is a multidimensional view of the data that enables you to find the most meaningful perspective.

Start the lesson

➤ In Microsoft Excel, open a new, empty workbook, and save the workbook with the name **Lesson6** in the folder containing the practice files for this book.

Building PivotTables

In Excel, each object class has its own list of methods and properties that you can use to manipulate objects belonging to that class. Many objects belong to collections, or link to other objects. The objects that support PivotTables are an elegant example of how objects work.

Create a default PivotTable

1   In the Lesson6 workbook, start recording a macro named **MakePivot**, and then immediately click the Stop Recording button and edit the macro.

2   Insert the following variable declaration statements at the beginning of the macro:

```
Dim myPivot As PivotTable
Dim myField As PivotField
Dim myItem As PivotItem
Dim myRange As Range
```

Assigning objects to these variables will enable Visual Basic to display Auto Lists to help you see methods and properties.

3   Press F8 twice to step down to the End Sub statement. From the View menu, click the Immediate Window command. Move and size the Immediate window so that you can see the Excel window in the background.

If the Orders.dbf file does not open, click the Open toolbar button, change to the folder containing the practice files for this book, and then click Cancel.

4   In the Immediate window, type **Workbooks.Open "Orders.dbf"** and press ENTER to open the database workbook.

The result of typing Workbooks.Open "Orders.dbf"

	A	B	C	D	E	F	G	H
1	DATE	STATE	CHANNEL	PRICE	CATEGORY	UNITS	NET	
2	11/1/94	WA	Wholesale	High	Seattle	40	110.00	
3	11/1/94	WA	Wholesale	High	Art	25	68.75	
4	11/1/94	WA	Retail	High	Art	3	16.50	
5	11/1/94	WA	Retail	Low	Environment	50	175.00	
6	11/1/94	WA	Wholesale	Low	Dinosaurs	40	70.00	
7	11/1/94	WA	Wholesale	Low	Seattle	35	61.25	
8	11/1/94	WA	Wholesale	Low	Environment	30	52.50	

In a few seconds, the database appears. The active sheet in the database workbook is a worksheet that contains a range named Database. The Worksheet object's PivotTableWizard can create a PivotTable from a range named Database.

5   In the Immediate window, type **Set myPivot = ActiveSheet.PivotTableWizard** and press ENTER.

The status bar momentarily displays the message, "Reading Data," and then a PivotTable appears.

If the PivotTable toolbar appears, close it.

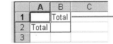

— The result of typing
Set myPivot = ActiveSheet.PivotTableWizard

Congratulations! You have just used Visual Basic commands to create a PivotTable. You also assigned a reference to the PivotTable object to the myPivot variable. Aren't you proud of yourself?

Manipulate pivot fields

I don't know quite how to tell you this, but your PivotTable looks somewhat, well, anemic. You may want to see some data, perhaps even some headings in the PivotTable.

A database usually consists of a list with a lot of rows and a few columns. Each column is called a *field*, and the label at the top of the column is the name of the field. The database in Orders.dbf has seven fields. Date, State, Channel, Price, and Category are fields that contain words. Units and Net are fields that contain numbers. A PivotTable typically summarizes number fields, sorting and grouping by the fields that contain words.

1   If necessary, position the windows so that you can see the Visual Basic editor and the PivotTable at the same time.

2   In the Immediate window, type **Set myField = myPivot.PivotFields("Units")** and press ENTER.

This assigns the Units pivot field to a variable.

3   Type **myField.Orientation = xlDataField** and press ENTER.

The label Sum of UNITS and a number appear in the body of the PivotTable. Since the Units field contains values, the PivotTable adds all the numbers in the Units column together.

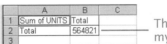

— The result of typing
myField.Orientation = xlDataField

The PivotFields collection contains one item for each of the seven fields in the database. You refer to a single item from the collection in the standard way, by name or by number. In this case, it's easier to remember the name of the Units field than to recall where it happens to fall in the database. Assigning xlDataField to the Orientation property summarizes the data in that field.

Now format the Units total.

4 Type **myField.NumberFormat = "#,##0"** and press ENTER.

	A	B	C
1	Sum of UNITS	Total	
2	Total	564,821	
3			

— myField.NumberFormat = "#,##0"

The number in the PivotTable looks much better with a comma. NumberFormat is a property of a PivotField object. It works exactly the same as the NumberFormat property of a Range object.

5 Type **Set myField = myPivot.PivotFields("State")** and press ENTER.

This assigns the State pivot field to the variable.

6 Type **myField.Orientation = xlRowField** and press ENTER.

Row headings appear, adding appropriate subtotals to the grand total that was already there.

	A	B	C
1	Sum of UNITS		
2	STATE	Total	
3	AZ	25,341	
4	CA	112,385	
5	ID	1,860	
6	NV	51,634	
7	OR	179,516	
8	UT	40,068	
9	WA	154,017	
10	Grand Total	564,821	
11			

— myField.Orientation = x1RowField

The gray box containing the word State is called a *field tile*. It serves as a visible heading for the pivot field.

By now you can probably guess how to turn the State field items into column headings.

7 Type **myField.Orientation = xlColumnField** and press ENTER.

The state codes move from the side to the top of Sheet1. The field tile moves above the state codes.

myField.Orientation = x1ColumnField

	A	B	C	D	E	F	G	H	I
1	Sum of UNITS	STATE							
2		AZ	CA	ID	NV	OR	UT	WA	Grand Total
3	Total	25,341	112,385	1,860	51,634	179,516	40,068	154,017	564,821
4									

Row and column fields group the data in the PivotTable. In the same way that you change pages in a magazine to select which part you wish to see, you can filter the data in a PivotTable by using a *page field*.

8 Type **myField.Orientation = xlPageField** and press ENTER.

The State field tile moves up to the top left corner of the worksheet.

To actually filter the data, by state for example, assign a state code to the CurrentPage property of the State page field.

The CurrentPage property works only with page fields.

9 Type **myField.CurrentPage = "WA"** and press ENTER. Then type **myField.CurrentPage = "CA"** and press ENTER.

The numbers change as you filter by different states.

To remove a field from one of the visible areas of the PivotTable, assign it to the *hidden* orientation.

10 Type **myField.Orientation = xlHidden** and press ENTER.

The State field tile disappears. The pivot table still contains a pivot field named State, but it no longer has a visible field tile.

The Orientation property of PivotFields is what makes the PivotTable "pivot."

Make multiple changes to a PivotTable

The PivotTable object also has a shortcut method that can assign several fields to the different PivotTable areas all at once.

1   Type **myPivot.AddFields "Category", "State", "Channel"** and press ENTER.

myPivot.AddFields "Category", "State", "Channel"

	A	B	C	D	E	F	G	H	I
1	CHANNEL	(All)							
2									
3	Sum of UNITS	STATE							
4	CATEGORY	AZ	CA	ID	NV	OR	UT	WA	Grand Total
5	Art	5,292	28,787	295	14,275	53,185	6,080	26,263	134,177
6	Dinosaurs	8,192	16,575	250	6,160	10,950	5,990	27,207	75,324
7	Environment	3,356	14,685	170	5,070	35,965	5,345	22,500	87,091
8	Humorous	1,577	6,970	290	1,784	7,466	8,140	1,423	27,650
9	Kids	3,020	37,733	226	11,490	53,288	2,402	15,067	123,226
10	Seattle					11,375		58,895	70,270
11	Sports	3,904	7,635	629	12,855	7,287	12,111	2,662	47,083
12	Grand Total	25,341	112,385	1,860	51,634	179,516	40,068	154,017	564,821
13									

The Category field becomes the row field, the State field becomes the column field, and the Channel field becomes the page field. The arguments to the AddFields method always appear in Row, Column, Page order.

To add more than one field to one of the orientations, you need to use multiple field names as a single argument. The Array function allows you to treat multiple field names as a single argument.

2   Type **myPivot.AddFields Array("State","Channel"), "Price", "Date"** and press ENTER.

myPivot.AddFields Array("State", "Channel"), "Price", "Date"

	A	B	C	D	E	F	G
1	DATE	(All)					
2							
3	Sum of UNITS		PRICE				
4	STATE	CHANNEL	High	Low	Mid	Grand Total	
5	AZ	Retail	783	2,869	3,789	7,441	
6		Wholesale	2,940	6,140	8,820	17,900	
7	AZ Total		3,723	9,009	12,609	25,341	
8	CA	Retail	6,152	5,229	10,414	21,795	
9		Wholesale	4,970	26,275	59,345	90,590	
10	CA Total		11,122	31,504	69,759	112,385	
11	ID	Retail	193	493	1,174	1,860	
12	ID Total		193	493	1,174	1,860	

Both State and Channel become row fields, Price becomes the column field, and Date becomes the page field.

When you have more than one field in a given area, you can swap the order of the fields using the Position property. The State field is still assigned to the myField variable.

3 Type **myField.Position = 2** and press ENTER to swap the order of the State and Channel fields.

	A	B	C	D	E	F	G
1	DATE	(All) ▼					
2							
3	Sum of UNITS		PRICE				
4	CHANNEL	STATE	High	Low	Mid	Grand Total	
5	Retail	AZ	783	2,869	3,789	7,441	
6		CA	6,152	5,229	10,414	21,795	
7		ID	193	493	1,174	1,860	
8		NV	13,419	8,785	15,305	37,509	
9		OR	6,336	22,291	30,094	58,721	
10		UT	380	1,376	1,867	3,623	
11		WA	3,341	12,489	17,072	32,902	
12	Retail Total		30,604	53,532	79,715	163,851	

— myField.Position = 2

In summary, use the AddFields method of the PivotTable object to make major changes to a PivotTable; use the Orientation, Position, and CurrentPage properties of the PivotField objects to fine-tune the table.

NOTE In addition to the PivotFields collection, the PivotTable object has subcollections that contain only PivotFields of a particular orientation. For example, the RowFields collection contains only the fields whose Orientation property is set to xlRowField. The subcollections are RowFields, ColumnFields, PageFields, DataFields, and HiddenFields. These collections do not have corresponding object classes. A member of the RowFields collection is still a PivotField object, not a RowField object. You never need to use any of these subcollections, but you may find them convenient. For example, if you know that there is only one row field, you can refer to it as RowFields(1), without worrying about its name or what its number is in the entire PivotFields collection.

Refining PivotTables

Manipulate pivot items

The unique values that appear in a PivotField are called *items*. You can manipulate individual items within a PivotField.

1 Type **Set myItem = myField.PivotItems("WA")** and press ENTER to assign the pivot item for Washington State to a variable.

Now that myItem refers to an individual pivot item, you can manipulate that item using its properties.

2 Type **myItem.Position = 1** and press ENTER.

	A	B	C	D	E	F	G
1	DATE	(All) ▼					
2							
3	Sum of UNITS		PRICE				
4	CHANNEL	STATE	High	Low	Mid	Grand Total	
5	Retail	WA	3,341	12,489	17,072	32,902	
6		AZ	783	2,869	3,789	7,441	
7		CA	6,152	5,229	10,414	21,795	
8		ID	193	493	1,174	1,860	

Set myItem = myField.PivotItems ("WA")
myItem.Position = 1

A pivot item has a Position property, just as a PivotField does.

3 Type **myItem.Name = "Washington"** and press ENTER.

	A	B	C	D	E	F	G
1	DATE	(All)	▼				
2							
3	Sum of UNITS		PRICE				
4	CHANNEL	STATE	High	Low	Mid	Grand Total	
5	Retail	Washington	3,341	12,489	17,072	32,902	
6		AZ	783	2,869	3,789	7,441	
7		CA	6,152	5,229	10,414	21,795	
8		ID	193	493	1,174	1,860	

myItem.Name = "Washington"

The name of the pivot item is what displays in the PivotTable. If you don't like the way the database designer abbreviated state names, you can fix the problem in the PivotTable. Of course, sometimes it's better to leave conventions alone. Fortunately, the PivotItem object remembers for you what its original name was.

4 Type **myItem.Name = myItem.SourceName** and press ENTER.

The name changes back to the original.

	A	B	C	D	E	F	G
1	DATE	(All) ▼					
2							
3	Sum of UNITS		PRICE				
4	CHANNEL	STATE	High	Low	Mid	Grand Total	
5	Retail	WA	3,341	12,489	17,072	32,902	
6		AZ	783	2,869	3,789	7,441	
7		CA	6,152	5,229	10,414	21,795	
8		ID	193	493	1,174	1,860	

myItem.Name = myItem.SourceName

For obvious reasons, the SourceName property is read-only.

Perhaps changing the spelling of the state name is not enough. Perhaps you don't like Washington state (I really do feel sorry for you), and want to eliminate it entirely.

5 Type **myItem.Visible = False** and press ENTER.

	A	B	C	D	E	F	G
1	DATE	(All) ▾					
2							
3	Sum of UNITS		PRICE				
4	CHANNEL	STATE	High	Low	Mid	Grand Total	
5	Retail	AZ	783	2,869	3,789	7,441	
6		CA	6,152	5,229	10,414	21,795	
7		ID	193	493	1,174	1,860	
8		NV	13,419	8,785	15,305	37,509	

myItem.Visible = False

Perhaps, however, you suddenly realize how foolish you are not to like Washington. Fortunately, you can put it back, the same way you got rid of it.

6 Type **myItem.Visible = True** and press ENTER.

Another useful thing you can do with a pivot item is to hide or show the detail to the right of a field. Try hiding the detail for the Retail channel.

7 Type **Set myItem = myPivot.PivotFields("Channel").PivotItems("Retail")** and press ENTER.

This assigns the pivot item to the myItem variable.

8 Type **myItem.ShowDetail = False** and press ENTER.

All the states for the Retail channel collapse into a single row.

	A	B	C	D	E	F	G
1	DATE	(All) ▾					
2							
3	Sum of UNITS		PRICE				
4	CHANNEL	STATE	High	Low	Mid	Grand Total	
5	Retail		30,604	53,532	79,715	163,851	
6	Wholesale	WA	26,430	60,255	34,430	121,115	
7		AZ	2,940	6,140	8,820	17,900	
8		CA	4,970	26,275	59,345	90,590	

myItem.ShowDetail = False

Manipulating pivot items is not generally as dramatic as manipulating PivotFields, but you can use the Position, Name, SourceName, Visible, and ShowDetail properties to refine the effect of the PivotTable.

Manipulate data fields

Data fields do the real dirty work of the PivotTable. This is where the numbers get worked over. Data fields are like other PivotFields in many ways, but they do have a few unique twists of their own. You can see how data fields are different from other fields when you add a second data field.

1 Type **Set myField = myPivot.PivotFields("Net")** and press ENTER to assign the Net field to the myField variable.

2 Type **myField.Orientation = xlDataField** and press ENTER to add a second data field.

	A	B	C	D	E	F	G	H
1	DATE	(All)						
2								
3				PRICE				
4	CHANNEL	STATE	Data	High	Low	Mid	Grand Total	
5	Retail		Sum of UNITS	30,604	53,532	79,715	163,851	
6			Sum of NET	117048.83	169646.7	282978.08	569673.61	
7	Wholesale	WA	Sum of UNITS	26,430	60,255	34,430	121,115	
8			Sum of NET	66975.08	96965.89	73780.08	237721.05	
9		AZ	Sum of UNITS	2,940	6,140	8,820	17,900	
10			Sum of NET	8085	10745	19677.55	38507.55	

Set myField = myPivot.PivotFields ("Net")
myField.Orientation = x1DataField

As soon as you have two data fields in the PivotTable, you get a new field tile, labeled Data. The Data field is not a field from the database. It is a temporary field that allows you to manipulate multiple data fields. The Data field begins as a row field, but you can change it into a column field.

3 Type **Set myField = myPivot.PivotFields("Data")** and press ENTER.

This assigns the temporary Data field to a variable. This statement will work only if you have more than one data field.

4 Type **myField.Orientation = xlColumnField** and press ENTER.

Set myField = myPivot.PivotFields ("Data")
myField.Orientation = x1ColumnField

	A	B	C	D	E	F
1	DATE	(All)				
2						
3			PRICE	Data		
4			High		Low	
5	CHANNEL	STATE	Sum of UNITS	Sum of NET	Sum of UNITS	Sum of NET
6	Retail		30,604	117048.83	53,532	169646.7
7	Wholesale	WA	26,430	66975.08	60,255	96965.89
8		AZ	2,940	8085	6,140	10745
9		CA	4,970	13374.78	26,275	44660.47
10		NV	4,440	11759.64	4,540	7945

When you made the State field into a row field, a tile labeled *State* appeared on the PivotTable. The same was true for the other row, column, and page fields. But when you made Units and Net into data fields, you didn't see tiles labeled Units and Net. Rather, you saw the labels Sum of UNITS and *Sum* of NET. These summary fields are new, derived fields that have been added to the PivotTable. In order to refer to one of these fields, you must use the new name.

5 Type **Set myField = myPivot.PivotFields("Sum of NET")** and press ENTER.

6 Type **myField.Orientation = xlHidden** and press ENTER.

myField.Orientation = x1Hidden

	A	B	C	D	E	F	G
1	DATE	(All) ▼					
2							
3	Sum of UNITS		PRICE				
4	CHANNEL	STATE	High	Low	Mid	Grand Total	
5	Retail		30,604	53,532	79,715	163,851	
6	Wholesale	WA	26,430	60,255	34,430	121,115	
7		AZ	2,940	6,140	8,820	17,900	
8		CA	4,970	26,275	59,345	90,590	
9		NV	4,440	4,540	5,145	14,125	

The Sum of NET column disappears—along with the Data tile, since there is now only one data field. To create a data field, you change the orientation of the database field. To remove a data field, you change the orientation of the derived field.

7 Type **Set myField = myPivot.PivotFields("Sum of UNITS")** and press ENTER to assign the data field to a variable.

The default calculation for a number field is to sum the values. The Function property of a data field allows you to change the way the PivotTable aggregates the data.

8 Type **myField.Function = xlAverage** and press ENTER.

myField.Function = x1Average

	A	B	C	D	E	F	G
1	DATE	(All) ▼					
2							
3	Average of UNITS		PRICE				
4	CHANNEL	STATE	High	Low	Mid	Grand Total	
5	Retail		111	92	111	104	
6	Wholesale	WA	287	354	167	259	
7		AZ	72	66	77	72	
8		CA	106	237	430	306	
9		NV	159	69	64	81	

The values change to averages, and the label changes to Average of UNITS. If you don't want the label switching around on you, you can use the Name property to control it yourself.

147

9   Type **myField.Name** = "**Avg Units**" and press ENTER.

The label changes to "Avg Units."

myField.Name = "Avg Units"

	A	B	C	D	E	F	G
1	DATE	(All)					
2							
3	Avg Units		PRICE				
4	CHANNEL	STATE	High	Low	Mid	Grand Total	
5	Retail		111	92	111	104	
6	Wholesale	WA	287	354	167	259	
7		AZ	72	66	77	72	
8		CA	106	237	430	306	
9		NV	159	69	64	81	

TIP   Once you replace the default name for the derived data field, Excel will not automatically change the name, even if you change the Function property. To have Excel automatically adjust the name, change the Name property to what the automatic name would be for the current function. For example, if the data field currently displays averages for the Units field, change the name to "Average of Units."

When you assign xlDataField to a field's Orientation property, you do not actually change the Orientation property for that field; rather, you create a new, derived field that does have xlDataField as its Orientation property. These derived fields allow you to create multiple data fields from a single source field. Then you can set one derived data field to show sums, another derived field to show averages, and so forth.

The umbrella Data field, which exists only when the PivotTable has more than one data field, acts like an ordinary PivotField, except that it can be assigned only to the row or column orientation.

Find PivotTable ranges

A PivotTable resides on a worksheet. It does not use ordinary worksheet formulas to perform its calculations, but it does take up worksheet cells. If you want to apply a special format to a specific part of a PivotTable, or if you want to add formulas to cells outside the PivotTable that align with cells in the PivotTable, you need to know which cells contain which parts of the PivotTable. Fortunately, all the objects relating to PivotTables have properties to help you find the cells that contain the various parts of the PivotTable.

1 In the Immediate window, type **Set myRange = myPivot.DataBodyRange** and press ENTER.

When you type the period after the word *myPivot*, Visual Basic displays the list of methods and properties. Several of the properties have names with the suffix *-Range*. For example, ColumnRange, DataBodyRange, DataLabelRange, and PageRange. All these properties that end in *-Range* return a range object of some kind.

2 Type **myRange.Select** and press ENTER.

Excel selects the range containing the body of the data, that is, the DataBodyRange.

	A	B	C	D	E	F	G
1	DATE	(All) ▾					
2							
3	Avg Units		PRICE				
4	CHANNEL	STATE	High	Low	Mid	Grand Total	
5	Retail		111	92	111	104	
6	Wholesale	WA	287	354	167	259	
7		AZ	72	66	77	72	
8		CA	106	237	430	306	
9		NV	159	69	64	81	
10		OR	316	320	222	276	
11		UT	264	346	383	350	
12	Wholesale Total		226	254	217	232	
13	Grand Total		171	177	166	171	
14							

Set myRange = myPivot.DataBodyRange
myRange.Select

You can also go the other way: you can find a PivotTable element that resides on a particular cell in Excel.

3 Type **Range("D4").Select** and press ENTER to select cell D4.

	A	B	C	D	E	F	G
1	DATE	(All) ▾					
2							
3	Avg Units		PRICE				
4	CHANNEL	STATE	High	Low	Mid	Grand Total	
5	Retail		111	92	111	104	
6	Wholesale	WA	287	354	167	259	
7		AZ	72	66	77	72	

Range ("D4").Select

4 Type **Set myItem = ActiveCell.PivotItem** and press ENTER.

The Low item from the Price field is assigned to the variable.

149

5 Type **myItem.DataRange.Select** and press ENTER to select the data cells "owned" by the Low Price item.

Set myItem = ActiveCell.PivotItem
myItem.DataRange.Select

	A	B	C	D	E	F	G
1	DATE	(All)					
2							
3	Avg Units		PRICE				
4	CHANNEL	STATE	High	Low	Mid	Grand Total	
5	Retail		111	92	111	104	
6	Wholesale	WA	287	354	167	259	
7		AZ	72	66	77	72	
8		CA	106	237	430	306	
9		NV	159	69	64	81	
10		OR	316	320	222	276	
11		UT	264	346	383	350	
12	Wholesale Total		226	254	217	232	
13	Grand Total		171	177	166	171	
14							

When you see a property for a PivotTable object with the suffix *-Range*, then you know that it returns a Range object of some kind. When you see a property for a Range object with the prefix *Pivot-*, you know that it returns an object that is on that cell.

Save your work

You have done a lot of exploring in the Immediate window. When you quit Excel, everything you have done will evaporate. You can save your explorations from the Immediate window by copying them into the MakePivot macro.

1 Press F8 to finish the macro.

2 Select the entire contents of the Immediate window. (Scroll to the top and click before the first word, and then scroll to the bottom and hold down the SHIFT key as you click below the last line.)

3 Press CTRL+C to copy the contents of the Immediate window.

4 Click in the Module window, on a blank line just above the End Sub statement and below the Dim statements.

5 Press CTRL+V to paste the contents of the Immediate window.

```
Sub MakePivot()
    Dim myPivot As PivotTable
    Dim myField As PivotField
    Dim myItem As PivotItem
    Dim myRange As Range
    Workbooks.Open "orders.dbf"
    Set myPivot = ActiveSheet.PivotTableWizard
    Set myField = myPivot.PivotFields("Units")
    myField.Orientation = xlDataField
    myField.NumberFormat = "#,##0"
    Set myField = myPivot.PivotFields("State")
    myField.Orientation = xlRowField
```

Paste the contents of the Immediate window into the macro.

The new lines are not indented the way proper statements in a macro ought to be.

6 Click in the middle of the first line that needs indenting, scroll to the bottom, and hold down SHIFT as you click in the middle of the last line that needs indenting. Then press TAB to indent them all at once.

*Save
button*

7 Save the Lesson6 workbook by clicking the Save button in the Visual Basic Editor, and close the Orders.dbf workbook without saving changes.

8 With the insertion point anywhere in the MakePivot macro, press F8 repeatedly to repeat (and review!) everything you did in this lesson.

> **NOTE** In this exploration, you assigned several different objects in turn to each of the object variables. You may find your macros easier to read if you create a unique variable with a descriptive name each time you need to assign an object to a variable.

Here, for your reference, is the entire macro you created in this lesson:

```
Sub MakePivot()
    Dim myPivot As PivotTable
    Dim myField As PivotField
    Dim myItem As PivotItem
    Dim myRange As Range

    Workbooks.Open "Orders.dbf"
    Set myPivot = ActiveSheet.PivotTableWizard
    Set myField = myPivot.PivotFields("Units")
    myField.Orientation = xlDataField
    myField.NumberFormat = "#,##0"
    Set myField = myPivot.PivotFields("State")
    myField.Orientation = xlRowField
    myField.Orientation = xlColumnField
    myField.Orientation = xlPageField
    myField.CurrentPage = "WA"
    myField.CurrentPage = "CA"
    myField.Orientation = xlHidden
    myPivot.AddFields "Category", "State", "Channel"
    myPivot.AddFields Array("State", "Channel"), "Price", "Date"
    myField.Position = 2

    Set myItem = myField.PivotItems("WA")
    myItem.Position = 1
    myItem.Name = "Washington"
    myItem.Name = myItem.SourceName
    myItem.Visible = False
    myItem.Visible = True
    Set myItem = myPivot.PivotFields("Channel").PivotItems("Retail")
    myItem.ShowDetail = False
```

```
        Set myField = myPivot.PivotFields("Net")
        myField.Orientation = xlDataField
        Set myField = myPivot.PivotFields("Data")
        myField.Orientation = xlColumnField
        Set myField = myPivot.PivotFields("Sum of Net")
        myField.Orientation = xlHidden
        Set myField = myPivot.PivotFields("Sum Of Units")
        myField.Function = xlAverage
        myField.Name = "Avg Units"

        Set myRange = myPivot.DataBodyRange
        myRange.Select
        Range("D4").Select
        Set myItem = ActiveCell.PivotItem
        myItem.DataRange.Select
    End Sub
```

This macro may not do much useful work, but now you understand how PivotTables work, and how you can manipulate them using Visual Basic.

Lesson Summary

To	Do this
Create a new default PivotTable and save a pointer to it	Use the statement *Set myPivot = ActiveSheet.PivotTableWizard.*
Make a field appear in the row, column, or page areas of a PivotTable	Assign xlRowField, xlColumnField, or xlPageField to the Orientation property of the PivotField object.
Change which field appears first within an area	Assign a number to the Position property of the PivotField object.
Change the name of a PivotField or a pivot item	Assign a new text string to the Name property of the object.
Restore a PivotField or pivot item to the name that appears in the database	Assign the value of the SourceName property to the Name property.
Refer to a data field that sums the value in the Units field	Use the expression *myPivot.PivotFields("Sum of Units").*
Refer to the range where the body of data from a PivotTable is located	Use the expression *myPivot.DataBodyRange.*
Refer to a PivotTable element on the active cell	Use the expression *ActiveCell.PivotItem.*

For online information about	Ask the Assistant for help using the words
Working with PivotTables	"PivotTables"
Working with PivotFields	"PivotFields"
Working with pivot items	"Pivot Items"

Preview of the Next Lesson

In the past four lessons, you have explored a variety of Excel objects. You have used Visual Basic to control Excel, but for all practical purposes, Visual Basic has done nothing but execute Excel methods and properties. In the next part, you will learn additional programming features that let you control how the Visual Basic statements run, making your macros even more powerful.

Exploring
Visual Basic

Part
3

Lesson

7

Controlling Visual Basic

In this lesson you will learn how to:

- Use conditional statements.
- Create loops using three different structures.
- Retrieve the names of files in a folder.
- Create breakpoints to debug long loops.
- Show progress while a macro executes a loop.

Estimated time
30 min.

Walk outside and stand in front of your car. Look down at the tread on the right front tire. See that little piece of gum stuck to the tread? Well, imagine you are that little piece of gum. Imagine what it feels like when the car first starts to move. You climb up, higher and higher, like you are on a Ferris wheel. Whee! Then the pure thrill as you come back down the other side. Who needs Disneyland, anyway? But don't you think that just possibly by the five hundredth or the five thousandth or the five millionth revolution, you might start to get a little tiny bit bored? Thwack, thwack, thwack, thwack. It really could get old after a while.

Just about anything you do is interesting—the first few times you do it. Repetition, however, can bring boredom. When you start doing the same task over and over, you start wanting somebody—or something—else to do it. This lesson will teach you how to record repetitive tasks as Visual Basic macros, and then turn them into machines that work relentlessly to improve your life.

Start the lesson

 Start Microsoft Excel, change to the folder containing the practice files for this book, open the Flow workbook, and save a copy as **Lesson7**.

Using Conditionals

Recorded macros are, to put it bluntly, rather dumb. They can repeat what you did when you recorded the macro, but they can't behave differently in different circumstances. They can't make decisions. The only way that you can make your macros "smart" is to add the decision-making ability yourself.

Make a decision

In the Lesson7 workbook, there is a macro named MoveRight. The MoveRight macro looks like this:

```
Sub MoveRight()
    ActiveCell.Offset(0, 1).Select
End Sub
```

This macro simply selects the cell to the right of the active cell. It has the keyboard shortcut CTRL+SHIFT+R assigned to it. This macro works fine—most of the time.

1 With cell A1 selected, press CTRL+SHIFT+R.

The macro selects cell B1.

2 Press CTRL+RIGHT ARROW to select cell IV1, the rightmost cell on the first row, and press CTRL+SHIFT+R.

Visual Basic displays an error.

> **Microsoft Visual Basic**
>
> Run-time error '1004':
>
> Application-defined or object-defined error
>
> [Continue] [End] [Debug] [Help]

You cannot select the cell to the right of the rightmost cell. This is an ugly error message. You would rather have your macro simply do nothing if it can't move to the right.

Reset button

3 Click the Debug button to jump to the code, and then click the Reset button to stop the macro.

4 Insert the statement **If ActiveCell.Column < 256 Then** after the Sub statement, indent the main statement, and insert the statement **End If** before the End Sub statement.

The revised macro should look like this:

```
Sub MoveRight()
    If ActiveCell.Column < 256 Then
        ActiveCell.Offset(0, 1) .Select
    End If
End Sub
```

An If statement (a statement that begins with the word *If*) pairs with an End If statement. The group of statements from the If to the End If are called, collectively, an *If structure*.

Visual Basic looks at the expression immediately after the word *If* and determines whether it is true or false. This true-or-false expression is called a *conditional expression*. If it is true, then in a simple If structure such as this example, Visual Basic executes all the statements between the If statement and the End If statement. If the expression is false, then Visual Basic jumps directly to the End If statement. You must always put the word *Then* at the end of the If statement.

5 Switch back to Excel, select cell IS1, and press CTRL+SHIFT+R four or five times.

The macro moves the active cell to the right until it gets to the last cell. After that it does nothing, precisely according to your instructions.

You can make your macro smart enough to avoid an error.

You cannot use the macro recorder to create an If structure. This kind of decision is pure Visual Basic and you must add it yourself. Fortunately, adding an If structure is easy.

1 Figure out a question with a "yes or no" answer. In this example, the question is, "Is the column of the active cell less than 256?" You can then turn this question into the true-or-false conditional expression in an If statement.

2 Put the word *If* in front of the conditional expression, and put the word *Then* after it.

3 Figure out how many statements you want to execute if the conditional expression returns a True value.

4 Put an End If statement after the last statement that you want controlled by the If structure.

Using If structures makes your macro "smart."

Make a double decision

Sometimes—such as when you are preventing an error—you want your macro to execute only if the conditional expression is true. Other times, you want the macro to simply behave differently based on the answer to the question.

For example, suppose that you want a macro that moves the active cell to the right, but only within the first five columns of the worksheet. When the active cell gets to the fifth column, you want it to move back to the first cell of the next line, like a typewriter. In this case, you want the macro to carry out one action if the cell column is less than five (move to the right), and a different action if it is not (move down and back).

1 Switch to Visual Basic and change the number *256* to **5** in the If statement.

2 Add the statement **Else** before the End If statement. Then press TAB and add the statement **Cells(ActiveCell.Row+1,1).Select** after the Else statement.

The revised macro should look like this:

```
Sub MoveRight()
    If ActiveCell.Column < 5 Then
        ActiveCell.Offset(0, 1).Select
    Else
        Cells(ActiveCell.Row + 1, 1).Select
    End If
End Sub
```

The Else statement simply tells Visual Basic which statement(s) to execute if the conditional expression is false.

3 Press F5 repeatedly to execute the macro.

You see it move to the right and then scroll back to column A, much like a typewriter.

After you move here...

...the macro moves here.

If structures can contain a single part, only executing statements when the conditional expression is true, or they can have two or more parts, executing one set of statements when the conditional expression is true, and a different set when it is false.

NOTE If structures can also become much more complex than either of these two alternatives. Ask the Assistant for information using the words "if then" to find out more about If structures.

Ask yourself a question

In Lesson 2, you created a macro that asked you to enter a date. You used Visual Basic's InputBox function to do that. The InputBox function is excellent for asking a question, but you must be careful about what happens when you click the Cancel button.

In the Lesson7 workbook is a macro named TestInput that prompts for the date. The code in this macro should look familiar:

```
Sub TestInput()
    Dim myDate As String
    myDate = InputBox("Enter Month in MMM-YY format")
    MsgBox "Continue the macro"
End Sub
```

The macro prompts for a date. It then displays a simple message box indicating that it is running the rest of the macro.

1   Click in the TestInput macro. Press F5 to run the macro, type **Nov-97** for the date, and click OK.

    The message box appears, simulating the rest of the macro.

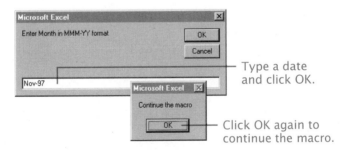

— Type a date and click OK.

— Click OK again to continue the macro.

2   Click OK to close the message box.

3   Press F5 to run the macro again, but this time click Cancel.

    The message box still appears, even though your normal expectation when you click Cancel is that you will, uh, cancel what you started.

4   Click OK to close the message box.

    You need a question whose answer is "yes" if the macro should continue. An appropriate question is, "Did you enter anything in the box??" Clicking Cancel is the same as leaving the box empty. In either case, the InputBox function returns an empty string (equivalent to two quotation marks with nothing between them). The operator <> (a less-than sign followed by a greater-than sign) means "not equal"; it is the opposite of an equal sign.

5   Before the MsgBox statement, enter the statement **If myDate <> ""** **Then**. Before the End Sub statement, enter **End If**. Indent the statement inside the If structure.

The revised macro should look like this:

```
Sub TestInput()
    Dim myDate As String
    myDate = InputBox("Enter Month in MMM-YY format")
    If myDate <> "" Then
        MsgBox "Continue the macro"
    End If
End Sub
```

6   Press F5 to run the macro. Type a date and click OK.

The macro "continues."

7   Click OK to close the message box.

8   Now run the macro again, but this time click Cancel.

The macro stops quietly.

9   Run it again, but this time type **hippopotamus** in the input box and click OK.

The macro continues, the same as if you had entered a date.

Typing an invalid date...

...still continues the macro.

10   Click OK to close the message box.

This could be a problem. You need to check for whether the box is empty, but you also need to check for a valid date. Visual Basic has an IsDate function that will tell you whether Visual Basic can interpret a value as a date. However, you only want to check for a date if the user did not click Cancel. This calls for super-duper, special-deluxe, *nested* If structures.

11   Change the macro to look like this:

```
Sub TestInput()
    Dim myDate As String
    myDate = InputBox("Enter Month in MMM-YY format")
    If myDate <> "" Then
        If IsDate(myDate) Then
            MsgBox "Continue the macro"
        Else
            MsgBox "You didn't enter a date"
        End If
    End If
End Sub
```

Be sure to indent each statement in such a way as to make it clear which statement is governed by which If or Else statement. Visual Basic does not require proper indentation, but indentation is critical to help you (or someone following after you) interpret the macro the same way that Visual Basic does.

12   Run the macro at least three times. Test it with a valid date, an invalid entry, and by clicking Cancel.

The valid and invalid entries should display the appropriate messages. Clicking Cancel or leaving the box empty should display no message.

Using the InputBox function can be a valuable way of making a macro useful across a wide range of circumstances. You must be careful, however, to check the result of the InputBox before you continue the macro. Typically you need to check for three possibilities: valid input, invalid input, and Cancel. An If structure—and sometimes a nested If structure—can make your macro smart enough to respond to all the possible options.

Ask with a message

Visual Basic's MsgBox function is handy for displaying simple messages. As the name implies, it displays a message box. The MsgBox function can do much, much more than that. It can ask questions, too. Many times, when a macro needs to ask a question, all it needs is a simple yes-or-no answer. The MsgBox function is perfect for yes-or-no answers.

Suppose that you have two macros. One is a long, slow macro named PrintMonth, and the other is a short, quick macro named ProcessMonth. You find that you often accidentally run the slow one when you meant to run the quick one. One solution would be to add a message box to the beginning of the slow macro asking you to confirm that you really did intend to run the slow one.

In the Lesson7 workbook, there is a macro named CheckRun. You will enhance this macro to see how to use a MsgBox function to ask a question. This is what the macro looks like before you start:

```
Sub CheckRun()
    MsgBox "This takes a long time. Continue?"
    MsgBox "Continue slow macro..."
End Sub
```

1 Click in the CheckRun macro and press F5 to run it. Click OK twice to close each of the message boxes.

The original macro displays two message boxes.

The first message box appears to ask a question, but it has only a single button. In order to ask a question, you must add more buttons.

2 Move the cursor to the end of the first MsgBox statement. Immediately after the closing quotation marks, type a comma.

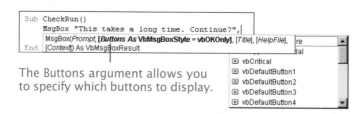

The Buttons argument allows you to specify which buttons to display.

As soon as you type the comma, Visual Basic displays the Quick Info for the MsgBox function. The first argument is named Prompt. That's the one where you enter the message you want to display. The second argument is named Buttons. This is an enumerated list of values. The default value for Buttons is vbOKOnly, which is why you saw only a single OK button when you ran the macro before.

Along with the Quick Info box, Visual Basic also displays the Auto List of possible values for the Buttons argument. You want the buttons to ask the question in terms of yes or no.

3 Scroll nearly to the bottom of the list, select vbYesNo, and press the TAB key.

4 Press F5 to run the macro. The first message box now has two buttons.

The message box now asks a question, but it totally ignores your answer. You need to get the answer from the MsgBox function, and then use that answer to control the way the macro runs.

5 Click Yes and then OK to close both message boxes. Then type the statement **Dim myCheck As Integer** at the beginning of the macro.

6 At the beginning of the first MsgBox statement, type **myCheck = ,** and then put parentheses around the argument list of the MsgBox function.

The revised statement should look like this:

```
myCheck = MsgBox("This takes a long time. Continue?",vbYesNo)
```

> **IMPORTANT** When you use the return value of a function such as MsgBox, you must put parentheses around the argument list. When you do not use the return value, you must not use parentheses.

7 Insert these three statements before the second MsgBox statement:

```
If myCheck = vbNo Then
    Exit Sub
End If
```

When you create a conditional expression using the result of the MsgBox function, you must not check for True or False. MsgBox has many different types of buttons it can display, so it has many different types of answers. If you use vbYesNo as the Buttons type, MsgBox will always return either vbYes or vbNo.

The Exit Sub statement causes Visual Basic to stop the current macro immediately. To avoid making your macros hard to read, you should use Exit Sub very sparingly. One good use for Exit Sub is when you cancel the macro right at the beginning, as in this case.

8 Test the macro. Run it and click Yes, and then run it and click No. Make sure that the rest of the macro runs only when you click Yes.

A message box is a powerful tool for asking simple questions. Be very careful to compare the answer to the correct constant, rather than to True or False. The MsgBox function is also a good example of when and when not to use parentheses around argument lists: use the parentheses if you use the return value of the function, and don't if you don't.

Creating Loops

In the classic book, *The Wealth of Nations*, the economist Adam Smith asked how much it would cost to make a single straight pin compared with how much it would cost to make 10,000 straight pins. The cost of one pin is almost as great as the cost of all 10,000. Similarly, writing a macro that runs once is almost as much work as writing a macro that runs thousands of times in a loop.

Loop through a collection using a For Each loop

Excel allows you to protect a worksheet so that nobody can change anything in any cells that are not specifically unlocked. You must, however, protect each sheet individually. Suppose that you have a workbook containing budgets for ten different departments, and that you want to protect all the worksheets.

In the Lesson7 workbook, there is a macro named ProtectSheets. Here's what it looks like:

```
Sub ProtectSheets()
    Dim mySheet As Worksheet
    Set mySheet = Worksheets(1)
    mySheet.Select
    mySheet.Protect "Password", True, True, True
End Sub
```

This macro assigns a reference to the first worksheet to the mySheet variable, then selects that sheet (selecting the sheet really isn't necessary, but makes it easier to see what the macro is doing), and then protects it. Now see how you can convert this macro to protect all the worksheets in the workbook.

1   Click in the ProtectSheets macro and press F8 repeatedly to step through the macro. Make sure you understand everything that the original macro does.

2   In the third line, replace *Set* with **For Each**, replace the equal sign with **in**, and remove the parentheses and the number between them.

3   Indent the next two statements, add a line break at the end of the second one, and type the statement **Next mySheet**.

The revised macro should look like this:

```
Sub ProtectSheets()
    Dim mySheet As Worksheet
    For Each mySheet In Worksheets
        mySheet.Select
        mySheet.Protect "Password", True, True, True
    Next mySheet
End Sub
```

For Each acts just like Set. It assigns an object reference to a variable. But instead of assigning a single object to the variable, it assigns each object from a collection to the variable. Then, for each (get it?) object in the collection, Visual Basic executes all the statements down to the Next statement. Statements beginning with For Each and ending with Next are called *For Each structures* or *For Each loops*.

(Technically, you don't need to put the variable name after *Next*. If you do use it, Visual Basic requires that it match the variable name after *For Each*. Always using a variable after *Next* can help you avoid errors.)

4 Press F8 repeatedly to step through the macro, watching as it works on each worksheet in turn.

5 Switch to Excel and try typing a value into a cell on any worksheet. (Close the error message box.)

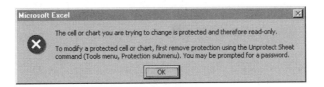

6 Create a new macro named **UnprotectSheets** that unprotects all the worksheets. (Hint: you will need to use the Unprotect method of the worksheet object, with a single argument that gives the password.)

Here's what your macro should look like:

```
Sub UnprotectSheets()
    Dim mySheet As Worksheet
    For Each mySheet In Worksheets
        mySheet.Select 'This statement is optional
        mySheet.Unprotect "Password"
    Next mySheet
End Sub
```

7 Save the workbook, press F5 to test the UnprotectSheets macro, and try changing a value on a worksheet.

Looping through a collection is as easy as assigning a single value to an object. Just replace Set with For Each, specify the collection, and add a Next statement.

TIP A For Each loop is a handy way of browsing collections in the Immediate window. However, in the Immediate window, everything you type must be on a single line. You can put multiple statements on a single line by separating the statements with colons. For example, here's what you would type in the Immediate window to see the names of all the Worksheets in the active workbook: *For Each x in Worksheets: ?x.Name: Next x.* (In the Immediate window it's all right to use short, meaningless names for variables.)

Loop with a counter using a For loop

Sometimes you want to do actions repeatedly, but can't use a For Each loop. For example, For Each loops only act on a single collection. If you want to compare two parallel collections—such as two ranges—you can't use a For Each loop. In that situation, Visual Basic has another, more generalized way to loop: a *For loop.*

The Compare worksheet in the Lesson7 workbook contains two named ranges.

	A	B	C	D	E	F	G	H
1								
2	Original				Revised			
3	143	116	110		106	133	115	
4	133	136	114		123	105	121	
5	123	113	120		116	102	120	
6	103	148	129		126	137	114	
7								

The Revised numbers are random sample numbers.

The one on the left is named Original, and the one on the right is named Revised. You can think of these as being an original forecast and a revised forecast. The cells in the Original range contain values. The cells in the Revised range contain a formula that will calculate a random number each time you press F9 to recalculate the workbook. (The formula is =ROUND(RAND()*50+100,0), which tells Excel to calculate a random number between 0 and 1, multiply it by 50, add 100, and round to the nearest whole number.)

In the Lesson7 Visual Basic module, there is a macro named CompareCells. This is what it looks like:

```
Sub CompareCells()
    Dim i As Integer
    Calculate
    i = Range("Revised").Cells.Count
    If Range("Revised").Cells(i) > Range("Original").Cells(i) Then
        Range("Revised").Cells(i).Interior.Color = vbYellow
    Else
        Range("Revised").Cells(i).Interior.Color = vbCyan
    End If
End Sub
```

The macro first executes the Calculate method, which is like pressing the F9 function key. It calculates new values for all the cells in the Revised range. Then the macro compares only the last cell in the Revised range with the last cell in the Original range. If the Revised value is greater than the Original, it turns yellow; otherwise it turns blue. The macro assigns the Count of cells in the range to the variable i. The macro uses that number several times, and *i* requires less typing than *Range("Revised").Cells.Count*.

Now see how you can convert this macro to compare all the cells at once.

If you are not comfortable with any of the Range methods and properties, review Lesson 4. If you are not comfortable with If structures, review the first half of this lesson.

1 Click in the CompareCells macro and press F8 repeatedly to step through the macro. Make sure you understand everything the original macro does.

	A	B	C	D	E	F	G	H
1								
2	Original				Revised			
3	143	116	110		104	110	134	
4	133	136	114		142	113	118	
5	123	113	120		138	111	133	
6	103	148	129		150	144	135	
7								

The original macro compares the last cell of each range.

2 In the statement that assigns the Count to the variable, insert the word **For** in front of the variable, then insert **1 To** after the equal sign.

3 Type **Next i** before the End Sub statement, and indent all the statements between *For* and *Next*.

The revised macro should look like this:

```
Sub CompareCells()
    Dim i As Integer
    Calculate
    For i = 1 To Range("Revised").Cells.Count
        If Range("Revised").Cells(i) > _
            Range("Original").Cells(i) Then
                Range("Revised").Cells(i).Interior.Color = vbYellow
        Else
                Range("Revised").Cells(i).Interior.Color = vbCyan
        End If
    Next i
End Sub
```

The keyword For works just like a simple assignment statement. It assigns a number to the variable. (The For keyword assigns a number to a variable, while For Each assigns an object reference to a variable.) The variable that gets assigned the number is called a *loop counter*. You specify the first value For should assign (in this case, 1), and the last value it should assign (in this case, the number of cells in the range).

169

Each time For assigns a number to the loop counter, Visual Basic executes all the statements down to the Next statement. Then For adds 1 to the loop counter and executes all the statements again, until the loop counter is greater than the value you specified as the last value.

4   Press F8 repeatedly to watch the macro work. Step through at least two or three loops, and then press F5 to finish the macro.

	A	B	C	D	E	F	G	H
1								
2	Original				Revised			
3	143	116	110		129	119	113	
4	133	136	114		129	104	111	
5	123	113	120		110	108	105	
6	103	148	129		132	101	121	
7								

A For loop allows you to loop through two collections at once.

In many cases, using a For Each loop is more convenient than using a For loop. However, a For loop is a more general tool, in that you can always use a For loop to reproduce the behavior of a For Each loop. For example, here is how you could write the ProtectSheets macro without using For Each:

```
Sub ProtectSheets()
    Dim mySheet As Worksheet
    Dim i as Integer
    For i = 1 to Worksheets.Count
        Set mySheet = Worksheets(i)
        mySheet.Select
        mySheet.Protect "Password", True, True, True
    Next i
End Sub
```

If you were going to be marooned on a desert island and could take only one of these two looping structures with you, you would probably be better off choosing For. Fortunately, however, you do not have to make the choice. In the many cases where For Each loops can work, use them happily. In cases where you need a counter, however, use For loops.

Loop indefinitely using a Do loop

A For Each loop works through a collection. A For loop cycles through numbers from a starting point to an ending point. In some situations, however, neither of these options will work. For example, Visual Basic has a function that will tell you the names of files in a folder. The function is named Dir, after the old MS-DOS operating system command of the same name. The first time you use Dir, you give it an argument that tells which kind of files you want to look at. To retrieve the name of one Excel workbook, you use the statement *myFile=Dir("*.xls")*. To get additional files that match the same pattern, you use Dir without any arguments at all. You must run Dir repeatedly because it returns only one file name at a time. When Visual Basic cannot find any more matching files, the Dir function returns an empty string.

Suppose that you want to create a macro that retrieves the names of all the Excel files in the current folder. The list of files in the directory is not a collection, so you can't use a For Each loop. You can't use a For loop either, because you don't know how many files you will get until you are finished. Fortunately, Visual Basic has one more way of controlling a loop: a *Do loop*.

In the Lesson7 workbook, there is a macro named ListFiles that retrieves the first two Excel files from the current directory and puts their names into the first two cells in the first column of the active worksheet. Here is the original macro:

```
Sub ListFiles()
    Dim myRow As Integer
    Dim myFile As String

    myRow = 1
    myFile = Dir("*.xls")
    Cells(myRow, 1) = myFile

    myRow = myRow + 1
    myFile = Dir
    Cells(myRow, 1) = myFile
End Sub
```

Aside from the variable declaration statements, this macro consists of two groups of three statements. In each group, the macro assigns a row number to myRow, retrieves a file name using the Dir function, and then puts the file name into the appropriate cell. The first time the macro uses Dir, it specifies the pattern to match. The next time, the macro simply uses Dir without an argument to retrieve the next matching file.

The names of the files your macro retrieves may differ from these.

Now see how you can convert this macro to loop until it has found all the files in the folder.

1   In the Lesson7 workbook, activate the Files worksheet. From the File menu, click Open, change to the folder containing the practice files for the book, and then click Cancel. Doing this ensures that the current folder contains Excel workbooks.

2   In Visual Basic, click on the ListFiles macro and press F8 repeatedly to step through the macro. Make sure you understand the original macro.

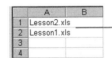
The original macro retrieves two file names.

> **TIP** As you step through the macro, move the mouse pointer over a variable name to see the current value stored in that variable.

3 Type **Do Until myFile = ""** on a new line after the first statement that contains a Dir function.

4 Type **Loop** on a new line after the second statement that contains a Dir function, and then delete the second *Cells(myRow, 1) = myFile* statement.

5 Indent the three statements between the Do and the Loop statements.

The revised macro should look like this:

```
Sub ListFiles()
    Dim myRow As Integer
    Dim myFile As String

    myRow = 1
    myFile = Dir("*.xls")
    Do Until myFile = ""
        Cells(myRow, 1) = myFile

        myRow = myRow + 1
        myFile = Dir
    Loop
End Sub
```

The phrase after *Do Until* is a conditional expression, precisely like one you would use with an If structure. The conditional expression must be something that Visual Basic can interpret as either True or False. Visual Basic simply repeats the loop over and over until the conditional expression is True.

If you want to increment a number during the loop, you must enter a statement to increment it. You must always be careful to cause something to happen during the loop that will allow the loop to end. In this case, you retrieve a new file name from the Dir function.

6 Press F8 repeatedly to watch the macro work. Step through at least two or three loops, and then press F5 to finish the macro.

	A	B
1	Lesson2.xls	
2	Lesson1.xls	
3	Control.xls	
4	Objects.xls	
5	BUDGET.XLS	
6	Ranges.xls	
7	Graphics.xls	
8	Lesson4.xls	
9	Lesson5.xls	
10	Lesson6.xls	

A Do loop allows you to loop as many times as necessary.

If you run a macro that contains an infinite loop, stop the macro by pressing CTRL+BREAK.

A Do loop is very flexible, but it is also a little bit dangerous because you have to be sure you provide a way for the loop to end. For example, if you forgot to add the statement to retrieve a new file name, or if you had included the argument to the Dir function inside the loop (so that Dir would keep returning the first file name over and over), then you would have what is called an *infinite loop*.

> **NOTE** Do loop structures have several useful variations. You can loop *until* the conditional expression is true, or *while* the expression is true. You can put the conditional expression at the top of the loop, or at the bottom of the loop. To find out more about Do loop structures, ask the Assistant for information using the words "do loop."

Managing Large Loops

A loop that executes only two or three times is not much different from a program without a loop. It runs fast, and it's easy to step through to watch how each statement works. Once you start repeating a loop hundreds or thousands of times, however, you need some additional techniques to make sure the macro works the way you want it to.

Set a breakpoint

In the Lesson7 workbook is a macro named PrintOrders. You can think of this macro as one that your predecessor wrote just before leaving the company. Or you can think of it as one that you almost finished three months ago. In either event, you have a macro that you don't understand and that doesn't work quite right.

The PrintOrders macro is supposed to print a copy of the entire Orders database, but sorted by product Category. You give each Category manager the section of the report that shows only orders for that one category, so you need a new page every time the Category changes. Unfortunately, the macro doesn't work quite right. You need to find and fix the problem. Here is the macro as you first receive it:

```
Sub PrintOrders()
    Dim myRow As Long
    Dim myStop As Long
    Workbooks.Open FileName:="orders.dbf"
    Columns("E:E").Cut
    Columns("A:A").Insert Shift:=xlToRight
    Range("A1").CurrentRegion.Sort Key1:="Category", _
        Order1:=xlAscending, Header:=xlYes
    myStop = Range("A1").CurrentRegion.Rows.Count
    For myRow = 3 To myStop
        If Cells(myRow, 1) <> Cells(myRow + 1, 1) Then
```

```
            Cells(myRow, 1).Select
            ActiveCell.PageBreak = xlPageBreakManual
        End If
    Next myRow
    Cells(myRow, 1).Select
    ActiveSheet.PageSetup.PrintTitleRows = "$1:$1"
    ActiveSheet.PrintPreview
    ActiveWorkbook.Close SaveChanges:=False
End Sub
```

Probably the best approach is to start stepping through the macro.

Open button

1   Make sure that the current folder is the one containing the practice files for this book. (From the File menu, click the Open button, change to the correct folder, and click Cancel.)

2   In Visual Basic, click in the PrintOrders macro, and then press F8 three times to jump over the variable declarations and open the database.

	A	B	C	D	E	F	G	H
1	DATE	STATE	CHANNEL	PRICE	CATEGORY	UNITS	NET	
2	11/1/94	WA	Wholesale	High	Seattle	40	110.00	
3	11/1/94	WA	Wholesale	High	Art	25	68.75	
4	11/1/94	WA	Retail	High	Art	3	16.50	
5	11/1/94	WA	Retail	Low	Environment	50	175.00	

In the original database, the Category field is in column E.

(The two variables are declared as Long, which means that they can hold whole numbers, but are not limited to the four-digit numbers of type Integer.)

3   Press F8 three more times.

	A	B	C	D	E	F	G	H
1	CATEGORY	DATE	STATE	CHANNEL	PRICE	UNITS	NET	
2	Art	11/1/94	WA	Wholesale	High	25	68.75	
3	Art	11/1/94	WA	Retail	High	3	16.50	
4	Art	11/1/94	WA	Wholesale	Mid	30	67.50	
5	Art	11/1/94	WA	Retail	Mid	20	90.00	

The macro moves the Category field to column A and sorts the database by Category.

These statements move the Category field over to column A, and then sort the list by Category.

4   Press F8 twice to assign a number to myStop and start the loop. Hold the mouse pointer over myStop and then over myRow to see the values that were assigned.

```
myStop = Range("A1").CurrentRegion.Rows.Count
For myRow = 3 To myStop
    myRow = 3 s(myRow, 1) <> Cells(myRow + 1, 1) Then
        Cells(myRow, 1).Select
```

The Data Tip box shows the value of the variable.

The value of myStop is 3300, and the value of myRow is 3. That appears correct. The loop will execute from row 3 to row 3300.

5 Press F8 several times.

Visual Basic keeps checking for whether the cell in the current row matches the cell below it. How many rows are in the Art category? This could take a very long time. But if you just press F5 to run the rest of the macro, you can't watch what happens when the condition in the If statement is true. If only there were a way to skip over all the statements until the macro moves into the inside of the If structure...

6 Click in the gray area to the left of the statement starting with *ActiveCell*.

Click in the left margin to create a breakpoint. —

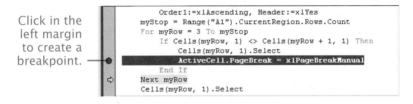

```
            Order1:=xlAscending, Header:=xlYes
        myStop = Range("A1").CurrentRegion.Rows.Count
    For myRow = 3 To myStop
        If Cells(myRow, 1) <> Cells(myRow + 1, 1) Then
            Cells(myRow, 1).Select
            ActiveCell.PageBreak = xlPageBreakManual
        End If
    Next myRow
    Cells(myRow, 1).Select
```

A dark red circle appears in the margin, and the background of the statement changes to dark red. This is a *breakpoint*. When you set a breakpoint, the macro starts stepping just before it would execute the breakpoint statement.

7 Press F5 to continue the macro.

Visual Basic stops when it reaches the breakpoint. —

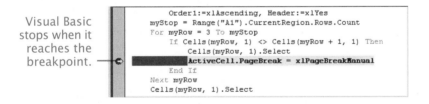

```
            Order1:=xlAscending, Header:=xlYes
        myStop = Range("A1").CurrentRegion.Rows.Count
    For myRow = 3 To myStop
        If Cells(myRow, 1) <> Cells(myRow + 1, 1) Then
            Cells(myRow, 1).Select
            ActiveCell.PageBreak = xlPageBreakManual
        End If
    Next myRow
    Cells(myRow, 1).Select
```

The macro stops at the breakpoint. The active cell is the first one that the If statement determined is different from the cell below it.

8 Press F8 to execute the statement that assigns a manual page break.

Press F8 to execute the statement with the breakpoint. —

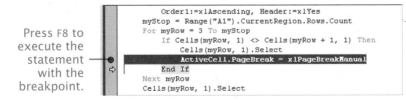

```
            Order1:=xlAscending, Header:=xlYes
        myStop = Range("A1").CurrentRegion.Rows.Count
    For myRow = 3 To myStop
        If Cells(myRow, 1) <> Cells(myRow + 1, 1) Then
            Cells(myRow, 1).Select
            ActiveCell.PageBreak = xlPageBreakManual
        End If
    Next myRow
    Cells(myRow, 1).Select
```

The page break appears above the row, not below the row. This is a problem. The macro should not set the page break on the *last* cell of a Category; rather, it should set the break on the *first* cell of a Category.

The If statement should check to see if the cell is different from the one *above* it.

9 Change the plus sign (+) in the If statement to a minus sign (-).

The revised statement should look like this:

```
If Cells(myRow, 1) <> Cells(myRow - 1, 1) Then
```

10 Press F5 and F8 to watch the macro work—properly this time—as it assigns page breaks to the next couple of Categories.

Setting a breakpoint is an invaluable tool for finding a problem in the middle of a long loop. Read on to learn an exceptionally easy way to set a temporary breakpoint if you only need to use it once.

Set a temporary breakpoint

Suppose you are now stepping through the middle of the PrintOrders macro. The code to assign a page break seems to be working properly. There are still some statements at the end of the macro, however, that you would like to step through.

1 Click the red circle in the margin to turn off the breakpoint.

2 Click anywhere in the *Cells(myRow,1).Select* statement after the end of the loop.

```
For myRow = 3 To myStop
    If Cells(myRow, 1) <> Cells(myRow - 1, 1) Then
        Cells(myRow, 1).Select
        ActiveCell.PageBreak = xlPageBreakManual
    End If
Next myRow
Cells(myRow, 1).Select
ActiveSheet.PageSetup.PrintTitleRows = "$1:$1"
```

Click in the statement where you want a temporary breakpoint.

You want a breakpoint on this statement, but one that you only need to use once. '

3 From the Debug menu, click the Run To Cursor command.

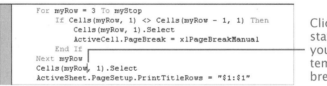

Use the Run To Cursor command to create a "one-time" breakpoint.

4 Press F8 three times to scroll to the bottom of the list, set the print titles, and preview the report.

5 Review the report.

The end of the Art category should have come on page 11, but there is an extra page break because of the original error in the macro.

6 Close Print Preview, and press F8 twice more to finish the macro.

7 Save the Lesson7 workbook.

Turning off a breakpoint is just as easy as turning one on: just click in the margin. But if turning a breakpoint on and off is still too much work, you can create a temporary one by running to the cursor.

Show progress in a loop

Even if the loop in a macro is working perfectly, if the macro takes a long time to execute, you might get nervous about whether something has gone wrong. The best way to feel comfortable when a long loop is running (particularly if you are wondering whether you have time to go get a cup of coffee), is to show the progress in the loop.

You can show progress with any kind of loop, but a For loop lends itself particularly well to showing progress because at any point in the loop your macro can determine both the current value of the loop counter and also what its final value will be.

1 In the PrintOrders macro, immediately following the For statement, insert this statement:

```
Application.StatusBar = "Processing row " & myRow & " of " & myStop
```

The status bar is the gray strip at the bottom of Excel that usually says "Ready." The StatusBar property of the Application object allows you to make the status bar say whatever you want. The best message is one that shows progress and also gives you an idea of how long the task will take.

The statement above creates this message when it enters the loop the first time: "Processing row 3 of 3300." By using an ampersand (&) to join together message text with the numbers in the myRow and myStop variables, you can create a very useful message. Just be careful to include an extra space before and after the numbers.

2 Press F5 to run the macro. Watch the status bar to see how the macro is progressing.

The status bar shows progress.

3 Close the Print Preview screen to let the macro finish.

The status bar indicates that the macro is still running. The status bar does not automatically reset when your macro ends. To return control of the status bar to Excel, you must assign the value False to it.

4 After the Next statement, insert the statement:

```
Application.StatusBar = False
```

5 Run the macro again, close the Print Preview screen at the appropriate time, and then look at the status bar.

Before the macro finishes, reset the status bar.

It is back to normal.

Visual Basic provides extremely powerful tools for repeating statements in a loop. Coupled with the decisions that you can make using If structures, they let you create macros that are very smart and very powerful.

Lesson Summary

To	Do this
Execute statements only if a condition is true	Insert the statements between an If statement and an End If statement.
Execute a first group of statements if a condition is true and a second group of statements if a condition is false	Insert the first group of statements between an If statement and an Else statement, and the second group of statements between the Else statement and an End If statement.
Execute statements for each item in a collection	Insert the statements between a For Each statement and a Next statement.
Execute statements a specific number of times	Insert the statements between a For statement and a Next statement.
Execute statements until a condition becomes true	Insert statements between a Do statement and a Loop statement.
Stop a macro while it is running	Press CTRL+BREAK.
Turn a breakpoint on or off	Click in the gray margin to the left of a statement in the Visual Basic Editor.
Display a message in the status bar	Assign a string to the Application.StatusBar property.
Restore the default message to the status bar	Assign False to the Application.StatusBar property.

For online information about	Ask the Assistant for help using the words
Using conditionals	"If Then"
Using For Each loops	"For Each"
Using For loops	"For Next"
Using Do loops	"Do Loop"
Conditional expressions	"Comparison operators"
Breakpoints and other debugging tools	"Breakpoints" or "Debugging"

Preview of the Next Lesson

So far, all of the macros you have created in this book have been simple, stand-alone procedures. In the next lesson you will learn how to create a whole new kind of macro: specialized macros that you can use in worksheet formulas or as extensions to Visual Basic's built-in capabilities.

Extending Microsoft Excel and Visual Basic

Estimated time
30 min.

In this lesson you will learn how to:

- Create and use custom functions.
- Handle errors that occur while a macro is running.

Single-cell organisms are all small. Bacteria, amoebas, paramecia—none are even large enough to see with the naked eye. Still, they work fine. Large, sophisticated organisms, however, require multiple cells. Cells give structure and add specialization to living things.

Recorded macros are like single-cell organisms. The macro recorder puts everything you do into a single procedure. And, like single-cell organisms, single-procedure macros should be small. Large, sophisticated applications work best when you break them up into smaller procedures. Also, just as large, complex organisms need an immune system to deal with diseases, sophisticated applications need a mechanism for dealing with error conditions. In this lesson, you will learn how to create custom functions, use arguments in procedures, and handle errors—tools you will need to make more powerful applications.

Start the lesson

 Start Microsoft Excel, change to the folder containing the practice files for this book, open the Function workbook, and save a copy as **Lesson8**.

Creating Custom Functions

Once you assign a value to a variable, you can use that value in any expression. For example, after you assign the number 25 to the variable myAge, then the value of the conditional expression myAge > 20 would be True. You can use the variable as if it were the value that it contains.

A function is like a variable, except that a function is smarter. A function is a variable that figures out its own value whenever you use it. For example, Microsoft Visual Basic has a function named Time. When you use the conditional expression *Time > #8:00 PM#*, the Time function checks the time on your computer's clock at the time you use the expression.

Visual Basic has many built-in functions. Excel also has many built-in functions. You can even create your own functions.

Use a custom function from a worksheet

Both Excel and Visual Basic have functions that return a random number between 0 and 1. Excel's function is named RAND(), and Visual Basic's function is named Rnd. You can use Excel's function in a worksheet cell, but you can use Visual Basic's function only in a Visual Basic macro.

You can also create a custom random number function—let's call it Random—that you can use from Excel. Why would you want to create your own random function when you could use the built-in one for free? So you can customize it. Once you create your own function, you can make it do whatever you want.

1 In the Lesson8 workbook, select the TestFunction sheet, and enter the formula =**Random()** into cell A12.

Using a function before it exists produces the #NAME? error.

Excel displays the #NAME? error value because the Random function does not exist yet.

2 Start recording a macro named **Random**, immediately stop the recorder, and then edit the macro.

3 Double-click the word *Sub* at the beginning of the macro and replace it with **Function**.

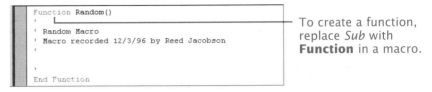

```
Function Random()
'
'  Random Macro
'  Macro recorded 12/3/96 by Reed Jacobson
'


End Function
```

To create a function, replace *Sub* with **Function** in a macro.

The End Sub statement changes to End Function. You have now created a function. Next you need to tell Excel what to use as the value of the function.

4 Type the statement **Random = Rnd** as the body of the function.

The revised function should look like this:

```
Function Random()
     Random = Rnd
End Function
```

The way you tell a function what value to return is by assigning a value to the name of the function, as if the function name were a variable. This function simply takes the value of Visual Basic's Rnd function and assigns it to the Random function.

5 Switch back to Excel, select cell A12, and click the Edit Formula button next to the formula bar.

Edit Formula button

```
Random
                                         = 0.705547512
Macro recorded 12/18/96 by Reed Jacobson.

            This function takes no arguments.

[?]    Formula result =0.53342402              OK      Cancel
```

Excel displays the Formula Editor, which explains to you that the Random function doesn't take any arguments.

Click OK to enter the random number into cell A12.

That's all there is to creating a simple worksheet function. In Visual Basic, you replace the word *Sub* with *Function*, and then somewhere in the function, assign a value to the function name. In Excel, you put the function name into a formula, followed by parentheses.

Add arguments to a custom function

Suppose that you want random whole numbers equal to 100, plus or minus 25. Or that you want random whole numbers equal to 1000, plus or minus 100. Excel's RAND() function cannot give you that kind of random number. Neither, for that matter, can yours, but since yours is a custom function, you can add additional capabilities to it by adding arguments.

To specify the random number ranges mentioned above, you need three arguments: one to specify the midpoint, one to specify the plus or minus range, and one to specify whether or not to round the final number. You can add those arguments to your function.

1 In Visual Basic, type **Midpoint, Range, Round** between the parentheses after the name of the function. The statement that contains the function name and its arguments is called the *function declaration* statement. In this statement you declare the name of the function and also the names of all the arguments.

The revised function declaration statement should look like this:

```
Function Random(Midpoint, Range, Round)
```

These three words are arguments to the function. You can use them inside the function as variables that have been pre-filled with values.

2 Change the statement that assigns a value to the function name to this:

```
Random = Rnd * (Range * 2) + (Midpoint - Range)
```

The Rnd function returns a random number between 0 and 1. If Range is equal to 25, that means that you want numbers from 25 below the midpoint to 25 above the midpoint, for a total range of 50. Multiplying Rnd by Range * 2 would then give you a random number between 0 and 50. If the target midpoint is 100, you then need to add 75 (that is, 100 – 25), to the random number. That's what this statement does.

3 Insert these three statements to round the number if necessary.

```
If Round Then
    Random = CLng(Random)
End If
```

To see other functions that convert between data types, click on CLng and press F1.

In Visual Basic, a *Long* is a whole number that can include large numbers. The Visual Basic function CLng converts a number to a Long, rounding it along the way. You only round the random number if the value of the Round argument is True. (Since the value of the Round argument already equals True or False, you don't need to compare it to anything to get a conditional expression.)

4   In Excel, enter **100** into cell B12, **25** into cell C12, and **TRUE** into
    cell D12.

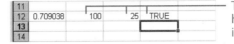

These cells will control
how the random number
is calculated.

You will use these values for the Midpoint, Range, and Random
arguments to your function.

*Edit Formula
button*

5   Select cell A12, and click the Edit Formula button next to the
    formula bar.

Random		
Midpoint		=
Range		=
Round		=
		=

Macro recorded 12/3/96 by Reed Jacobson.

Midpoint

Formula result =   [OK] [Cancel]

The Formula Editor
displays the custom
arguments you
created.

The Formula Editor box appears, showing you the three new arguments
to your function.

6   Click in the Midpoint box, and then click cell B12. Click in the Range
    box, and then click cell C12. Click in the Random box, and then click
    cell D12. Then click OK.

random		
Midpoint	B12	= 100
Range	C12	= 25
Round	D12	= TRUE
		= 116

Macro recorded 1/23/97 by Michael A. Brown.

Round

Formula result = 104   [OK] [Cancel]

Link the arguments
to worksheet cells.

Cell A12 contains a random number between 75 and 125. You use
arguments to pass values to a function.

7   Change cell B12 to **1000** and cell C12 to **100**.

The function
uses these
values...

11				
12	1052	1000	100	TRUE
13				
14				

...to create this
random number.

185

The value of cell A12 changes to a random number between 900 and 1100. Whenever you change the value of a cell that the function refers to, the function calculates a new answer.

Adding arguments is a way to make functions more flexible.

Make a function volatile

Most functions recalculate only when the value of a cell that feeds into the function changes. Other functions (such as Excel's RAND() function), called *volatile functions*, recalculate whenever any cell on the worksheet changes, or whenever you press F9. You can make your function volatile; then it will calculate a new random number whenever you press F9.

1   In Visual Basic, insert this statement after the statement containing the name of the function:

```
Application.Volatile True
```

2   Switch back to Excel and press F9. The random number in cell A12 changes. Press F9 several times to verify that the function generates random numbers in the appropriate range.

Most of the time you do not want custom functions to be volatile. You want the function to recalculate only when a value that feeds into it changes. For those few cases where you do want the formula to recalculate, just use the Application object's Volatile method with True as an argument.

Make arguments optional

The only problem with your new, enhanced Random function is that it is now more complicated to use in those simple cases where you do not need the new arguments. If you put =Random() into a cell, omitting the arguments, Excel will display the #VALUE! error value. To avoid this error message, you can tell Visual Basic that you want the arguments to be optional. Then you specify default values to use if the argument is not supplied.

1   In Visual Basic, type the word **Optional** in front of each of the three argument names.

The revised statement should look like this:

```
Function Random(Optional Midpoint, Optional Range, Optional Round)
```

You do not have to make all the arguments optional, but once you make one argument optional, all the arguments that follow it must be optional as well. In other words, you place optional arguments at the end of the argument list.

2   Type = **0.5** after the word *Midpoint*, = **0.5** after the word *Range*, and = **False** after the word *Round*. Break the statement into two lines after the first comma.

The resulting statement should look like this:

```
Function Random(Optional Midpoint = 0.5, _
    Optional Range = 0.5, Optional Round = False)
```

You can specify a default value for any optional argument. You assign the default value to the argument name the same way you would assign a value to a variable, using a simple equal sign.

3 In Excel, enter **=Random()** into cell A13. A random number between 0 and 1 appears.

Optional arguments allow you to add powerful features to a function, while keeping it easy to use in those cases where you do not need the extra features. To make an argument optional, add *Optional* before the argument name. To add a default value for an optional argument, assign the value to the argument name the same way as if it were a variable.

Use a custom function from a macro

You can use a custom function from a macro just as easily as you can use it from a worksheet cell.

1 In Visual Basic, at the bottom of the module, type **Sub TestRandom** and press ENTER to start creating a macro.

2 Type **MsgBox** and a space.

Visual Basic shows the Quick Info box with the arguments for MsgBox.

3 Press CTRL+SPACEBAR to show the list of global methods and properties, and then press R to scroll down to the words that begin with an R.

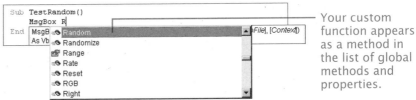

Your custom function appears as a method in the list of global methods and properties.

Your Random function is automatically included in the list. Your function has the icon for a method next to it. Excel methods are simply functions that are built into Excel. You create new global methods simply by writing new functions.

4 Press the TAB key to insert the function name into the statement, and then type an opening parenthesis to begin the argument list.

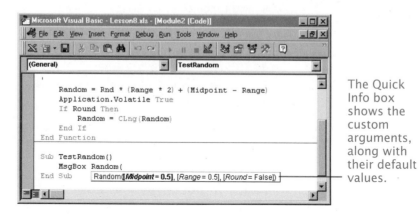

The Quick Info box shows the custom arguments, along with their default values.

Visual Basic displays the Quick Info box with the arguments for your custom function. The Quick Info box even shows the default values for the optional arguments.

5 Type **200, 5, True** as the list of arguments, and then type a closing parenthesis.

6 Press F5 to run the macro. Click OK when your random number appears.

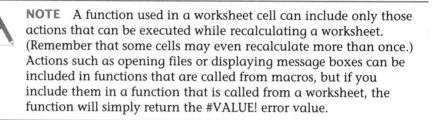

You can run a custom function from a macro.

A function is a procedure like a Sub procedure, except that it returns a value that you can use either in a cell in Excel, or from a Visual Basic macro.

> **NOTE** A function used in a worksheet cell can include only those actions that can be executed while recalculating a worksheet. (Remember that some cells may even recalculate more than once.) Actions such as opening files or displaying message boxes can be included in functions that are called from macros, but if you include them in a function that is called from a worksheet, the function will simply return the #VALUE! error value.

Handling Errors

Believe it or not, computer programs do not always work perfectly. Every now and then you may actually write a macro that doesn't quite do what you want. These errors come in several different types:

Syntax errors   These are mistakes such as using an opening quotation mark and leaving off the closing quotation mark. When you type a statement into a procedure, the Visual Basic Editor checks the statement for syntax errors as soon as you leave the statement.

Compiler errors   Some mistakes cannot be detected on a single-line basis. For example, you might start a For Each loop but forget to put a Next statement at the end. The first time you try to run a procedure, Visual Basic translates that procedure (along with all the other procedures in the module) into internal computer language. Translating to computer language is called *compiling*, and errors that Visual Basic detects while translating are called *compiler errors*. Syntax errors and compiler errors are usually easy to find and fix.

 TIP   Visual Basic can check for spelling errors when you use variables. From Visual Basic's Tools menu, select the Options command and select the Require Variable Declarations check box. After you do this, Visual Basic will add the statement *Option Explicit* to any new module that you create. When *Option Explicit* appears at the top of a module, Visual Basic will display a compiler error any time you use a variable that you did not explicitly declare.

Logic errors   The computer can never detect some mistakes. For example, if you mean to change a workbook caption to "My Workbook," but you accidentally spell the caption "My Werkbook," the computer will never complain. Or if you compare the new values with the wrong copy of the old values, the computer won't find the error for you. You can toggle breakpoints, step through the procedures, and watch values, but you still have to find the problem on your own.

Run-time errors   Sometimes a statement in a procedure works under some conditions, but fails under others. For example, you might have a statement that deletes a file on the hard disk. As long as the file exists and can be deleted, the statement works. If, however, the file does not exist, Visual Basic doesn't know what else to do but quit with an error message. These errors cannot be detected until you run the procedure, so they are called *run-time* errors. Some run-time errors indicate problems. Other run-time errors are situations that you can anticipate and program Visual Basic to deal with automatically. Visual Basic has tools that can help you deal with any kind of run-time error.

Ignore an error

Suppose that you want to create a macro that creates a temporary report worksheet. The macro will give the name Report to the report worksheet, and it will replace any existing Report worksheet in the active workbook. The Lesson8 workbook contains a macro named MakeReport that creates and names the Report worksheet. Here is the original macro:

```
Sub MakeReport()
    Dim mySheet As Worksheet
    Set mySheet = Worksheets.Add
    mySheet.Name = "Report"
End Sub
```

The macro adds a worksheet, assigning a reference to the new worksheet to the mySheet variable. It then changes the Name property of the sheet.

1 Go to the MakeReport macro, and then press F5 to run it.

The macro created a new worksheet.

You should see a new worksheet named Report in the active workbook. The macro works fine. Or at least it seems to work fine. What happens if you run the macro again?

2 Press F5 again to run the macro a second time.

Unless you specify otherwise, a run-time error displays a dialog box like this.

Visual Basic displays an error message informing you that you can't rename a sheet to the name of an existing sheet. The solution is simple: all you have to do is delete the old Report sheet before you rename the new one.

3 Click End to remove the error message, and insert these two statements before the one that renames the worksheet:

```
Application.DisplayAlerts = False
Worksheets("Report").Delete
```

Turning off alert messages keeps Excel from asking if you really want to delete the sheet.

4 Press F8 repeatedly to step through the macro. You may see the macro step through the Random function, because a volatile function often recalculates when you rename the worksheet.

The macro creates a new worksheet, deletes the old Report worksheet, and then renames the new worksheet. Once again the macro works fine. Or at least it seems to work fine. What happens if there is no Report worksheet in the workbook?

5 Switch to Excel, delete the Report worksheet, switch back to Visual Basic, and press F5 to run the macro.

```
Microsoft Visual Basic

Run-time error '9':

Subscript out of range




   Continue      End      Debug      Help
```

Once again, you get an error message, this time informing you that the subscript is out of range. In other words, there is no item named Report in the Worksheets collection.

The interesting thing about this error is that you really don't care. You were just going to delete the worksheet anyway. If it already doesn't exist, so much the better.

6 Click the End button to clear the error message, and insert this statement above the one that deletes the worksheet:

```
On Error Resume Next
```

This statement tells Visual Basic to ignore any run-time errors and simply continue with the next statement.

7 Press F5 to test the macro. Test it again now that the Report worksheet exists.

Finally, the macro seems to work properly. Some errors simply deserve to be ignored.

Ignore an error safely

When you use an On Error Resume Next statement, Visual Basic ignores all run-time errors until you turn error checking back on, or until Visual Basic gets to an End Sub or End Function statement. You should be very careful when you tell Visual Basic to ignore errors, that you don't ignore errors that you didn't mean to ignore.

If the statement Option Explicit appears at the top of the module, delete it.

1 In the MakeReport macro you created in the previous section, remove the quotation marks from around the word "*Report*" in the statement that gives the worksheet a new name. This will create a run-time error.

The revised, erroneous statement should now look like this:

```
mySheet.Name = Report
```

2 Press F5 to test the macro.

The macro should have named the sheet *Report*.

The macro appeared to run just fine, but you do not have a Report worksheet when you are done. Visual Basic interpreted the word *Report*, without the quotation marks, as a new (empty) variable, and was unable to assign that empty name to the worksheet. Unfortunately, since you had told Visual Basic to ignore errors, it didn't even warn you of a problem. (Of course, if you had inserted *Option Explicit* at the top of the module, Visual Basic would have complained about using an undefined variable.)

The best way to ignore errors for just one or two statements is to put the statements into a Sub procedure of their own. When Visual Basic gets to an End Sub or End Function statement, it cancels the effect of the On Error Resume Next statement.

3 Create a new Sub procedure named DeleteSheet. This procedure will quietly delete the Report worksheet if it exists.

4 Move the three statements that delete the worksheet into the DeleteSheet macro. The new macro should look like this:

```
Sub DeleteSheet()
    Application.DisplayAlerts = False
    On Error Resume Next
    Worksheets("Report").Delete
End Sub
```

The On Error Resume Next statement loses its effect at the End Sub statement, so you only ignore a possible error in the single Delete statement. This is a much safer way to ignore a run-time error.

5   In the MakeReport macro, type **DeleteSheet** where the three statements had been.

The revised MakeReport macro (still containing the error) should look like this:

```
Sub MakeReport()
    Dim mySheet As Worksheet
    Set mySheet = Worksheets.Add
    DeleteSheet
    mySheet.Name = Report
End Sub
```

The MakeReport macro no longer contains an On Error Resume Next statement, so Visual Basic should be able to alert you to the error.

6   Press F5 to run the macro, click End to close the error box, replace the quotation marks around the sheet name, and test the macro when the report file exists as well as when it does not.

You want the macro to warn you about unexpected errors.

This time, the macro really does work well. It ignores the error you want to ignore, and warns you of other, inadvertent errors.

Generalize the DeleteSheet routine

The DeleteSheet macro you created in the previous section quietly deletes the Report worksheet if it happens to exist. Unfortunately, it will delete only the Report worksheet. What if you sometimes need to delete a sheet named Report and other times need to delete a sheet named Analysis? This DeleteSheet procedure has too much potential to limit it to deleting only one specific sheet. You can add an argument to generalize the DeleteSheet routine, in much the same way that you added an argument to the Random function earlier in this lesson.

1   Type **SheetName** as an argument name between the parentheses after the DeleteSheet macro name.

2   Replace *"Report"* with **SheetName** in the body of the DeleteSheet macro. *SheetName* should not have quotation marks around it.

193

3 Type "**Report**" after *DeleteSheet* in the MakeReport macro.

Here's what the two revised macros should look like:

```
Sub MakeReport()
    Dim mySheet As Worksheet
    Set mySheet = Worksheets.Add
    DeleteSheet "Report"
    mySheet.Name = "Report"
End Sub

Sub DeleteSheet(SheetName)
    Application.DisplayAlerts = False
    On Error Resume Next
    Worksheets(SheetName).Delete
End Sub
```

The DeleteSheet macro now knows absolutely nothing about the name of the sheet it will delete. It will simply delete whatever sheet it is given, without asking any questions, and without complaining if it discovers its services are not really needed.

4 Press F5 to test the MakeReport macro.

5 Make a new macro named MakeAnalysis. Make it an exact copy of the MakeReport macro, except have it create a sheet named Analysis.

The macro should look like this:

```
Sub MakeAnalysis()
    Dim mySheet As Worksheet
    Set mySheet = Worksheets.Add
    DeleteSheet "Analysis"
    mySheet.Name = "Analysis"
End Sub
```

6 Test the MakeAnalysis macro.

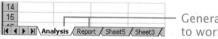
Generalize a sub procedure
to work with any worksheet.

The DeleteSheet macro now not only avoids the inconveniences associated with deleting a worksheet, it is a generalized tool—an enhancement to Excel's built-in capabilities—that you can use from any macro you want.

Check for an error

When you use the On Error Resume Next statement in a macro, Visual Basic allows you to do more than merely ignore the error. Visual Basic contains a special debugging object named Err. The Err object has properties that you can check to see whether an error has occurred and, if so, what the error is.

Suppose that you want to create a Report worksheet, but without deleting any existing Report sheets. Rather, you want to put a suffix on the worksheet name, much as Excel does when you add a new worksheet. In the Lesson8 workbook, there is a macro named MakeNextReport. This macro will create a sheet named Report1 or, if that already exists, it will create a sheet named Report2. Here is the original MakeNextReport macro:

```
Sub MakeNextReport()
    Dim mySheet As Worksheet
    Dim myBase As String
    Dim mySuffix As Integer

    Set mySheet = Worksheets.Add
    myBase = "Report"
    mySuffix = 1

    On Error Resume Next
    mySheet.Name = myBase & mySuffix
    If Err.Number <> 0 Then
        mySuffix = mySuffix + 1
        mySheet.Name = myBase & mySuffix
    End If
End Sub
```

This macro creates a new worksheet and then tries to name it using *Report* as the base name and *1* as the suffix. The On Error Resume Next statement tells Visual Basic not to stop if Excel is unable to rename the sheet. The If statement, however, checks to see if the Err object's Number property is equal to 0. Zero as an error number means that there was no error. If there was an error, the macro increases the suffix to *2* and tries again.

1 Go to the MakeNextReport macro, and then press F8 repeatedly to watch the macro work. Once again, Visual Basic may step through the Random function as the worksheet recalculates.

The macro adds a suffix to the worksheet name.

The new worksheet should rename properly the first time, so the macro never has to increment the suffix.

2 Step through the macro a second time, and then run it a third time.

Sometimes you need to check for more than one error.

195

The second time, the macro does have to increment the suffix number, and the third time it simply fails, leaving the new sheet with the wrong name. The Number property of the Err object is the key to knowing whether an error has occurred.

It would be nice if this macro could be smart enough to keep incrementing the suffix until it finds one that works. That sounds like a job for a loop structure, and since you can't know when the loop begins or how many times you will have to repeat the loop, you will need to use a Do loop.

3   Replace the word *If* with **Do Until**, remove the *Then* at the end of the statement, and change the not equal sign (<>) to an equal sign (=). Then change *End If* to **Loop**.

The last few lines of the macro should look like this:

```
On Error Resume Next
mySheet.Name = myBase & mySuffix
Do Until Err.Number = 0
    mySuffix = mySuffix + 1
    mySheet.Name = myBase & mySuffix
Loop
```

The loop should check to see if the rename occurred successfully. If not, it increments the suffix, tries the rename again, and checks again until there is no error.

4   Press F8 repeatedly to step through the macro.

The first time the macro tries to name the report sheet, it fails, because Report1 already exists, so the macro proceeds into the loop. At the end of the loop, the macro tries to rename the sheet again, but fails again, because Report2 already exists, so the macro reenters the loop a second time. At the end of the loop, the macro tries a third time to rename the sheet. This time the sheet renames properly.

5   Keep stepping in the macro.

 The macro didn't stop when it created a valid name.

Something is wrong. The macro goes into the loop again, renaming the sheet as Report4, then as Report5. This could go on forever.

The macro does not realize that the error is over. The Err.Number value did not automatically change back to 0, just because the macro successfully renamed the worksheet. You need to tell the macro that the error is no longer relevant.

*Reset
button*

6 Click the Reset button to stop the macro. Then, on the line immediately following the Do statement, type the statement **Err.Clear**.

Clear is the name of a method for the Err object. It resets the error number to 0 and makes Visual Basic forget that an error ever occurred.

> **IMPORTANT** Some macro statements change the Err.Number value back to 0 when they complete successfully. Others do not. To be safe, you should clear the Err object before a statement that you want to check, and then inspect the value of Err.Number immediately after that statement executes.

7 Press F5 to test the macro. Test it again. And again. The macro is now able to create a new report sheet, incrementing as much as necessary—but no more!

The macro works once
it clears the old error.

It is only meaningful to check the value of Err.Number after you use an On Error Resume Next statement, since otherwise Visual Basic would have halted with an error message box. Looking at the properties of the Err object is a good way to gain control over the way your macro handles errors.

Trap an error

So far, you have seen three ways to handle a run-time error: you can let Visual Basic display the error dialog box, you can ignore the error altogether, or you can check for a non-zero error number after each statement.

Having Visual Basic display an error message may not be a bad alternative if you are writing macros for yourself, but if you want to give a macro to someone else, you probably want more control over what the error message says. Checking for a nonzero error value after every statement, however, can make your macros hard to read. Fortunately, Visual Basic can monitor the error value for you. This is called *trapping* an error.

Suppose, for example, that you had a macro that opens, prints, and closes several workbooks. It is possible that one of the workbooks might be missing when the macro runs. In the Lesson8 workbook is a macro named CheckFiles that opens and closes several practice workbooks that came with the book. In the interest of conserving trees, the macro does not actually print the workbooks.

One of the workbook file names, however, has been misspelled. Here is the original macro:

```
Sub CheckFiles()
    Workbooks.Open "Graphics"
    ActiveWorkbook.Close
    Workbooks.Open "Ranges"
    ActiveWorkbook.Close
    Workbooks.Open "Bad File Name"
    ActiveWorkbook.Close
    Workbooks.Open "Budget"
    ActiveWorkbook.Close
End Sub
```

You naturally can't tell which of the files will not be found until the macro actually runs. If you run this macro, you'll see Visual Basic's standard error message.

Microsoft Visual Basic

Run-time error '1004':

' Bad File Name .xls' could not be found. Check the spelling of the file name, and verify that the file location is correct.

If you are trying to open the file from your list of most recently used files on the File menu, make sure that the file has not been renamed, moved, or deleted.

| Continue | End | Debug | Help |

Here are the steps you follow to add special code that Visual Basic will run whenever an error occurs.

1. At the end of the macro, type the statement **CheckFiles_Err:** just before the End Sub statement.

   The statement *CheckFiles_Err:* is called a *label*. A label consists of a single word followed by a colon. You can indent it if you want, but you might want to keep it lined up with the Sub and End Sub statements because it behaves like an appendix to the macro. A label must always end with a colon.

    NOTE You can use any name you want for a label within the macro. You may like to use the name of the macro plus the suffix *_Err*. That makes it easy to know that the label is part of the macro, and that it exists to help handle errors.

2 After the error label, type the statement **MsgBox Err.Number**.

The statements below the label are the ones that the macro will execute when it detects an error. These statements are called an *error handler*. The simplest error handler is a message box that displays the number of the error.

3 Immediately before the error label, type the statement **Exit Sub**.

You do not want the statements in the error handler to execute if the macro completes normally. If the macro gets to the Exit Sub statement, that means that no error was detected.

4 At the top of the macro, just under the Sub statement, type the statement **On Error GoTo CheckFiles_Err**.

This statement tells Visual Basic that if it sees a run-time error, it should drop whatever it is doing and jump immediately to the label you specify. You do not put a colon after the label name here. You only use a colon when you create the actual label.

5 Press F5 to test the macro.

— Use Err.Number to find the number of the most recent error.

Visual Basic should display a simple message box showing only the message number. You can make the message more elaborate. The Err object has a Description property that gives a longer text description of the error. That description is often a useful addition to an error message box.

6 Click OK. Delete the statement *MsgBox Err.Number* and replace it with these statements:

```
MsgBox "Please notify Reed Jacobson with this error number: " & _
"Error Number: " & Err.Number & _
vbCrLf & vbCrLf & Err.Description
```

You can string many pieces together to form an error message. Just put an ampersand in between each piece. The word *vbCrLf* is a built-in Visual Basic constant that means "Carriage Return Line Feed," or CRLF. A CRLF is a computer term for a new line. You can put vbCrLf into a string anytime you want to force the message to go to a new line. (When you create your own macros, I would be most grateful if you substitute your own name for mine in the error message. Thanks.)

7 Press F5 to run the macro and see the more elaborate error message.

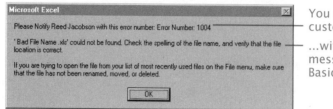

You can combine a custom message...

...with the error message Visual Basic provides.

The finished macro should look like this:

```
Sub CheckFiles()
    On Error GoTo CheckFiles_Err
    Workbooks.Open "Graphics"
    ActiveWorkbook.Close
    Workbooks.Open "Ranges"
    ActiveWorkbook.Close
    Workbooks.Open "Bad File Name "
    ActiveWorkbook.Close
    Workbooks.Open "Budget"
    ActiveWorkbook.Close
    Exit Sub
CheckFiles_Err:
    MsgBox "Please notify Reed Jacobson with this error number: " & _
    "Error Number: " & Err.Number & _
    vbCrLf & vbCrLf & Err.Description
End Sub
```

If you are creating an application for someone else to use and you do not want that person to ever see Visual Basic's default error dialog box, you should always include an error handler in every macro that the user launches directly. If you have some statements where the error should be handled differently—either ignored or checked on a statement-by-statement basis—put those statements into a separate procedure and use an On Error Resume Next statement within that procedure. Visual Basic will automatically restore the error handler when the procedure ends. Visual Basic gives you a great deal of control over how you can handle errors.

Lesson Summary

To	Do this
Create a custom function	Replace the word *Sub* at the beginning of a macro with the word *Function*.
Determine the return value for a function	Create a statement inside the function that assigns a value to the function name.
Add arguments to a function	Put names for the arguments inside the parentheses after the function name, and then use the arguments as if they were pre-filled variables.
Make a custom function recalculate each time the worksheet recalculates	Use *Application.Volatile True* at the beginning of the function.
Make an argument optional	Use *Optional* in front of the argument name in the function declaration statement.
Create a default value for an optional argument	Assign a value to the argument name in the function declaration statement.
Ignore a run-time error	Use *On Error Resume Next* before the statement that may have an error.
Ignore an error for only certain statements	Create a separate Sub procedure or function that contains the statements with the error you want to ignore, and put an On Error Resume Next statement in that procedure.
Check to see if an error has occurred in a macro that uses an On Error Resume Next statement	Look for a nonzero value in the Number property of the Err object.
Reset the Err object when an error has occurred	Use the statement *Err.Clear* after the statement with the error.
Make the macro jump to the label *Routine_Err:* when a run-time error occurs	Use the statement *On Error GoTo Routine_Err* at the top of the macro.

For online information about	Ask the Assistant for help using the words
Creating a function procedure	"Writing a function procedure"
Using arguments	"Arguments"
Handling errors	"Handling errors"

Preview of the Next Lesson

So far, you have launched macros by clicking the Run Macro button on the Visual Basic toolbar, pressing a shortcut key, or pressing F5 in Visual Basic. In the next lesson, you will learn how to launch macros using events, an exciting feature that is brand-new in Excel 97.

Making Macros Easy to Use

Part 4

Launching Macros with Events

Estimated time

30 min.

In this lesson you will learn how to:

- Create custom toolbar buttons.
- Create custom menu commands.
- Create custom command buttons.
- Create worksheet and workbook event handlers.

My grandmother used to use her sewing machine to embroider names on outfits for us. She had a powerful old sewing machine, with lots of pulleys and levers and loops. When she changed the thread, she had to poke the new thread up and over and through what seemed like countless turns and spools and guides, before even getting to the needle. I still don't know how she managed embroidering the names. She would move levers and twist the fabric and the name somehow appeared. She was very good, and the result was beautiful. Very few people could create embroidered names the way she did.

Now even I can embroider names onto clothes. I flip the thread around a couple of guides and the machine is threaded. I type in the name, select the lettering style, and push another button to embroider the name. The machine sews in all directions so I don't even have to turn the fabric. Anyone can use a sewing machine these days.

One purpose of macros is to make your own life simpler. An even more important one may be to enable others to accomplish tasks that they would not be able to do without your help. In this lesson and the lessons that follow, you will learn how to make macros easy for others to use.

Start the lesson

 Start Microsoft Excel, change to the folder containing the practice files for this book, open the Events workbook, and save a copy as **Lesson9**.

Creating Custom Toolbars and Menus

You might feel perfectly comfortable running a macro by pressing a shortcut key combination or even pressing F5 in the Visual Basic Editor. If you are going to give a macro to somebody else, however, you want to make it as easy to run as possible. One way to make a macro easy to run is to integrate it into the Excel environment. Most built-in commands can be initiated by choosing a menu command or clicking a toolbar button. By adding your macros to menus and toolbars, you can make them seem as if they are integral parts of Excel.

Try out the ZoomIn and ZoomOut macros

The Lesson9 workbook already contains two simple macros, ZoomIn and ZoomOut, that will change the size of your display. These are macros that you will assign to custom toolbar buttons and menu commands. Here are the macros:

```
Sub ZoomIn()
    Dim myZoom As Integer
    myZoom = ActiveWindow.Zoom + 10
    If myZoom <= 400 Then
        ActiveWindow.Zoom = myZoom
    End If
End Sub

Sub ZoomOut()
    Dim myZoom As Integer
    myZoom = ActiveWindow.Zoom - 10
    If myZoom >= 10 Then
        ActiveWindow.Zoom = myZoom
    End If
End Sub
```

Each macro considers a new value for the Zoom property of the active window. If the new value is within the acceptable limits (between 10% and 400%, the range of zoom factors in Excel), it changes the property; otherwise it does nothing.

1   Go to the ZoomIn macro. Press F5 a few times to see how the worksheet zooms in. Step through the macro if you want, to feel comfortable with how it works.

The ZoomIn macro enlarges the worksheet.

	A	B	C
1			
2			
3			

2   Go to the ZoomOut macro. Press F5 as necessary to redisplay the window at a normal size.

These are typical macros. In this lesson you will learn new ways to run them.

Create a custom toolbar

A toolbar button is a convenient way to launch a macro. A toolbar is small, and easy to show or hide. An icon can make a tool easy to find, and a ToolTip can make it easy to remember.

1   Activate the Excel window, right-click any toolbar, and click the Customize command.

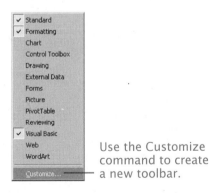

Use the Customize command to create a new toolbar.

2   In the Customize dialog box, click the Toolbars tab.

3   Click the New button, type **Zoom** as the name for the toolbar, and click OK.

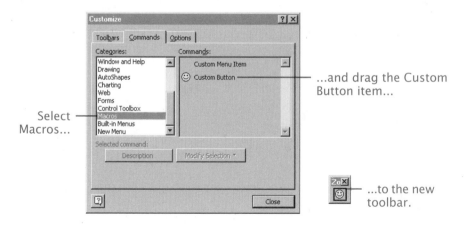

The toolbar name will appear on the toolbar's caption.

A new, empty toolbar appears. The Customize dialog box is still open and available to help you fill the toolbar.

4   Click the Commands tab in the Customize dialog box, and select Macros from the Categories list.

Select Macros...

...and drag the Custom Button item...

...to the new toolbar.

5 Drag the Custom Button item (complete with its happy face) from the Commands list onto the Zoom toolbar.

When you drag the item onto the toolbar, the Modify Selection button becomes available.

6 Click the Modify Selection button, press N to select the Name box, and type **Zoom &In** as the new name. Do not press ENTER.

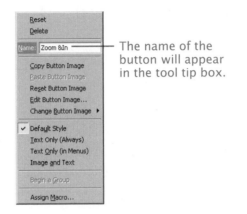

The name of the button will appear in the tool tip box.

The value in the Name box determines what the ToolTip for the button will be. The ampersand (&) precedes the letter that will be underlined if you use this command on a menu. The ampersand has no effect on the toolbar button, but put it there anyway.

If the menu disappeared, click the Modify Selection button again to redisplay it.

7 Click the Change Button Image command, and click the up arrow icon.

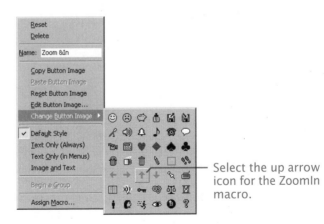

Select the up arrow icon for the ZoomIn macro.

The icon on the button changes, and the menu disappears.

209

8 Click the Modify Selection button, and click the Assign Macro command. Select the ZoomIn macro, and click OK.

Assign Macro	? X
Macro Name:	
ZoomIn	OK
ZoomIn	Cancel
ZoomOut	
	Edit
	Record...
Macros in:	All Open Workbooks
Description	

If you don't see the Zoom toolbar, try moving the Customize dialog box out of the way.

9 Repeat steps 4 to 8, but this time give the button the name **Zoom &Out**, select the down arrow icon, and assign the ZoomOut macro to the button.

10 Click the Close button, and then try out the toolbar buttons. Hold the mouse over the button to see the ToolTip appear. Hide and redisplay the toolbar.

The custom button displays a ToolTip the same as a built-in button does.

Once you have a macro, it is easy to assign it to a toolbar button. Use the Customize dialog box to create and add buttons to the toolbar. Use the Modify Selection button to change the name, icon, and macro for a button.

Create a custom menu

A menu command is another convenient way to launch a macro. A menu command stays out of the way, reducing clutter on the desktop, but the menu it belongs to is always available, whereas a toolbar can be temporarily hidden. In Microsoft Office 97, a menu is really just a specialized toolbar. That means that adding a command to a menu is just as easy as adding it to a toolbar.

1 Right-click any toolbar, and click the Customize command to display the Customize dialog box.

2 Click the Commands tab, and select New Menu from the Categories list.

Select the New
Menu category to
add a new menu
to a menu bar.

The New Menu category has only a single item: New Menu. You can use this item to create a new menu on a menu bar, or a new submenu on an existing menu.

3 Drag the New Menu item up to Excel's menu bar, dropping it between the Window and Help menus.

The new menu appears
in Excel's menu bar.

4 Click the Modify Selection button, change the value in the Name box to **&Zoom**, and press ENTER.

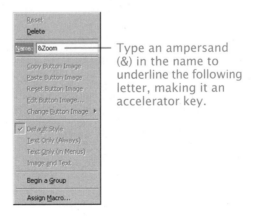

Type an ampersand
(&) in the name to
underline the following
letter, making it an
accelerator key.

If you look closely at the Zoom menu, you can see that the letter *Z* is underlined. That's because there is an ampersand (&) in front of the *Z* in the menu item name. The underlined letter, which lets you execute the command by pressing the ALT key followed by that letter, is called an *access key* or an *accelerator key*.

You could add brand new commands to the Zoom menu, but since you already have the toolbar buttons on the Zoom toolbar, you can copy them to the Zoom menu. (It is often a good idea to put commands on both a toolbar and a menu bar, giving a user the choice of which to use.)

In this step, be careful not to release the mouse button too soon.

5 Drag the Zoom In toolbar button (the one with the up arrow icon) up to the Zoom menu. A small, blank menu appears. Drag the button onto the menu, and then hold down the CTRL key as you release the mouse button.

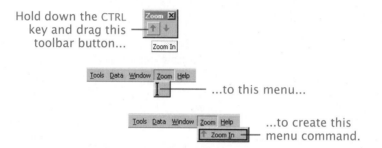

If you do not hold down the CTRL key when you release the mouse button, you will move the toolbar button rather than make a copy. If you do accidentally move the button, simply hold down the CTRL key as you drag it back from the menu to the toolbar.

The command name for the new menu item is the same as the ToolTip for the toolbar button. The command name has the letter *I* underlined. When you add a name to a toolbar button, think about what letter you want underlined if you move the button to a menu, and insert an ampersand in front of the letter when you first name the button.

6 Drag the Zoom Out toolbar button up to the Zoom menu, holding down the CTRL key as you release the mouse.

7 Close the Customize dialog box and try out the menu commands. Test them using the keyboard shortcuts. Press ALT, Z, I, and ALT, Z, O to make sure the accelerator keys work properly.

When you add a command to a toolbar, you can easily copy it to a menu, or if you add a command to a menu, you can easily copy it to a toolbar. The general term that includes both toolbars and menus is *command bar*. The new Customize dialog box for command bars makes moving between toolbars and menus delightfully simple.

Run macros from a closed workbook

Normally, you can run a macro only when the workbook that contains the macro is open. Toolbar buttons and menu commands, however, have a unique capability: they remember where to find a macro, even when that macro's workbook is closed.

New button

1   Save and close the Lesson9 workbook. Click the New button to create a new workbook.

2   Click the Zoom In toolbar button on the Zoom toolbar.

The Lesson9 workbook automatically opens and hides behind the active workbook, and the macro runs.

3   Close the temporary workbook that you created, revealing the Lesson9 workbook.

Remove menus and toolbars

Toolbar buttons and menu commands customize a user's workspace. Once you create a custom menu or toolbar, it will remain a part of Excel on that computer until you remove it. Since you probably will not be using the Zoom toolbar or menu on an ongoing basis, you should remove them now. Here's how:

1   Right-click any toolbar and click Customize to show the Customize dialog box.

2   Click the Toolbars tab, select the Zoom toolbar in the list, click the Delete button, and click OK.

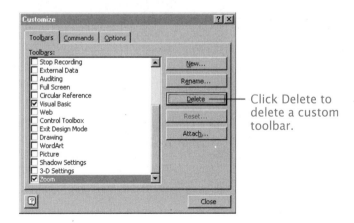

Click Delete to delete a custom toolbar.

3 Click on the Zoom menu, and holding down the mouse button, drag the menu off onto the Excel worksheet.

While the Customize dialog box is visible, drag the menu off the menu bar to delete the menu.

The menu permanently disappears.

4 Click the Close button in the Customize dialog box.

Toolbar buttons and menu commands are very effective tools for customizing a user's copy of Excel. They remain available and active even when you close the workbook containing the macros they are attached to.

Sometimes, however, you want to give someone a button that is available only when a specific workbook is open. A command button is such a tool.

Creating Custom Command Buttons

Toolbar buttons and menu commands respond to a single event: a click. You tell the button or command which macro to run by using the Assign Macro command. Command buttons, on the other hand, can not only trigger an event when you click them, but also respond to additional events as well, such as the simple movement of the mouse above the button. Because command buttons can respond to a complex set of events, they require a whole new way of linking a macro to the button. This new approach uses what are called *event handler procedures*. Event handler procedures are special macros that are linked to an object such as a command button. First create a command button, and then you can see how to add event handler procedures to make it work.

Create a custom command button

A command button is useful for running macros that relate to a specific sheet. Command buttons are usually large and easy to click, with a label describing what the button will do.

[Control Toolbox button icon]

Control Toolbox button

1 With the Lesson9 workbook open, click the Control Toolbox button on the Visual Basic toolbar to display the Control Toolbox toolbar.

Control Toolbox

— The Control Toolbox toolbar

*You will put
controls on a
worksheet in
Lesson 10 and
controls on
a form in
Lesson 11.*

*Command
Button button*

The Control Toolbox is a toolbar that contains a number of controls that you can use on a worksheet or on a form. These controls are called *ActiveX controls*. An ActiveX control is a special kind of drawing object that carries out an action when you click it. The ActiveX control we will work with in this lesson is the command button control.

2   Click the Command Button button and drag a rectangle on the worksheet from the top-left corner of cell A1 to the bottom-right corner of B2.

> **TIP**   You can easily "snap" any drawing object to align with the corners of a cell by holding down the ALT key as you drag a rectangle for the object. You can also hold down the ALT key to snap to cell gridlines as you move or resize an existing drawing object.

A command button appears on the worksheet. It has white handles on the edges, showing that it is currently selected.

While the command button is selected, you can change its properties. Up to now you have changed properties using Visual Basic commands. ActiveX controls, however, have a special Properties window that allows you to change properties directly.

*Properties
button*

3   On the Control Toolbox toolbar, click the Properties button.

Properties	✕
CommandButton1 CommandButton	▾

Alphabetic	Categorized

(Name)	CommandButton1
Accelerator	
AutoLoad	False
AutoSize	False
BackColor	☐ &H8000000F&
BackStyle	1 - fmBackStyleOpaqu
Caption	CommandButton1
Enabled	True
Font	MS Sans Serif

The Properties window appears. The box at the top shows you which object's properties are being displayed. In this case, it is CommandButton1, which is a CommandButton object.

215

This window shows various properties of the command button. One important property of the command button is its name. This property appears as *(Name)* in the Properties window. The parentheses make the Name property sort to the top of the list. The Name property affects how you use the button in your macros.

4   Replace the default value of the Name property with **btnZoomIn**.

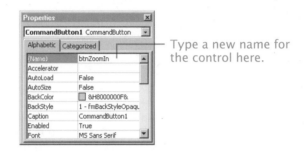

Type a new name for the control here.

You cannot put spaces into the name. Many people use three-letter prefixes when naming controls. The three-letter prefix helps identify what kind of control it is; in this case, *btn* stands for "button."

Changing the name of the button does not change the label displayed on it, however. That is the function of the Caption property.

5   Replace the default value of the Caption property with **Zoom In**.

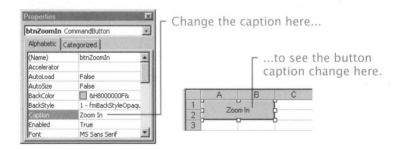

Change the caption here...

...to see the button caption change here.

The caption on the button changes as soon as you change the Caption property. With ActiveX controls, you do not use an ampersand to specify the accelerator; instead, there is a separate Accelerator property for that purpose.

6   We want the letter *I* to be the accelerator key. Type **I** as the value of the Accelerator property.

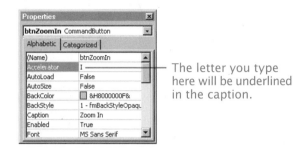

The letter you type here will be underlined in the caption.

As soon as you assign I to the Accelerator property, the letter *I* in the caption becomes underlined.

There is one more property that you should set when you create a custom command button. It affects the active cell in Excel. Suppose cell B4 is the active cell when you click the command button. You would normally expect cell B4 to be the active cell even after clicking the button (unless the button runs a macro that changes the active cell.) But the default behavior of a command button is to remove the dark border around the active cell, making it impossible to see which cell is active.

7   Scroll down to the TakeFocusOnClick property and change it to False in the resulting drop-down list.

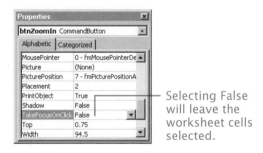

Selecting False will leave the worksheet cells selected.

TakeFocusOnClick is a complicated name for a simple property. Setting it to False simply means, "Leave the active cell alone when you click this button."

You now have created and customized the command button. All that is left is to link it to a macro and make it run.

Link a command button to a macro

You do not assign a macro to a command button. Instead, you create a macro with a special name, in a special place, and the macro automatically links to the button. Fortunately, the Control Toolbox has a button that will do all the work for you.

View Code button

1 With the command button still selected, click the View Code button.

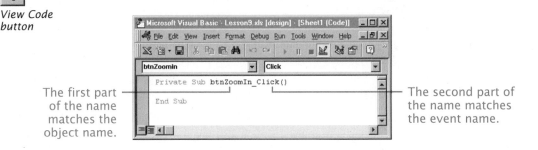

The first part of the name matches the object name.

The second part of the name matches the event name.

The Visual Basic Editor window appears with a new macro. The word *Private* before the macro name means that this macro will not appear in the Run Macro dialog box. The macro name is btnZoomIn_Click. The name is very important. The part of the name before the underscore matches the command button. The part of the name after the underscore matches the name of the event that this macro will handle. In this example, the macro will run whenever you click the button. A macro linked to an event like this is called an *event handler*.

> **NOTE** The word *procedure* is a more technical synonym for a macro. Excel uses the word *macro* because "macro recorder" is less intimidating than "procedure recorder." In general, this book will use *macro* to refer to those procedures that you can run from the Macro dialog box, and *procedure* to refer to functions and event handlers.

You could copy the code from the ZoomIn macro into the btnZoomIn_Click procedure, but it is easier to simply run that macro (since it already exists) from this one.

2 Type **ZoomIn** as the body of the procedure.

```
Private Sub btnZoomIn_Click()
    ZoomIn
End Sub
```

You are now ready to try clicking the button.

3   Switch back to Excel, click on any cell in the worksheet to deselect the button, and then click the button.

The procedure does not run. You simply reselected the button.

You need some way of letting Excel know whether clicking an ActiveX control should run the event handler or simply select the control. You do that by controlling *design mode*. When Excel is in design mode, clicking a control selects it. When Excel is not in design mode (a condition called *run mode*), clicking a control runs the event handler procedure. Whenever you put an ActiveX control on a worksheet, Excel automatically switches to design mode.

Exit Design Mode button

4   Click the Exit Design Mode button.

The selection handles disappear from the command button.

Design Mode button

5   Try out the button: click it. Press ALT+I to try out the accelerator key.

6   Click the Design Mode button to turn design mode back on, and click the command button.

It becomes selected.

Attaching an event handler procedure to a control is different from attaching a macro to a toolbar button:

- With a toolbar button, you can name the macro whatever you want, and then use the Assign Macro dialog box to link the macro to the button. With an event handler, the name and location of the procedure creates the link to the control.

- With a toolbar button, you make Excel ignore events by opening the Customize dialog box. With a control, you do this by clicking the Design Mode button.

Create an event handler on your own

You can create an event handler for a control by clicking the View Code button. You might find it enlightening to see how you can also create an event handler directly in the Visual Basic Editor.

1   Repeat steps 2 to 7 of the section, "Create a custom command button," to create a Zoom Out command button. Drag a rectangle on the worksheet from the top-left corner of cell A3 to the bottom-right corner of cell B4. In the Properties window, give it the name **btnZoomOut**, the caption **Zoom Out**, and the letter **O** as its accelerator. Also, set the TakeFocusOnClick property to False. Do not create an event handler procedure.

2   Switch to Visual Basic, and click anywhere in the btnZoomIn_Click procedure.

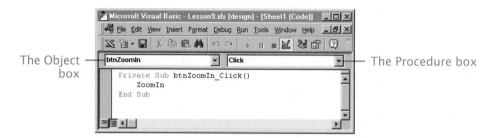

The Object box — The box on the left contains btnZoomIn — The Procedure box

Above the code portion of the window are two boxes. The box on the left contains the first half of the procedure name (*btnZoomIn*) and the box on the right contains the second half of the procedure name (*Click*). These two boxes are named Object and Procedure, respectively.

3   Click the arrow next to the Object list.

The list shows all the objects related to the current worksheet that can have event handlers: here, btnZoomIn, btnZoomOut, and Worksheet.

4   Select btnZoomOut from the list.

A new procedure appears. Click is the default event for a button, so the new procedure is named btnZoomOut_Click, precisely what you need.

5   Type **ZoomOut** as the body of the procedure.

6   Switch to Excel, turn off design mode, and try out both buttons.

The lists at the top of the code window can help you build event handlers by combining an object with an event.

Make a button respond to mouse movements

The command button actually has several different events that it can recognize. Three of the most useful events are a click (the Click event), a double-click (the DblClick event), and a mouse movement (the MouseMove event). The MouseMove event is especially useful because it provides information to the procedure in the form of arguments.

1   In Visual Basic, select btnZoomOut from the Object list, and then select MouseMove from the Procedure list.

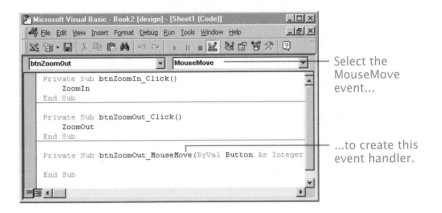

Select the MouseMove event...

...to create this event handler.

The declaration for the new procedure is relatively long. This is what it looks like when divided into shorter lines:

```
Private Sub btnZoomOut_MouseMove( _
    ByVal Button As Integer, _
    ByVal Shift As Integer, _
    ByVal X As Single, _
    ByVal Y As Single)
```

This event handler procedure has four arguments: Button, Shift, X, and Y. (The word *byVal* means that Excel will ignore any changes the procedure makes to an argument.) The arguments communicate information to you that you can take advantage of as you write the macro. The Button argument indicates whether a mouse button is down as the mouse moves. The Shift argument indicates whether the SHIFT, CTRL, or ALT keys are pressed. The X and Y arguments indicate the horizontal and vertical position of the mouse.

2   Insert **ZoomOut** as the body of the new procedure, switch to Excel, and move the mouse over the Zoom Out button.

Just move the mouse over the button to zoom out.

You don't even have to click. Just moving the mouse over the button causes the procedure to run. Events can happen very fast.

You can use the arguments that the MouseMove event provides you to control the procedure. Specifically, if Shift is equal to 1, the SHIFT key is down. If it is equal to 2, then the CTRL key is down. You can change the procedure so that it zooms in when the SHIFT key is down and zooms out when the CTRL key is down.

3   Replace the body of the btnZoomOut_MouseMove procedure with these statements:

```
If Shift = 1 Then
    ZoomIn
ElseIf Shift = 2 Then
    ZoomOut
End If
```

 NOTE   The ElseIf keyword allows you to combine Else and If statements into a single statement.

4   Switch to Excel and try out the event handler. Try moving the mouse by itself. Then try holding down the SHIFT key as you move it. Then try holding down the CTRL key as you move it.

As you move the mouse over the button, you can practically see the procedure running over and over. Each time the button detects the mouse moving, it triggers another event and the event handler procedure runs again. Event handler procedures can be a very powerful way to make things happen.

Explore the Visual Basic project

You may wonder where all these event handlers are stored, and how they relate to the macros that you create with the macro recorder. When you use the macro recorder to create a macro, the macro is stored in a module. You can have multiple macros in a single module, and you can have multiple modules in a workbook. (Each time you close and reopen a workbook, the macro recorder creates a new module for any new macros you record.) Event handler procedures for a command button are attached to the worksheet that contains that button. Visual Basic refers to all the code in a single workbook—whether the code is in a module or attached to a worksheet—as a *project*. Visual Basic has a special window that allows you to explore the project.

*Project Explorer
button*

1   In Visual Basic, click the Project Explorer button.

The Project window appears. The name of the project is VBAProject and the name of the workbook (Lesson9.xls) appears in parentheses. Procedures can be stored either on module sheets (grouped under Modules in the Project window), or attached to workbooks and worksheets (grouped under Microsoft Excel Objects in the Project window).

Behind each worksheet is a hidden page that contains any code for that worksheet, or for objects on that worksheet. When you create a new worksheet, a new code page appears in the Project window. When you delete a worksheet, the worksheet's code page disappears.

2   Double-click the entry labeled Module1.

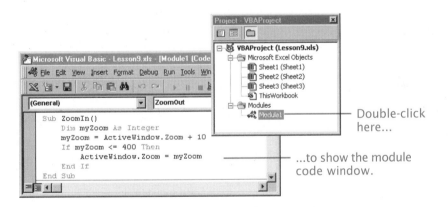

Double-click here...

...to show the module code window.

The main Visual Basic window displays the macros stored in Module1.

3 Double-click the entry labeled Sheet1.

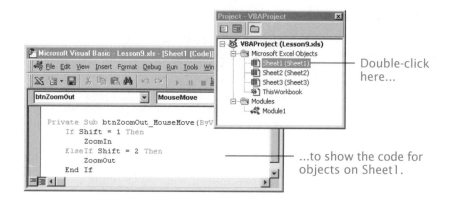

Double-click here...

...to show the code for objects on Sheet1.

The main Visual Basic window displays the event handlers for the objects on Sheet1.

4 In Excel, drag the sheet tab for Sheet1 to the right and hold down the CTRL key as you release the mouse.

Create a new sheet in Excel.

Excel creates a copy of the sheet. The copy's name is Sheet1 (2), and it has its own copy of the command buttons.

5 Switch to Visual Basic and look at the Project window now.

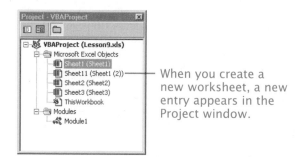

When you create a new worksheet, a new entry appears in the Project window.

There is a new sheet in the list under Microsoft Excel Objects. The name in parentheses, Sheet1 (2), matches the name on the worksheet tab. The name in front of the parentheses, Sheet11, is a unique name that Visual Basic generates.

6 Double-click the Sheet11 worksheet item in the Project window.

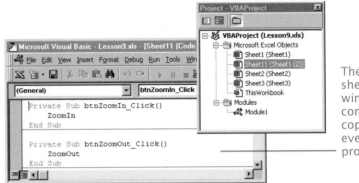

The new sheet's code window contains copies of the event handler procedures.

The main Visual Basic window now shows the event handler procedures for the copies of the command buttons. These procedures look just like the procedures that are linked to the command buttons on Sheet1, but they are now separate entities. Even if you change the btnZoomIn_Click procedure on Sheet11, the btnZoomIn_Click procedure on Sheet1 remains unchanged.

7 In Excel, delete the Sheet1 (2) worksheet. Then switch back to Visual Basic and look at the Project window.

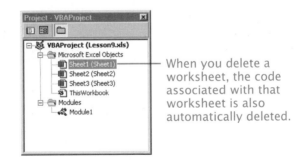

When you delete a worksheet, the code associated with that worksheet is also automatically deleted.

As you probably anticipated, the entry for Sheet11 has disappeared, along with the procedures that were associated with it.

IMPORTANT When you delete a worksheet that has event handler procedures associated with it, all the procedures are destroyed with the worksheet. Save your work frequently when you write event handlers for worksheets, so you can recover your work if you accidentally delete a worksheet.

Handling Worksheet and Workbook Events

ActiveX controls aren't the only objects in Excel that can have events. Worksheets and workbooks have events, too. Each of these objects has different events that it can respond to.

Run a procedure when the selection changes

1 In Visual Basic, activate the Sheet1 code window. (Activate the Project window and double-click Sheet1.)

2 From the Objects list, at the top-left of the code window, select Worksheet.

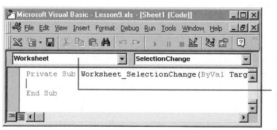

A worksheet object can respond to events.

A new procedure appears with the name Worksheet_SelectionChange. This event happens whenever you change the selection on the worksheet. It doesn't matter whether you click on a cell or use the arrow keys to move around; the event happens either way.

Just to see what events are available for a worksheet, click the arrow next to the Procedure list, at the top right of the code window.

This list shows the available events for the Worksheet object.

The list shows the seven events that a worksheet can respond to. SelectionChange is the default event for a worksheet, just as Click is the default event for a command button.

3 Press ESC to close the list of events, and enter these statements as the body of the Worksheet_SelectionChange procedure:

```
If ActiveCell.Interior.Color = vbCyan Then
    Selection.Interior.Color = vbYellow
Else
    Selection.Interior.Color = vbCyan
End If
```

The procedure will now change all the selected cells to light blue unless the active cell already happens to be blue.

4   Activate Sheet1 in Excel and click several different cells. Press arrow keys to move between cells. Drag a selection rectangle through several cells.

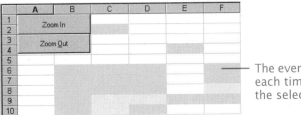

The event handler runs each time you change the selection.

The cell colors change every time you change which cells are selected.

5   Now activate Sheet2 and select a cell.

Nothing happens. The Worksheet_SelectionChange event handler is active only for the original worksheet.

Handle an event on any worksheet

When you create an event handler for Sheet1's SelectionChange event, that handler applies only to that worksheet. If you activate Sheet2 and change the selection, nothing happens. Worksheet event handlers respond to events only on their own worksheet. To handle an event on any worksheet, you must use a workbook-level event handler.

1   In Visual Basic, activate the Project window and double-click the ThisWorkbook item.

2   From the Object list, select Workbook.

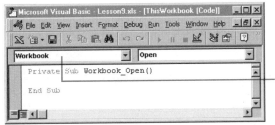

A workbook can respond to events.

A new procedure appears with the name Workbook_Open. Open is the default event for a workbook. This is the event you would use if you wanted to run a procedure every time you opened the workbook.

3   Click the Procedures list to see the events available for a workbook.

This list shows the events available for a workbook object.

A workbook can respond to any of 19 different events. It just happens that seven of the events begin with *Sheet*. These seven workbook Sheet events correspond to the seven events for a worksheet, except that they apply to any worksheet in the workbook, even worksheets that don't exist yet.

4   Select the SheetSelectionChange event. This creates a new Workbook_SheetSelectionChange procedure.

5   Delete the Workbook_Open procedure. You won't need this one.

6   Type **Selection.Interior.Color = vbRed** as the body of the procedure.

```
Private Sub Workbook_SheetSelectionChange(ByVal
    Selection.Interior.Color = vbRed
End Sub
```

7   Switch to Excel, activate Sheet2, and click various cells.

The cells change to red.

8   Activate Sheet1, and click various cells.

The cells change to red. What happened to the SelectionChange event handler procedure for this sheet?

It may seem that the event handler for the workbook replaces the one for an individual sheet, but that is not quite true. In fact, they both ran. The workbook one just ran last. The property for the interior color of the cell changed to blue (or yellow) and then very quickly changed to red. You didn't see the intermediate color because Windows does not refresh the screen until the macro finishes. So all you ever see is the final color.

You can create event handler procedures for events that take place on a worksheet. Worksheet event handler procedures can exist either at the worksheet level or at the workbook level. If the procedure is at the workbook level, it handles events for all worksheets, regardless of whether a worksheet has an event handler of its own.

Suppress a workbook event

It may seem strange that a worksheet event handler would not override a workbook event handler for the same event. In fact, having the worksheet event occur first gives you a great deal of control over how to take advantage of events.

If you want both event handlers to run, you don't have to do anything. If you want the worksheet event handler to suppress the workbook event handler, you can make the worksheet event handler tell the workbook event handler to do nothing. The way you do that is by creating a custom property at the workbook level.

1 Double-click ThisWorkbook in the Project window. At the top of the code window, enter this statement above the event handler procedure:

```
Public ProcessingEvent As Boolean
```

This declares ProcessingEvent as a *public* variable in ThisWorkbook. A public variable is essentially a very simple property. Declaring the variable as Boolean means that it can be only True or False. If you don't assign something to it, it will be False.

2 Change the body of the event handler to this:

```
If ProcessingEvent = True Then
    ProcessingEvent = False
Else
    Selection.Interior.Color = vbRed
End If
```

The event handler will now change the color of the selection only if the ProcessingEvent variable is not True. If ProcessingEvent is True, it changes it back to False. (Otherwise, suppressing the event handler once would suppress it until you close the workbook.)

3 Double-click Sheet1 in the Project window. At the bottom of the SelectionChange event handler, type **ThisWorkbook.ProcessingEvent = True** just before the End Sub statement.

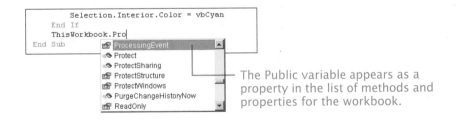

The Public variable appears as a property in the list of methods and properties for the workbook.

The new ProcessingEvent property is in the list of members. It even has a standard Property icon next to it. With this statement, the worksheet event handler tells the workbook event handler not to do anything.

229

4 Activate Sheet1 in Excel and change the selection.

The selection should change to yellow or blue. The worksheet event handler is suppressing the workbook event handler.

5 Activate Sheet3 and change the selection.

The selection should change to red. The workbook event handler still functions properly as long as it is not overridden by the worksheet.

Creating a simple custom property inside ThisWorkbook in the form of a public variable allows you to suppress the workbook event handler. You now have total control over which event handlers function at which time. You can have an event handler run only at the worksheet level, only at the workbook level, at both levels, or as a mixture.

Cancel an event

Some events are made to be canceled. For example, Excel displays a shortcut menu when you right-click on a worksheet. What if you want to prevent the shortcut menu from appearing? You can create an event handler procedure that cancels that event.

Events that can be canceled all have the word *Before* in front of the event name. A worksheet has a BeforeDoubleClick event and a BeforeRightClick event. A workbook has corresponding SheetBeforeDoubleClick and SheetBeforeRightClick events, and also BeforeClose, BeforeSave, and BeforePrint events. Each event procedure that can be canceled has a Cancel argument. To cancel the corresponding event, assign True to the Cancel argument.

1 In the Sheet1 code window, select Worksheet from the Object list and BeforeRightClick from the Procedures list.

2 In the event handler procedure that appears, type **Cancel = True** as the body.

```
Private Sub Worksheet_BeforeRightClick(ByVal Tar
    Cancel = True
End Sub
```

3 Activate Excel and select Sheet1. Try right-clicking on a cell.

The color changes, but the shortcut menu does not appear. The event handler executed before the actual event occurred, and you prevented the event from happening.

Toolbars and menus can be linked to macros. Command buttons, worksheets, and workbooks can be linked to event handlers. All these tools allow you to create applications that are easy for anyone to use.

Lesson Summary

To	Do this	Button
Customize toolbars or menu bars	Display the Customize dialog box by right-clicking any toolbar and clicking Customize.	
Add a command to a toolbar or a menu	In the Customize dialog box, click the Commands tab, select the Macros category, and drag one of the commands to the menu or toolbar.	
Assign a macro to a custom toolbar button or menu	With the Customize dialog box open, click the button or command, click the Modify Selection button, click the Assign Macro command, and select the macro.	
Copy a toolbar button or menu command	Hold down the CTRL key as you drag the item to a new location.	
Add a custom command button to a worksheet	Click the Control Toolbox button on the Visual Basic toolbar, click the Command Button button, and drag a rectangle on the worksheet.	
Make a command button snap to cell gridlines as you move or resize it	Hold down the ALT key as you drag or resize the button.	
Create an event handler that will run when you click a command button	First give the command button a name you like, then click the View Code button on the Control Toolbox toolbar.	
Enable a command button	Click the Exit Design Mode button.	
Select a command button without running its event handler	Click the Design Mode button.	
Create an event handler that will run whenever you change the selection on a specific worksheet	In the Project window, double-click the worksheet name, then select Worksheet from the Object list and SelectionChange from the Procedure list.	

Lesson Summary, *continued*

To	Do this	Button
Create an event handler that will run whenever you change the selection on any worksheet in a workbook	In the Project window, double-click ThisWorkbook, then select Workbook from the Object list and SheetSelectionChange from the Procedure list.	
Prevent an event from occurring	Look for an event that has the word *Before* as part of the name. In the event handler, assign True to the Cancel argument.	

For online information about	Ask the Assistant for help using the words
Creating custom toolbars and menus	"Overview of command bars"
Creating command buttons	"Command buttons"
Using events	"Events"

Preview of the Next Lesson

You typically think of list boxes, scroll bars, and other graphical controls in connection with dialog boxes. Excel, however, allows you to add these active controls directly to worksheets. In the next lesson you will learn how to make a worksheet easy to use by adding active controls, the same controls you will later use in custom dialog boxes.

Using Dialog Box Controls on a Worksheet

Estimated time
30 min.

In this lesson you will learn how to:

- Add ActiveX controls to a worksheet.
- Link the value of a control to a worksheet cell.
- Link a list box to a worksheet range.
- Create a list box with multiple columns.
- Protect a worksheet that uses ActiveX controls.

Microsoft Excel is a great program. Many people purchase it to use at work. At least, people *say* they're going to use it at work. Of course we all know the real reason most of us buy it: to calculate car payments. (The rest of us buy it for figuring out mortgage payments.) It's *after* buying it that we discover that it's also good for one or two other projects as well.

Anyway, say you have a friend who just bought Excel to calculate loan payments, but who doesn't know how to use it very well yet. You want to help out by building a model your friend can use for calculating the payments. You want your friend to be able to try out several possible prices, interest rates, and repayment periods, but you want to eliminate the chance for mistakes. Happily for both of you, Excel has some very powerful tools to help you do just that.

Start the lesson

 Start Excel, change to the folder containing the practice files for this book, open the Loan workbook, and save a copy as **Lesson10**.

Using a Loan Payment Calculator

When you interact with Excel, you do so through Excel's graphical user interface. A graphical user interface includes menus, dialog boxes, list boxes, scroll bars, buttons, and other graphical images. A graphical user interface makes a program easier to learn and also helps reduce errors by restricting choices to valid options.

Historically, creating a graphical user interface has been the domain of professional computer scientists. More recently, users of advanced applications have been able to add graphical controls to custom dialog boxes. Now, with Excel, you can take advantage of dialog box-style controls directly on the worksheet, without doing any programming at all. These controls are called ActiveX controls. For example, the command button you created in Lesson 9 was an ActiveX control.

In this lesson, you will create a worksheet model to calculate a car loan payment. You will add ActiveX controls to the worksheet to make it easy to use for a friend who is unfamiliar with worksheets. In the process, you will become familiar with how ActiveX controls work, which will be useful when you create custom forms, as you will do in Lesson 11.

Create a loan payment model

The Loan sheet of the practice workbook contains labels that will help you create a model for calculating the monthly payments for a car loan.

	A	B	C	D
1				
2		Price		
3		Down		
4		Loan		
5		Interest		
6		Years		
7		Payment		
8				

These are the labels for the loan payment calculator.

There are no named ranges on this worksheet.

Cells B2 through B7 contain the labels Price, Down, Loan, Interest, Years, and Payment. Go through the following steps to create a fully functional loan payment calculator.

1 Type **$5000** in cell C2 (to the right of Price), type **20%** in cell C3 (to the right of Down), type **8%** in cell C5 (to the right of Interest), and type **3** in cell C6 (to the right of Years).

	A	B	C	D
1				
2		Price	$ 5,000	
3		Down	20%	
4		Loan		
5		Interest	8.00%	
6		Years	3	
7		Payment		
8				

These are the constant values for a sample loan payment.

2 In cell C4 (to the right of Loan), type **=Price*(1-Down)** and press ENTER.

	A	B	C	D
1				
2		Price	$ 5,000	
3		Down	20%	
4		Loan	$ 4,000	
5		Interest	8.00%	
6		Years	3	
7		Payment		
8				

The formula =Price*(1-Down) calculates the loan amount.

The value $4,000 appears in the cell. Excel interprets which cells contain the price and down payment by looking at the labels next to the cells.

TIP If you want to make sure that Excel is using the correct cells in the formula, select cell C4, and click in the formula bar. The word *Price* in the formula changes to blue, and a blue border appears around cell C2, the price value. The word *Down* also changes to green, and a green border appears around cell C3, the down payment value. You can now feel confident that Excel is using the correct cell references. Press the ESC key to return Excel to its normal mode.

3 In cell C7 (to the right of Payment), type **=PMT(Interest/ 12,Years*12,Loan)** and press ENTER.

	A	B	C	D
1				
2		Price	$ 5,000	
3		Down	20%	
4		Loan	$ 4,000	
5		Interest	8.00%	
6		Years	3	
7		Payment	($125.35)	
8				
9				

The formula =PMT(Interest/12,Years*12,Loan) calculates the loan payment.

The payment amount, $125.35, appears in the cell. Once again, Excel uses the labels next to the cells to determine which cells you meant to use.

This is the monthly payment amount for this hypothetical car. The red text and the parentheses around the number in the worksheet indicate a negative number. You don't receive this amount, unfortunately; you pay it. (If you want to change the monthly payment to a positive number, put a minus sign in front of *Loan* in the formula.)

Use the loan payment model

1   Enter **$12000** in cell C2. The loan amount should change to $9,600 and the payment should change to $300.83.

	A	B	C	D
1				
2		Price	$12,000	— A new price...
3		Down	20%	
4		Loan	$ 9,600	
5		Interest	8.00%	
6		Years	3	...results in a new
7		Payment	($300.83)	— payment amount.
8				

This simple model calculates monthly loan payments for a given set of input variables. You change the input variables to anything you like and the payment changes accordingly. You can even enter outlandish values.

2   Enter **$1500000** as the price of the car. This is a very expensive car. The payment formula bravely calculates the monthly payment, but you can't read it because it is too big.

	A	B	C	D
1				
2		Price	######	— A price that's
3		Down	20%	too big...
4		Loan	######	
5		Interest	8.00%	
6		Years	3	...produces an
7		Payment	######	— unusable result.
8				

3   Press CTRL+Z to change the price back to $12,000. (The monthly payment for the expensive car, in case you are interested, would be $37,603.64.)

One of the problems with this model is that it is *too* flexible. You can enter ridiculously large prices, even ridiculously high interest rates. (Try **500%**.) You can even enter something totally useless as the number of years, such as "Dog."

The wide spectrum of choices available, only a few of which are meaningful, may be confusing when your friend is using the model. You can add controls to the worksheet that will eliminate any possible confusion.

Creating an Error-Resistant Loan Payment Calculator

Excel has tools that enable you to make an error-resistant loan payment calculator. By restricting options to valid items, you can make your model less likely to produce erroneous results, and also much easier to use. The Control Toolbox, the same toolbar you used to create a command button in Lesson 9, contains all kinds of useful ActiveX controls that you can put on a worksheet: list boxes, spin buttons, combo boxes, and so on.

Restrict the years to a valid range

Start by making it difficult to enter an invalid number of years. Typically, for car loans you can borrow for up to five years in units of a year. Just to be safe, allow values from 1 to 6 for the number of years. A spin button is an effective way to specify such integer values.

Control Toolbox button

1 Activate the Control Toolbox. (Click the Control Toolbox button on the Visual Basic toolbar.)

2 Click the Spin Button button on the Control Toolbox.

3 Hold down the ALT key and click close to the top-left corner of cell E6. (Holding down the ALT key makes the control snap to the cell grid line.)

Spin Button button

4 Release the ALT key and drag the bottom-right corner of the new spin button to the center of the bottom of cell E6. This makes the spin button rotate sideways and fit on the row.

	A	B	C	D	E
1					
2		Price	$12,000		
3		Down	20%		
4		Loan	$ 9,600		
5		Interest	8.00%		
6		Years	3		◄ ►
7		Payment	($300.83)		
8					

Add a spin button control to change the number of years.

Properties button

5 Click the Properties button to display the Properties window.

6   Type **1** as the value of the Min property, and type **6** as the value of the Max property.

— Change the Max and the Min properties.

You want the spin button to control the value in cell C6.

7   For the LinkedCell property, type **C6** and press ENTER.

An ActiveX control has many properties. For most of the properties, you can simply accept the default values. Only change the properties for which you need a custom value.

— Enter a cell reference as the LinkedCell property to cause the control to change the value of that cell.

Exit Design Mode button

8   Click the Exit Design Mode button, and try clicking the spin button.

The number in cell C6 changes as you click the spin button, and the payment amount changes accordingly. Your friend will now be able to easily select only valid loan duration values.

Restrict the down payment to valid values

Unfortunately, your friend can still enter an invalid value for the down payment percentage; -50%, for example, or "Dog." You need to help out. A reasonable range of values for the down payment would be anywhere from 0 percent to 100 percent, counting by 5 percent. Even though you specify the down payment as a percentage (which is a fraction, not an integer), you can still use a spin button as long as you utilize an extra cell to hold the intermediate value.

Design Mode button

Copying the control makes both controls exactly the same size.

1 Click the Design Mode button to switch back to design mode.

2 Hold down both the ALT key and the CTRL key, and drag the spin button from cell E6 to cell E3. When you release the mouse button, a copy snaps to the top-left corner of cell E3.

	A	B	C	D	E
1					
2		Price	$ 12,000		
3		Down	20%		
4		Loan	$ 9,600		
5		Interest	8.00%		
6		Years	3		
7		Payment	($300.83)		
8					

— Create a second spin button to control the down payment percentage.

3 In the Properties window, type **100** as the value of the Max property, **0** as the value of the Min property, and type **H3** as the value of the LinkedCell property.

4 As the value of the SmallChange property, type **5** and press ENTER. This property controls how much the number will change each time you click the control.

The SmallChange property controls how much the spin button changes when you click it.

Exit Design Mode button

5 Click the Exit Design Mode button and click the control.

The value in cell H3 changes between 0 and 100. Now you need a value in cell C3 that changes between 0% and 100%.

6 Select cell C3, type **=H3/100**, and press ENTER.

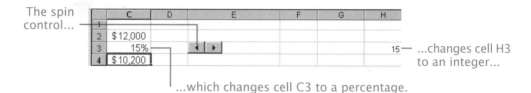

The spin control... ...which changes cell C3 to a percentage. ...changes cell H3 to an integer...

A percentage value appears in the cell.

7 Click the spin button to see both the integer in cell H3 and the derived value in cell C3 change in tandem.

The spin button can increment only in integers, but the down payment needs to be entered as a percentage. Dividing the value in cell H3 by 100 allows the spin button to use integers and you to specify the down payment as a percentage.

Restrict the interest rate to valid values

The interest rate is another input value your friend might make a mistake entering. The interest rate is similar to the down payment rate; both are percentages. You probably want to allow interest rates to vary by as little as 0.25 percent, and within a range from 0 percent through about 20 percent. Because you're allowing so many possible values, you will have many more steps than with the down payment rate, so you'll use a scroll bar control instead of a spin button. Like a spin button, the scroll bar only returns integers, so you will still need to link the control to an intermediate cell.

Scroll Bar button

1 Click the Scroll Bar button on the Control Toolbox, and then hold down the ALT key as you click the top left corner of cell E5.

2 Continue holding down the ALT key as you drag the bottom-right corner of the new scroll bar to the bottom-right corner of cell E5.

	B	C	D	E	F
1					
2	Price	$12,000			
3	Down	15%			
4	Loan	$10,200			
5	Interest	8.00%			
6	Years	3			

Create a scroll bar to set the interest rate.

3 In the Properties window, type **2000** as the value of the Max property, type **25** as the value of the SmallChange property, type **100** as the value of the LargeChange property, and type **H5** as the value of the LinkedCell property. Press ENTER.

*Exit Design
Mode button*

4 Click the Exit Design Mode button and try out the scroll bar control by clicking on the arrows as well as the area in between.

If you click one of the arrows on either end, the number in cell H5 changes by 25 (the SmallChange value). If you click between the box and the end, the number changes by 100 (the LargeChange value).

5 Select cell C5, type **=H5/10000**, and press ENTER. You divide by 100 to turn the number from H5 into a percentage and by another 100 (100 * 100 = 10000 total) to allow for hundredths of a percent.

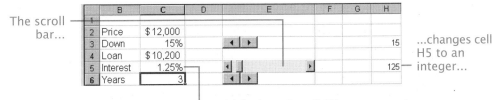

The scroll bar... ...changes cell H5 to an integer...

...which changes cell C5 to a percentage.

Now your friend can easily modify the number of years for the loan (using one spin button), the down payment percentage (using the other spin button), or the interest rate (using the scroll bar control). Everything is easy except the price of the car.

Retrieving a Value from a List

You could specify the price of the car by creating another scroll bar, but the price of a car is actually determined by which car you want to buy. You know that your friend has been looking through the want-ads and has come up with a list of used cars to consider. You can make the model very friendly to use by allowing your friend to select the description of the car and have the price automatically appear in the Price cell.

Prepare a list of cars

The Lesson10 practice file contains a hypothetical list of your friend's cars and their prices. The list starts in cell K2.

	I	J	K	L	M
1					
2			91 Mercury Sable	$10,500	
3			88 Nissan Pulsar NX	$6,350	
4			90 Toyota Camry	$8,950	
5			88 Dodge Lancer ES	$6,299	
6			87 BMW 325	$7,959	
7			91 Chev Camaro	$6,796	
8			88 Mazda MX6	$8,500	
9					

You can create a list box that displays this list of cars.

1 Select cell K2 and press CTRL+SHIFT+* to select the entire block of cells.

2 From the Insert menu's Name submenu, click Define. Type **CarList** as the name of the list, and click OK. The defined name contains both the list of car names and the corresponding list of prices.

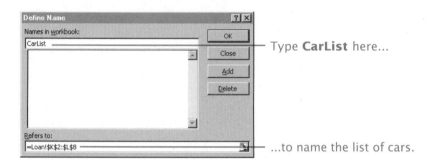

Type **CarList** here...

...to name the list of cars.

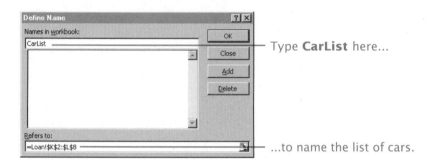

Combo Box button

3 In the Control Toolbox, click Combo Box, hold down the ALT key, and drag a rectangle from the top-left corner to the bottom-right corner of cell E2.

	B	C	D	E	F
1					
2	Price	$ 12,000			
3	Down	15%			
4	Loan	$ 10,200			
5	Interest	1.25%			
6	Years	3			
7	Payment	($288.83)			

Create a Combo Box control to select the desired car.

A combo box can have either of two styles. It can be a drop-down list box, allowing you to select only items from the list, or it can be a list box combined with an edit box, allowing you to enter new values as well as select from the list. Because you want to confine your friend to the existing list of cars, you want the combo box to be a drop-down list box.

4   In the Properties window, for the value of the Style property, select 2 - fmStyleDropDownList.

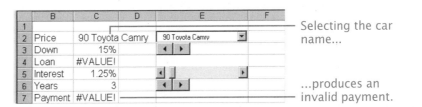

Select this style to
select only items
in the list.

5   Type **C2** as the value of the LinkedCell property and press ENTER.

The price from cell C2 appears as the value of the combo box.

6   Type **CarList** as the value of the ListFillRange property and press ENTER.

Nothing seems to happen, but the combo box now knows to get its list of values from the CarList range. You can also watch the value of cell C2 change when you select a new car from the combo box.

*Exit Design
Mode button*

7   Click the Exit Design Mode button, click the arrow on the combo box, and select *90 Toyota Camry* from the list.

	B	C	D	E	F
1					
2	Price	90 Toyota Camry		90 Toyota Camry	
3	Down	15%			
4	Loan	#VALUE!			
5	Interest	1.25%			
6	Years	3			
7	Payment	#VALUE!			

Selecting the car
name...

...produces an
invalid payment.

The name for the Toyota appears in the drop-down control, but also unfortunately in cell C2. The loan payment calculator does not seem to like having a car name entered as the price.

You can now select a car name from the combo box, but you want the combo box to put the price of the car into cell C2, not the name of the car. Since the ListFillRange, CarList, contains an extra column with the car prices, you can tell the combo box to get the value from that second column.

Retrieve the price from the list

Design Mode button

1 Click the Design Mode button, and click the combo box.

2 In the Properties window, type **2** as the value of the ColumnCount property.

The ColumnCount property informs the combo box that there really are two columns of values in the ListFillRange.

3 Type **2** as the value of the BoundColumn property and press ENTER.

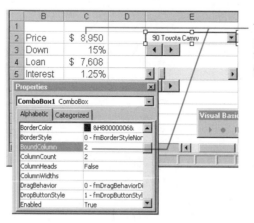

The BoundColumn property controls which column's value goes into the cell.

The BoundColumn property tells the combo box which column's value to put into the linked cell. And sure enough, the price of the Toyota, $8,950, appears in the cell.

4 Turn off design mode and click the arrow on the combo box.

	B	C	D	E	F
1					
2	Price	$ 8,950		90 Toyota Camry	
3	Down	15%		91 Mercury Sable $10,500	
4	Loan	$ 7,608		88 Nissan Pulsar I $6,350	
5	Interest	1.25%		90 Toyota Camry $8,950	
6	Years	3		88 Dodge Lancer $6,299	
7	Payment	($215.42)		87 BMW 325 $7,959	
				91 Chev Camaro $6,796	
				88 Mazda MX6 $8,500	

Select the car from the list to put the price into cell C2.

5 Select *87 BMW* from the drop-down list of cars.

	B	C	D	E
1				
2	Price	$ 7,959		87 BMW 325
3	Down	15%		

The price changes to $7,959.

Now your friend will not accidentally calculate the payment for a $1,000,000 car. Your friend can just select various cars from the list and Excel will automatically insert the correct price in the Price cell.

Set the column widths

The combo box works fine, but while the list was dropped down, there was a horizontal scroll bar across the bottom. Even though there is plenty of room for the price, the combo box makes the price column just as wide as the car name column. As a default, a combo box uses the same width for each column. If, as in this example, you want the columns to have different widths, you can manually control the column widths.

1   Turn on design mode and select the combo box.

A point is equal to 1/72 inch.

2   In the Properties window, type **1 in; .5 in** as the value of the ColumnWidths property (to specify 1 inch for the first column, and 0.5 inches for the second), and press ENTER.

The displayed value of the property changes to *72 pt; 36 pt*. This is the equivalent value in *points*. You can type the value of the property using inches (in), centimeters (cm), or points (pt), but the value will always be displayed in points.

3   Turn off design mode and click the combo box arrow.

Columns can have custom widths.

The combo box, complete with multiple columns, looks great!

Protecting the Worksheet

The model works fine now. It does not require any typing into cells. And you were able to create it without using any macros! The model is still not bulletproof, however. There is nothing in the model to prevent your friend from accidentally typing, say, "Dog" in cell C2 as the price of the car, thereby destroying the formula.

You might protect the worksheet. That would keep your friend from typing invalid values into the model, but it would also unfortunately keep the ActiveX controls from changing the values of the linked cells. You can, however, set the worksheet protection in such a way that Visual Basic procedures can still change the cells. All you need are five simple event handler procedures to effectively protect the model.

Create an event handler for the combo box

The first step is to convert the ActiveX controls from linking to the cells to using an event handler to put a new value into a cell.

View Code button

1 Turn on design mode and select the combo box.

2 In the Properties window, change the Name property to **cboPrice**. (The prefix *cbo* stands for "combo box.") Clear the LinkedCell property box, and then click the View Code button on the Control Toolbox.

A new event handler procedure named cboPrice_Change appears. Change is the default event for a combo box.

3 As the body of the macro, insert this statement:

```
Range("C2").Value = cboPrice.Value
```

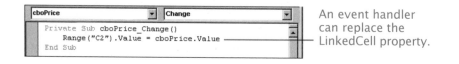

An event handler can replace the LinkedCell property.

This event handler procedure will change cell C2 to match the new value of the combo box whenever that value changes.

4 Activate Excel, turn off design mode, and try out the combo box.

The value in cell C2 should change to the correct price each time you select a new car.

5 Repeat steps 1 through 4 for the spin button that sets the down payment percentage. Give it the name **spnDown**, clear the LinkedCell property box, and in its event procedure enter the statement:

```
Range("C3").Value = spnDown.Value / 100
```

```
Private Sub spnDown_Change()
    Range("C3").Value = spnDown.Value / 100
End Sub
```

6 Repeat steps 1 through 4 for the scroll bar. Give it the name **scrRate**, clear the LinkedCell property box, and in its event procedure enter the statement:

```
Range("C5").Value = scrRate.Value / 10000
```

```
Private Sub scrRate_Change()
    Range("C5").Value = scrRate.Value / 10000
End Sub
```

7 Repeat steps 1 through 4 for the spin button that sets the number of years. Give it the name **spnYears**, clear the LinkedCell property box, and in its event procedure enter the statement:

```
Range("C6").Value = spnYears.Value
```

```
Private Sub spnYears_Change()
    Range("C6").Value = spnYears.Value
End Sub
```

8 Clear cells H3 and H5, since you don't need the values in them any more.

You now have an event handler procedure for each control, and none of the controls is linked to a cell. You are finally ready to protect the worksheet.

Protect the worksheet

For more information about locking cells, activate Excel and ask the Assistant for help using the words "locked cells."

You typically protect a worksheet by clicking the Protection command from the Tools menu and then clicking the Protect Sheet command. When you protect a worksheet this way, you can't subsequently change the value of any locked cells. On a worksheet that you protect with a menu command, nothing can change locked cells—not the user, ActiveX controls, or macros.

A macro, however, can protect a worksheet in such a way that a macro can still change locked cells. This special kind of protection does not last when you close and reopen the workbook, so you must protect the worksheet each time you open the workbook. Isn't there an event that runs each time you open a workbook? Yes, indeed, there is.

Project Explorer button

1 Activate Visual Basic, click the Project Explorer button, and double-click the ThisWorkbook object.

2 From the Object list (above the code window), select Workbook.

3 Insert this statement as the body of the Workbook_Open procedure:

```
Sheets("Loan").Protect UserInterfaceOnly:=True
```

```
Private Sub Workbook_Open()
    Sheets("Loan").Protect UserInterfaceOnly:=True
End Sub
```

The UserInterfaceOnly argument to the Protect method is what allows a macro to make changes even if a user or control cannot.

4 Save and close the Lesson10 workbook. Then reopen it.

5 Try typing numbers into the model.

With the worksheet protected, only the event handler procedures can change the cells.

Excel politely explains that the worksheet is protected.

6 Try changing the model using the ActiveX controls.

Everything works fine.

The loan payment calculator model is now robust and ready to give to your friend. Your friend can now experiment with various scenarios without having to worry about typing invalid inputs into the model. In fact, he can't type anything into the model—because the worksheet is protected. Besides, there is nothing to type. Your friend can control everything on the worksheet by just clicking controls with the mouse. One of the greatest benefits of a graphical user interface is the ability to restrict choices to valid values, thereby reducing or eliminating user error while also making a model easier to use.

Lesson Summary

To	Do this
Add ActiveX controls to a worksheet	Activate the Control Toolbox, click a control button, and drag a rectangle on the worksheet.
Link the value of a control to a cell	Assign the cell address to the LinkedCell property of the control.
Set limits for scroll bar and spin button controls	Assign minimum and maximum values to the Min and Max properties of the controls.
Link the list for a list box or combo box to a range on a worksheet	Assign the range address or its name to the ListFillRange property of the control.
Show multiple columns in a list box or combo box	Assign the number of columns to the ColumnCount property of the list box or combo box.
Protect the worksheet while still allowing ActiveX controls to change the value of cells	Use event handler procedures to assign the values of the controls to cells, and then run the worksheet's Protect method with the UserInterfaceOnly argument set to True.

For online information about	Ask the Assistant for help using the words
Using ActiveX controls on a worksheet	"ActiveX controls"
Protecting a worksheet	"Protect worksheet"

Preview of the Next Lesson

In this lesson, you learned how to use ActiveX controls on a worksheet. You can use the same controls, plus others that are unavailable on a worksheet, in a dialog box. In the next lesson you will learn how to create an effective dialog box for a Visual Basic application.

Creating a Custom Form

Estimated time
55 min.

In this lesson you will learn how to:

- Create a custom form.
- Initialize a form.
- Check for invalid input values in a text box.
- Run macros from a form.

Take a 3-foot by 4-foot piece of plywood and cans of blue, yellow, and orange paint. Drip, dribble, splash, and spread the paint on the plywood. You now have—a mess. But put a $500 frame around the painted plywood, and you now have—a work of art! Seriously, even serious art does not look serious without a good frame, and the best diamond brooch does not seem to be a precious gift if given in a paper bag.

Similarly, you can write macros that are practical, convenient, and useful, but until you put a frame around them, until you tighten up the edges and make them easy to use, until you package them, you do not have a truly valuable application. Creating a custom form is an excellent way to make functionality easy to use and valuable. In this lesson, you will learn how to create a custom form, create the functionality for the form, and link the two together into an integrated tool.

Start the lesson

➤ Start Microsoft Excel, change to the folder containing the practice files for this book, open the Budget workbook (the same one you used for Lesson 1), and save a copy as **Lesson11**.

Creating a Form's User Interface

The Budget worksheet shows detailed budget information for the year 1997. It includes both detail and summary rows.

	A	B	C	D	E	F
1	Summary		Rates	Jan-97	Feb-97	Mar-97
2	Projected Units			29000	30000	31000
3	Projected Revenues			71000	73000	75000
4	Projected Pre-tax Profit			26819.9	27057.9	30295.9
5						
6	Variable					
7	Ink		0.095	2755	2850	2945
8	Emulsion		0.012	348	360	372
9	Reducers		0.002	58	60	62
10	Rags		0.002	58	60	62

Suppose that you need to print different versions of the budget. The managers want a version that shows only the summary rows. The data entry person wants a version that shows only the detail rows, without the totals. The budget analyst wants both the detail and the summary rows, but does not want to see months that are completed.

To make it easy to print the various versions of the report, you can create a custom dialog box, or *user form*. Here's the strategy for creating the form:

1 Design what the form will look like. This is called the *user interface*. The easiest way to design a form in Visual Basic is to just jump in and create it.

2 Create the macros you need to make the form work. This is the form's *functionality*. Adding functionality may involve making changes to the worksheet that enable the macros to work.

3 Make the form run the macros, and provide a way to show the form. This is the final *implementation*.

The process of designing the form's user interface can help you figure out what functionality you need to develop.

Create the form

**Visual Basic
Editor button**

**Insert UserForm
button**

*The button may
have a different
picture
depending on
whether you
have previously
used it.*

1 With the Lesson11 workbook open, click the Visual Basic Editor button.

The second button from the left of Visual Basic's Standard toolbar is the Insert UserForm button.

2 Click the arrow next to the Insert UserForm button to display a list of objects that you can insert.

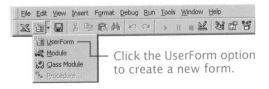

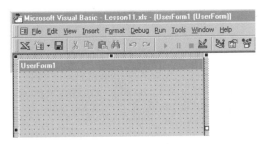

Click the UserForm option to create a new form.

3 Click the UserForm option to create a new, empty user form.

The form is stored in your project just like a module. You can "run" the form from Visual Basic in the same way that you run a macro.

**Close Window
button**

4 Press F5 to display the form, and then click the Close Window button to close it.

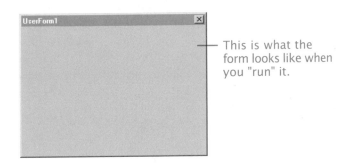

This is what the form looks like when you "run" it.

By default, the caption of the form is UserForm1. The caption is a property; you can change the caption using the Properties window.

Properties Window button

5 Click the Properties Window button, and change the value of the Caption property to **Print Options**.

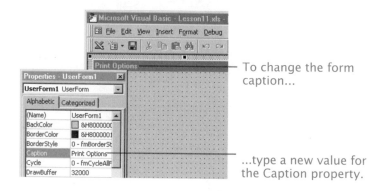

To change the form caption...

...type a new value for the Caption property.

The caption changes in the form as you change the value in the Properties window.

6 Change the value of the Name property to **frmPrint**. The prefix *frm-* is short for "form." The *Print* part of the name tells you the intended purpose of the form. If you ever need to refer to the form inside a procedure, you can use this meaningful name.

That's all there is to creating a user form! Of course, you might want to put something a little fancier inside it.

Add option buttons

When you print the report, you must choose one of three layouts: all the rows, only the summary rows, or only the detail rows. Option buttons provide a way to select a single item from a short, predefined list. Generally, option buttons go inside a frame.

When Visual Basic displayed the user form, it automatically displayed the Control toolbox for forms. This Control toolbox is very similar to the Control toolbox you use to add ActiveX controls to a worksheet.

1 Click the Form window.

2 In the Control toolbox, click the Frame button, and then click near the top-left corner of the form.

Frame button

If you do not see the Control toolbox, click the Toolbox button on the Standard toolbar to display it.

A large frame control appears on the form. You can move or resize the frame later. Next add the option buttons. You can avoid clicking the control button on the toolbox each time you add a button by double-clicking the control button. This activates that button until you click it again.

OptionButton button

3 Double-click the OptionButton button, click in three places on the form to create three buttons, and then click the OptionButton button again to turn it off.

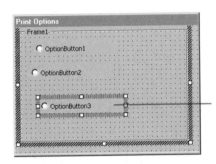

Double-click a control in the toolbox to create multiple controls quickly.

4 Activate the Properties window and select Frame1 from the drop-down list at the top.

5 Type **Rows** as the value of the Caption property, and type **grpRows** as the value of the Name property. (The prefix *grp-* is short for "group," which is an old name for a frame. The prefix *frm-* is already reserved for a form.)

6 Select the first option button and type **All** as the value of the Caption property, type **optAll** as the value of the Name property, and type **A** as the value of the Accelerator property. (You have probably guessed what the prefix *opt-* is short for.) With the optAll control still selected, type **True** as the value of the Value property.

Setting the Value property to True makes this the default option.

7 Give the second option button the caption **Summary**, the name **optSummary**, and the accelerator key **S**.

8 Give the third option button the caption **Detail**, the name **optDetail**, and the accelerator key **D**.

9 Select all three option buttons by clicking between the bottom option button and the bottom of the frame and dragging a rectangle that touches each of the option button captions.

10 From Visual Basic's Format menu, click Vertical Spacing and then click Remove. Then from the Format menu, click Align and then click Lefts. Again from the Format menu, click Size To Fit. Finally drag the group of controls up close to the top-left corner of the frame, and resize the frame to just fit around the option buttons.

Use commands on the Format menu to clean up the form.

The Format menu provides powerful tools for getting the controls on a form to line up properly.

11 Save the workbook, press F5 to see how the option buttons will look (try clicking the option buttons), and then close the Print Options window.

You can select only one option button from the group.

A frame with a set of option buttons is a good user interface for selecting a single option from a predefined list.

Add a check box with a related text box

Your form needs some way for you to specify whether to print all the months or only the remaining months. This is basically a "yes or no" choice. The best control for a "yes or no" choice is a check box. When the check box is selected, the macro will print starting with the current month.

Still, even though the budget analyst says that the report should start with the current month, you know that there will inevitably be exceptions. You should therefore add a text box that lets you specify a different start month, just to be prepared.

*CheckBox
button*

1 With the form window visible, click the CheckBox button in the Control toolbox, and then click below the frame on the form where you want the check box to appear.

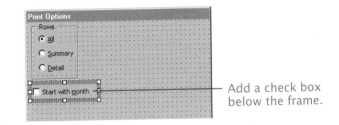

Add a check box
below the frame.

2 In the Properties window, change the caption for the check box to **Start with month**, change the name to **chkMonth**, and change the Accelerator to **m**.

3 Double-click the right size handle of the check box selection rectangle to shrink the rectangle to fit the caption.

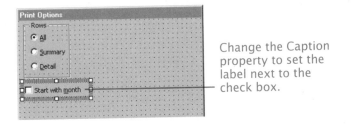

Change the Caption
property to set the
label next to the
check box.

You will now add the text box for the month right after the caption for the check box so that the contents appear to complete the "Start with month" caption.

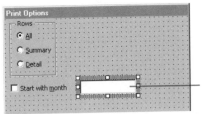

ab|

*TextBox
button*

4 Click the TextBox button in the toolbox, and then click to the right of the check box caption.

Add a text box to complete
the sentence started by the
check box caption.

5 Change the text box name to **txtMonth**, set the Value property to **7/1/1997**, and then change the Enabled property to **False**.

You won't need to change the value of the month if the check box is cleared. Setting the Enabled property to False makes the contents of the box appear gray. You want the text box to become enabled whenever the user selects the check box. This is a job for an event.

6   Double-click the chkMonth check box control.

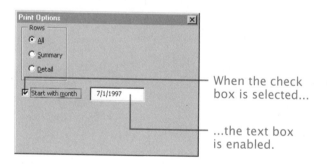

Double-click the check box to create an event handler for the default event.

A new window captioned frmPrint (Code) appears. It contains a new event handler procedure, chkMonth_Click. The Click event is the default event for a check box.

7   Insert the following statement as the body of the new chkMonth_Click procedure:

```
txtMonth.Enabled = chkMonth.Value
```

This statement will enable the text box whenever the check box is selected, and disable the text box whenever the check box is cleared.

8   Save the workbook, press F5 to run the form, and click the check box a couple of times. Then close the form.

When the check box is selected...

...the text box is enabled.

When the check box is cleared, you can't change the date. When it is selected, you can.

Adding an event to the check box control makes the user interface work better, but it doesn't change anything in Excel. Even though the event is Visual Basic code, it does not really contribute to the functionality of the application.

Initialize the text box

When you created the month text box, you assigned 7/1/1997 as a default date. Since most of the time you will want the current month in that box, you can make the form easier to use by initializing the text box with the current month. That means that you must calculate the appropriate date for the text box at the time that you display the form.

1 Double-click the background of the form.

```
UserForm ▼    Click ▼
    Private Sub chkMonth_Click()
        txtMonth.Enabled = chkMonth.Value
    End Sub

    Private Sub UserForm_Click()

    End Sub
```

Double-click the form to create an event handler for the default event.

A new procedure named UserForm_Click appears. The name of the object for a form is always UserForm. No matter what name you give the form, the event handler procedures always use the name UserForm. The default event for a form is Click, but you don't want to wait until the user clicks the form to initialize the month. You therefore need a different event.

2 From the Procedures list, select the Initialize event. After the UserForm_Initialize procedure appears, delete the UserForm_Click procedure.

3 Enter the following statement as the body of the procedure:

```
txtMonth.Value = Date
```

```
UserForm ▼    Initialize ▼
    Private Sub chkMonth_Click()
        txtMonth.Enabled = chkMonth.Value
    End Sub

    Private Sub UserForm_Initialize()
        txtMonth.Value = Date
    End Sub
```

Initialize the text box in the form's Initialize event handler.

Date is a built-in Visual Basic function that returns the current date, based on your computer's internal clock.

4 Press F5 to run the form.

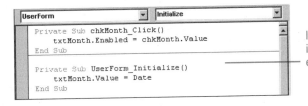

The text box is initialized with the current date.

The purpose of the date is to identify the month you want the report to start with. You will create a macro that searches the top row of the worksheet to find a date that matches the one in the text box. The dates in the top row of the worksheet are all for the first day of the month. In order to find a match, therefore, the date in the text box must be for the first day of the month as well.

The date that the macro puts into the text box, however, is the current date. Since it is highly unlikely that the current date is the first day of the month, you need a way to convert it to the first day of the current month.

5 Close the form, and then double-click the background to get back to the UserForm_Initialize procedure.

You are now going to create a custom function that will convert any date into the first day of the month.

6 Below the UserForm_Initialize procedure, add this custom function:

```
Function StartOfMonth(InputDate)
    If IsDate(InputDate) Then
        StartOfMonth = DateSerial(Year(InputDate), _
            Month(InputDate), 1)
    Else
        StartOfMonth = Empty
    End If
End Function
```

This function accepts an input date as an argument. It first checks to see if the input date is a date or can be turned into one. If it can, then the function extracts the year and the month from the input date, and uses the DateSerial function to create a new date. You give the DateSerial function a year, a month, and a day, and it gives you back the appropriate date. The StartOfMonth function ignores the day portion of the input date, and always uses 1 as the day instead.

If the input date cannot be interpreted as a date for some reason, the function returns the special value *Empty*. The Empty value is the same as when a variable has never been initialized. The Visual Basic Date function in the UserForm_Initialize procedure always returns a valid date, so if you only call the StartOfMonth function from the UserForm_Initialize procedure, it doesn't have to handle an invalid date. But whenever you write a custom function, you should write it to work in a variety of situations that might arise. Returning an Empty value when the argument is an invalid date is one way to make your function more flexible.

> **TIP** If you want to test the function, you can do so from the Immediate window. Because this function is part of the code for a form object, however, you must include the form name before the function name. For example, you could test the function in the Immediate window by entering the following statement: **?frmPrint.StartOfMonth("May 23, 1997")**.

7 Change the statement in the UserForm_Initialize procedure to **txtmonth.Value = StartOfMonth(Date)**.

8 Press F5 to run the dialog box, check the date in the month box, and close the form.

The text box is initialized with the first day of the current month.

The date should be the first day of the current month.

Many controls need to be initialized. Some controls, such as the option buttons, can be initialized when you create the form. Other controls, such as the month text box, need to be initialized when you run the form, and the Initialize event handler is the place to do it.

Add command buttons

Your form now allows you to specify what both the rows and columns of the report should look like. You still need a way to actually start printing. To do that, you add a command button. In theory, you don't need a cancel button, because you can always just click the Close Window button to close the form, but a cancel button is easier to understand and use, and the whole purpose of a good user interface is to make the form easy to understand and use.

1 Activate the Form window.

2 Click the CommandButton button in the Control toolbox and then click on the form, to the right of the Rows frame.

CommandButton button

3   Hold down the CTRL key and drag the new button down to make a copy of it.

Hold down the CTRL key and drag to clone a control.

The top button will print the report, and the bottom one will be a Cancel button.

4   Change the caption on the top button to **Print**, assign **P** as the accelerator key, change the name to **btnPrint**, and change the Default property to **True**.

Only one command button on a form can be the default. A default button is the one that gets "clicked" when you press ENTER.

5   Change the caption on the bottom button to **Cancel**, do not assign an accelerator key, change the name to **btnCancel**, and change the Cancel property to **True**.

Make one button into the default button...

...and one button into the cancel button.

Only one command button on a form can be a cancel button. A cancel button is the one that gets "clicked" when you press ESC.

Normally, when you click a cancel button, you expect the form to close. A cancel button by itself, however, does not close the form. First, you have to add an event handler to it.

6   Double-click the cancel button to create an event handler named btnCancel_Click, and enter the statement **Unload Me** as the body of the procedure.

The cancel button unloads the form without doing anything else.

The Unload command removes a form from memory. The Me keyword refers to the current form. The macro statement *Unload Me* therefore instructs Visual Basic to remove from memory the form that contains the control whose event handler is currently running.

Select btnPrint from the Objects list at the top of the code window to create a new procedure called btnPrint_Click, and enter these two statements as the body of the procedure:

```
Unload Me
MsgBox "Printing"
```

The print button unloads the form and then prints the report.

The first statement removes the form, and the second statement is a placeholder until you add the functionality to print the report.

7 Save the workbook, and run the form several times. Try clicking the Cancel and the Print buttons. Try pressing ESC or ENTER.

Press ENTER to "click" the default button.

Press ESC to "click" the cancel button.

Either pressing ENTER or clicking the Print button should display the *Printing* message. Either pressing ESC or clicking the Cancel button should make the form disappear quietly.

Set the tab order for controls

1 Run the form one more time. This time, press the TAB key repeatedly. Watch the small gray box move from control to control.

The gray border shows which control has the focus.

The gray box identifies the control that has the *focus*. When you use the keyboard, you can press the TAB key to move the focus from control to control.

2 Click Cancel to close the form.

Some people prefer to use the keyboard. For them, you should make sure that accelerator keys are properly defined and the tab order is logical. For this form, the tab order should be optAll, optSummary, optDetail, chkMonth, txtMonth, btnPrint, and btnCancel. If that is not the tab order for your controls, Visual Basic provides a simple way to change it.

If you do not see a Tab Order command, move the mouse over the arrow at the bottom of the View menu.

3 Click the background of the form. From the View menu, click the Tab Order command.

Select the control whose tab order is wrong...

...and move it up or down.

The Tab Order dialog box shows five controls: grpRows, chkMonth, txtMonth, btnPrint, and btnCancel. It treats the grpRows frame control (along with the controls it contains) as a single item. If a control is out of place in the sequence, you simply select the control and click the Move Up or Move Down button to put it in the right place.

4   After making any necessary adjustments, click OK to close the dialog box. Select the frame box (or any of the option buttons), and, from the View menu, click the Tab Order command again.

Controls inside a frame have their own tab order.

This time, the Tab Order dialog box shows only the controls inside the frame.

5   After making any necessary adjustments, click OK to close the dialog box. Save the workbook.

The tab order is easy to set, but remember that you need to set the order for the controls in each frame separately.

Preparing a Form's Functionality

The form now looks good. The next step is to build the functionality for printing the report. You need a way to change between the different row views, and you need a way to hide any unwanted columns. Excel can store different views of a worksheet that you specify, which you can then show later as needed. If you build some views into the worksheet, creating a macro to change between views will be easy.

Create custom views on a worksheet

A custom view allows you to hide rows or columns on a worksheet and then give that view a name so that you can retrieve it easily. You need to create three views. The first view shows all the rows and columns. That one is easy to create. The second view shows only the total rows. The third view shows only the detail rows. Hiding the rows can be a tedious process. Fortunately, you need to hide them only once. You can also use Excel's Goto Special command to help select the rows faster.

1   Activate Excel. From the View menu, click the Custom Views command.

2   In the Custom Views dialog box, click the Add button, type **All** as the name for the new view, clear the Print Settings check box, leave the Hidden Rows, Columns And Filter Settings check box selected, and click OK.

Create a custom view...

...that remembers which rows are hidden.

You just created the first view, the one with all rows and columns displayed. You now need to create the Summary view, showing only the total rows. That means that you need to hide the detail rows. You notice that only the detail rows have labels in column B.

3   Select column B. From the Edit menu, click Go To and then click Special. Select the Constants option and click OK.

The Constants option selects only cells containing constants.

Only the cells in the detail rows are still selected.

4   Hide the selected rows. (From the Format menu, click Row, and then click Hide.)

	A	B	C	D	E
1	Summary		Rates	Jan-97	Feb-97
2	Projected Units			29000	30000
3	Projected Revenues			71000	73000
4	**Projected Pre-tax Profit**			26819.9	27057.9
5					
6	Variable				
13	**Total Variable**			7598	7860

The rows with constants in Column B are hidden.

The only remaining rows that you want to hide all have blank cells in column D. Does that give you any ideas?

5 Select column D. Click Edit, Go To, Special. Select Blanks and click OK. Hide the selected rows as you did in step 4.

	A	B	C	D	E
1	Summary		Rates	Jan-97	Feb-97
2	Projected Units			29000	30000
3	Projected Revenues			71000	73000
4	Projected Pre-tax Profit			26819.9	27057.9
13	Total Variable			7598	7860
21	Total Salaries			16546	16546

The rows with constants in Column B or blanks in Column D are hidden.

This is the view for the managers.

6 With only these total rows visible, create another view named **Summary**. (From the View menu, click Custom Views, click Add, type **Summary**, clear Print Settings, and click OK.)

Now you need to create the detail view. For the detail view, you want to hide all the summary rows. The rows you want to hide have labels in the range A4:A68.

7 Show the All custom view to unhide all the rows. Select the range A4:A68, use Go To Special to select the cells with constants, and then hide the rows. Select column D and hide all the rows with blank cells.

	A	B	C	D	E
1	Summary		Rates	Jan-97	Feb-97
2	Projected Units			29000	30000
3	Projected Revenues			71000	73000
7		Ink	0.095	2755	2850
8		Emulsion	0.012	348	360
9		Reducers	0.002	58	60
10		Rags	0.002	58	60

The summary rows are hidden.

8 With these detail rows visible, create a new view named **Detail**, again clearing the Print Settings option.

9 Save the workbook, and try showing each of the three views. Finish with the All view.

Creating the views is bothersome, but you only have to do it once. Once the views are created, making a macro to switch between views is easy.

Create a macro to switch views

1 Start recording a macro named **ShowView**. Show the Summary view, turn off the recorder, and look at the macro. It should look like this:

```
Sub ShowView()
    ActiveWorkbook.CustomViews("Summary").Show
End Sub
```

Apparently, a workbook has a collection named CustomViews. You use the name of the view to retrieve an item from the collection. The item has a Show method. To switch between views, all you need to do is sub-stitute the name of the view in parentheses.

Rather than create three separate macros, you can pass the name of the view as an argument.

2   Type **ViewName** between the parentheses after *ShowView*, and then replace *"Summary"* (quotation marks and all), with **ViewName**. The revised macro should look like this:

```
Sub  ShowView(ViewName)
     ActiveWorkbook.CustomViews(ViewName).Show
End  Sub
```

Next you will test the macro and its argument using the Immediate window.

3   Press CTRL+G to display the Immediate window.

4   Type **ShowView "Detail"** and press ENTER.

Test the procedure using the Immediate window.

The worksheet should change to show the detailed view.

5   Type **ShowView "All"** and press ENTER. Then type **ShowView "Summary"** and press ENTER.

The macro works with all three arguments.

6   Close the Immediate window and save the workbook.

You now have the functionality to show different views. Creating the views may not have been fun, but it sure made writing the macro a lot easier. Also, if you decide to adjust a view (say, to include blank lines), you don't need to change the macro.

You still need to create the functionality to hide columns containing dates earlier than the desired starting month.

Dynamically hide columns

You don't want to create custom views to change the columns because you would need to create 36 different custom views: one for each month times the three different row settings. You need to change the columns dynamically, based on the choices in the dialog box. If you are going to hide columns, you will start with column C and end with an arbitrary month specified. One good way to find the month is to use Excel's Find method.

1   In Excel, select all of row 1, and then start recording a macro named **HideMonths**.

Be sure to type "1997," not "97," for the year.

2   From the Edit menu, click the Find command, type **5/1/1997** in the Find What box, select the Find Entire Cells Only check box, and make sure the Look In drop-down list box says Formulas.

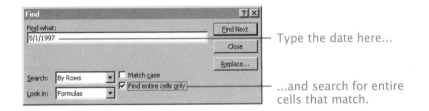

Type the date here...

...and search for entire cells that match.

By searching for the formula, you look for the underlying date in the cell, not the way it happens to be formatted. By searching only entire cells, you make sure that 1/1/1997, for example, will find only January (1/1/1997), and not November (11/1/1997).

3   Click Find Next, close the Find dialog box, stop the recorder, and then edit the HideMonths macro. Put a line continuation (a space, an under-score, and a new line) after every comma to make the statement read-able. It should then look like this:

```
Sub HideMonths()
    Selection.Find(What:="5/1/1997", _
        After:=ActiveCell, _
        LookIn:=xlFormulas, _
        LookAt:=xlWhole, _
        SearchOrder:=xlByRows, _
        SearchDirection:=xlNext, _
        MatchCase:=False).Activate

End Sub
```

The macro searches the selection (in this case, row 1), starting with the active cell (in this case, cell A1), searches for the specified date, and activates the matching cell.

You don't want the macro to change the selection, and you don't want the macro to activate the cell it finds. Rather, you want the macro to assign the found range to a variable so you can refer to it.

4   Make these changes to the macro: Declare the variable myFind as a Range. Change *Selection* to **Rows(1)** and *ActiveCell* to **Range("A1")**. Delete *.Activate* from the end of the second statement, and add **Set myFind =** to the beginning.

The revised macro will look like this:

```
Sub HideMonths()
    Dim myFind as Range
    Set myFind = Rows(1).Find(What:="5/1/1997", _
        After:=Range("A1"), _
        LookIn:=xlFormulas, _
        LookAt:=xlWhole, _
        SearchOrder:=xlByRows, _
        SearchDirection:=xlNext, _
        MatchCase:=False)

End Sub
```

If the Find method is successful, then myFind will contain a reference to the cell that contains the month. You want to hide all the columns from column C to one column to the left of myFind.

5 Before the End Sub statement, insert this statement:

```
Range("C1",myFind.Offset(0,-1)).EntireColumn.Hidden = True
```

This selects a range starting with cell C1 and ending one cell to the left of the cell with the month name. It then hides the columns containing that range.

6 Save the workbook, and press F8 repeatedly to step through the macro. Watch as columns C through H disappear.

You will be changing this subroutine to hide columns up to any date. You need some way of knowing whether the Find method finds a match or not. If the Find method does find a match, it assigns a reference to the variable. If it does not find a match, it assigns a special reference, *Nothing*, to the variable. You can check to see if the object is the same as Nothing. Because you are comparing object references and not values, you don't use an equal sign to do the comparison. Instead you use a special object comparison word, *Is*.

> **NOTE** A variable that is declared as a variant contains the value Empty when nothing else is assigned to it. A variable that is declared as an object contains the reference Nothing when no other object reference is assigned to it. *Empty* means "no value," and *Nothing* means "no object reference." To see if the variable myValue contains the Empty value, use the expression *IsEmpty(myValue)*. To see if the variable myObject contains a reference to Nothing, use the expression *myObject Is Nothing*.

7   Replace the statement that hides the columns with this If structure:

```
If Not myFind Is Nothing Then
    Range("C1", myFind.Offset(0, -1)).EntireColumn.Hidden = True
End If
```

The statement that hides the columns is unchanged. If the Find method fails, it assigns Nothing to myFind, so the conditional expression is False and no columns are hidden.

8   Test the macro's ability to handle an error by changing the value that the Find method searches for from *5/1/1997* to **Dog**. Then step through the macro and watch what happens when you get to the If structure. Hold the mouse pointer over the myFind variable and see that its value is Nothing.

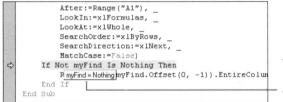

The Find method returns Nothing if it doesn't find a match.

If you search for a date that is in row 1, then myFind will hold a reference to the cell containing that date and the macro will hide the months that precede it. If you search for anything else, then myFind will hold a reference to Nothing, and the macro will not hide any columns.

9   Press F5 to end the macro.

The final step is to convert the date to an argument.

10   Type **StartMonth** between the parentheses after *HideMonths*, and replace "5/15/1997"or "Dog" (including the quotation marks) with **StartMonth**. The revised (and finished) procedure should look like this:

```
Sub HideMonths(StartMonth)
    Dim myFind As Range
    Set myFind = Rows(1).Find(What:=StartMonth, _
        After:=Range("A1"), _
        LookIn:=xlFormulas, _
        LookAt:=xlWhole, _
        SearchOrder:=xlByRows, _
        SearchDirection:=xlNext, _
        MatchCase:=False)
    If Not myFind Is Nothing Then
        Range("C1", myFind.Offset(0, -1)).EntireColumn.Hidden = True
    End If
End Sub
```

271

Be sure to type "1997," not "97," for the year.

11 Now test the macro. Press CTRL+G to display the Immediate window. Enter **ShowView "All"** and then enter **HideMonths "8/1/1997"**.

	A B	M	N	O
1	Summary	Aug-97	Sep-97	Qtr3
2	Projected Units	35000	36000	106000
3	Projected Revenues	85000	87000	255000
4	**Projected Pre-tax Profit**	39247.9	40985.9	117481.7

The months before August are hidden.

12 Close the Immediate window and save the workbook.

You now have macros that can handle the functionality of the form by hiding appropriate rows and columns. It is now time to put the form and the functionality together.

Implementing a Form

You have created a user interface for the form. The user interface allows you to specify which rows and columns to print. You have also created the functionality for the form. The ShowView and HideMonths macros show the appropriate rows and columns. You now need to make the user interface drive the functionality. You need to implement the form.

For this form, the Print button is what formats and prints the report. You will put all the code that links the form to the functionality into the btnPrint_Click procedure.

Implement option buttons

To implement the option buttons, you need a way to determine which option button value is True. The frame control has a Controls property that returns a collection of all the controls in the frame. You can loop through those controls and determine which option button value is True.

1 In Visual Basic, click the Project Explorer toolbar button, double-click the frmPrint form, and then close the Project window.

Project Explorer button

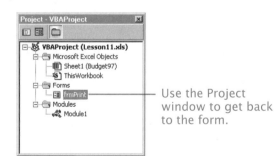

Use the Project window to get back to the form.

When you have a project with several components, the Project window is often the easiest way to get to the right place.

2 Double-click the Print button to show the btnPrint_Click event handler procedure.

3 Insert these statements at the beginning of the procedure, before the Unload Me statement:

```
Dim myOption As Control
Dim myView

For Each myOption In grpRows.Controls
    If myOption.Value = True Then
        myView = myOption.Caption
    End If
Next myOption
ShowView myView
```

This For Each loop inspects each control in the frame, looking for a value of True. You declare the loop variable as a Control (not as an OptionButton) because it is possible for a frame to contain other types of controls besides option buttons.

 NOTE If you loop through the controls of a frame that contains controls other than option buttons, you should check to see if the control is an option button. If you prefix each option button name with *opt-*, then you can use the conditional expression *Left(myOption.Name,3) = "opt"* to determine whether the control is an option button.

The loop stores the caption of the selected option in a variable and the macro later uses that variable as the argument when it runs the ShowView macro. How fortunate that we used the same names for the custom views and the captions of the option buttons.

4 Save the workbook, and press F8 to run the form. (Press F8 repeatedly to step through the initialization procedures.)

You can run the form by pressing F5 or F8 while either the form design window or the form code window is active. If you press F8 to run the form, then you can step through any event handler procedures that run while the form is visible.

5 Click the Summary option, and click Print. Press F8 repeatedly to step through the btnPrint_Click procedure. Close the message box as necessary.

An option button can be easy to implement if you plan ahead. In this example, giving the custom views in the worksheet the same names as the captions of the option buttons made the option buttons easy to implement.

Also, if you had to add a fourth view option, all you would have to do is define a new view on the worksheet, and add an option button with the appropriate caption to the form. You would not need to make any changes to any of the procedures.

Implement a check box

If the check box is selected, the Print button event handler should run the HideMonths macro. Actually, the HideMonths macro will do nothing if you give it a date that it doesn't find. You can take advantage of that by assigning to a variable either the date from the month box, or an invalid value.

1   Double-click the Print button to show the btnPrint_Click procedure, and add the following statements after *Dim myView*:

```
Dim myMonth

If chkMonth.Value = True Then
    myMonth = txtMonth.Value
Else
    myMonth = "no date"
End If
```

These statements assign to the myMonth variable either the value from the month text box or an obviously invalid value.

2   Insert the statement **HideMonths myMonth** after the statement *ShowView myView*.

You place this statement after the ShowView statement because you want to change the view before hiding the months; showing the custom view redisplays all the hidden columns.

Be sure to type "1997," not "97," for the year.

3   Save the workbook, and press F5 to run the form. Select the check box, type **9/1/1997** in the month box, and click Print.

	A	B	N	O	P
1	Summary		Sep-97	Qtr3	Oct-97
2	Projected Units		36000	106000	37000
3	Projected Revenues		87000	255000	89000
4	**Projected Pre-tax Profit**		40985.9	117481.7	43223.9

The date in the text box of the form determines the first visible month.

The worksheet shows only the months starting from September.

4   Click OK to close the message box.

Check for errors in an edit box

What if you run the form and type "4/15/97" as the date? The macro would simply not hide any columns. What if you type "Dog" as the date? The macro also would not hide any columns. The form would be far more helpful if it would automatically convert *4/15/97* to the appropriate *4/1/1997*. (Where could you find a function to convert a date to the start of the specified month?) And if the input box contains something like "Dog," the form should point out the error.

1 Double-click the Print button. In the btnPrint_Click procedure, replace *myMonth = txtMonth.Value* with **myMonth = StartOfMonth(txtMonth.Value)**.

The StartOfMonth function converts a date to the first of the month. If the input date is not a valid date, the function returns the Empty value. (Aren't you glad that you wrote the StartOfMonth function to handle invalid dates?) If the myMonth variable contains the Empty value, you will want to show a message and make the value easy to fix.

2 Insert these statements before the Else statement:

```
If myMonth = Empty Then
    MsgBox "Invalid Month"
    txtMonth.SetFocus
    txtMonth.SelStart = 0
    txtMonth.SelLength = 1000
    Exit Sub
End If
```

When you run the form, if you type an invalid date, the macro will appropriately display a message box explaining the problem. After you close the message box, you should be able to just start typing a corrected value. In order for that to happen, however, the macro must move to the text box and preselect the current, invalid contents.

The SetFocus method moves the focus to the text box. Setting the SelStart property to 0 starts text selection from the very beginning of the text box. Setting the SelLength property to 1000 extends text selection to however much text there is in the box. Using an arbitrarily large value like 1000 simply avoids having to calculate the actual length of the contents of the box.

3 Save the workbook, and press F5 to run the form. Try enabling the month, typing **Dog**, and clicking Print. Try typing **Jun 23, 97** and clicking Print. (Close the message box.)

When you put an edit box onto a form, you must think about what the macro should do if the user enters an invalid value. Many times, displaying an error message and pre-selecting the invalid entry is the best alternative. The SetFocus method and the SelStart and SelLength properties are the tools that allow you to do that.

Print the report

The Print form now does everything it needs to do—everything, that is, except print. If you make the report display the report in print preview mode, you can then decide whether to actually print it or just admire it.

1 Double-click the Print button. In the btnPrint_Click procedure, replace *MsgBox "Printing"* with **ActiveSheet.PrintPreview**.

After the report prints, you should restore the rows and columns in the worksheet.

2 After the statement *ActiveSheet.PrintPreview*, type the statement **ShowView "All"**.

3 Save the workbook, press F5 to run the form, select the Summary option, limit the months to August and later, click the Print button, and click Zoom to see the beautiful report.

Use Print Preview to see what the report will look like.

4 Close the Print Preview window.

The user interface of the form is now linked to its full functionality. All that is left is to provide a way for the user to run the form from Excel, instead of from Visual Basic.

Launch the form

To launch the form, you create a standard macro that displays the form. Once you have done that, you make event procedures that automatically add a menu command when the workbook opens and remove it when the workbook closes.

Project Explorer button

1 Click the Project Explorer button to show the Project window, double-click the Module1 module (that is, the module that contains the ShowView and HideMonths macros), activate the code window, and scroll to the bottom of the module.

2 Insert this macro:

```
Sub ShowForm()
    frmPrint.Show
End Sub
```

The Show method of a form displays the form. To refer to the form, simply use the name that you gave it when you created it.

3 In the Project window, double-click the ThisWorkbook object. Select Workbook from the Objects list, and insert these statements as the body of the Workbook_Open procedure:

```
Dim myButton As CommandBarButton
Set myButton = _
    Application.CommandBars("Worksheet Menu Bar").Controls.Add
myButton.Caption = "&Print Report"
myButton.Style = msoButtonCaption
myButton.BeginGroup = True
myButton.OnAction = "ShowForm"
```

The CommandBars collection works like any other collection; you specify an item using the name of the item. The Controls collection also works like other collections; you add an item—in this case a command bar button—using the Add method. The Add method returns a reference to the new object, which you can assign to an object variable. Unless you specify otherwise, the Add method adds the control to the end of the collection.

Assigning a value to the Caption property sets the text for the command. Assigning msoButtonCaption to the Style property makes the control display the caption, rather than an icon. The BeginGroup property adds a line before the command, separating it from the built-in commands. The OnAction property is the name of the macro you want to have run.

This menu item will appear on the main Excel menu bar whenever you open the workbook.

4 From the Procedures list at the top of the code window, select BeforeClose. Insert these statements as the body of the Workbook_BeforeClose procedure:

```
ActiveWorkbook.Save
On Error Resume Next
Application.CommandBars("Worksheet Menu Bar") _
    .Controls("Print Report").Delete
```

The first statement saves the workbook. This prevents Excel from asking whether or not to save the workbook. The second statement keeps Visual Basic from complaining if the Print Report command does not exist for some reason. The third statement deletes the new Print Report menu command. These statements will execute whenever the workbook closes, removing any trace of the Print Report command.

5 Switch to Excel; save and close the workbook.

6 Open the Lesson11 workbook.

   The new command appears on the main worksheet menu as soon as you open the workbook.

7 Click the new Print Report menu command, and then click Cancel.

8 Close the workbook.

   The new command disappears. Your custom form is completely integrated with Excel.

Creating a fully usable form entails three major steps: creating the user interface, creating the functionality, and joining them together into a working tool.

Lesson Summary

To	Do this
Add a form	Click the Insert UserForm button.
Test run an active form	Press F5 (or press F8 to step through the form's procedures).
Arrange controls on a form	Select multiple controls, and then choose commands from Visual Basic's Format menu.
Initialize a control when you design the form	Set the value of a property for the control in the Properties window.
Initialize a control when you run the form	Assign a value to a property for the control in the UserForm_Initialize event handler procedure for the form.
Make an event handler procedure close the form	Use the Unload Me statement.
Set the tab order for controls on a form or in a frame	Select the form or the frame, and click the Tab Order command from the View menu.
Check to see if the Find method found a matching cell	Assign the result of the Find method to an object variable, and use *Is Nothing* to examine the variable.
Determine which option button in a frame is selected	Use a For Each loop to search the Controls collection of the frame, looking for a True value.

To	Do this
Select the contents of a text box that contains an error	Use the SetFocus method to activate the text box, and then assign 0 to the SelStart property and 1000 to the SelLength property.
Show a form from a macro	Specify the form by name, and then use the Show method.
Add a command to the worksheet menu bar	Use the statement *Application.CommandBars("Worksheet Menu Bar").Commands.Add.*
Create procedures that run when the workbook opens or closes	Add procedures named Workbook_Open and Workbook_BeforeClose to the ThisWorkbook object in a workbook.

For online information about	Ask the Assistant for help using the words
Creating a custom form	"User form"
Using option buttons	"Option buttons"
Using menus and toolbars	"Command bars"

Preview of the Next Lesson

In the next lesson, you will create a management reporting tool. You will create an effective user interface, use a pivot table and a chart, and retrieve information dynamically from an external database.

Creating an Enterprise Information System

Estimated time
50 min.

In this lesson you will learn how to:

- Retrieve data from an external database.
- Create a graphical front end to an application.
- Create an animated logo.
- Change and restore workbook settings.

While I was in college, I spent two years in Japan. Before departing, I spent two months in an intensive language training program. At the end of the two months, I was reasonably satisfied with my ability to speak Japanese. Then I arrived in Tokyo. For the first two weeks, I was unable to detect *any* similarity between the language I had studied and the language the local inhabitants were speaking. It was, shall we say, a humbling experience.

Within a few weeks, however, I began to be able to pick out words, and within a few months I was able to communicate reasonably well. By the end of the two years, I once again felt reasonably satisfied with my ability to speak Japanese. And I learned along the way that classroom practice is not the same as real-world experience.

Learning to write macros is in some ways similar to learning a new foreign language. Once again, classroom practice is not the same as real-world experience. In this lesson, you will build a simple but complete Enterprise Information System (EIS) that will allow people in all parts of a hypothetical enterprise to look at orders for the past two years. Creating a packaged application turns up numerous new real-world challenges that you don't encounter when building macros for yourself. This lesson will show you how to solve many such challenges.

Most of the concepts in this lesson have been introduced earlier in this book. This lesson shows how to put those concepts to work in packaging an application, and also introduces a few new tricks that you may need.

Start the lesson

 Start Microsoft Excel.

Examining an Existing Enterprise Information System

In this lesson you will create an EIS that displays order information for each state in the Miller Textiles territory. It will be easier for you to understand the pieces that you have to build if you have a vision of what you will end up with. So let's take a look at the finished product before you start building it yourself.

Look at the application

Open button

1 Click the Open button, change to the Finished folder under the folder containing the practice files for this book, and open Lesson12.

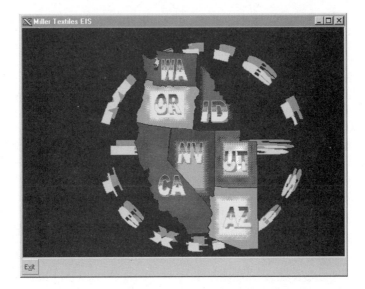

The workbook opens, displays an introductory animation, and shows you a colored, shaded map of the western United States.

2 Click the map for California.

The screen switches to display quarterly orders for the past two years, complete with a graph.

3 Click the Return To Main command at the bottom-left corner of the Workbook window to return to the map.

4 Click the Exit command at the bottom of the window to close the workbook.

This is a simple EIS. It displays information from one of the company's databases in an easy-to-use, visually powerful way.

Take a closer look at the application

Many small details make the difference between an application that is intuitive and easy to use, and one that is frustrating. Take another look at the Miller Textiles EIS, and notice some details worth including in yours.

1 Before reopening the EIS workbook, open and position several toolbars. Make the Excel window short and wide so you can tell if the application puts it back to the original size when it finishes.

Resize the window so you can tell if the application restores it properly.

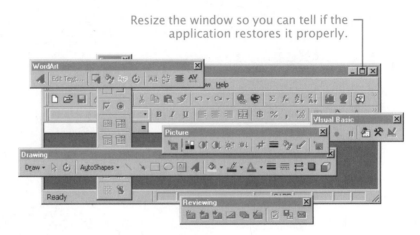

2 Open the finished Lesson12 workbook again. Wait for the animation to begin, but before it ends, press CTRL+BREAK.

The animation stops, and the procedure that controls it jumps directly to its end, and then displays the map. Animations are good for attracting attention, but they can be annoying to an impatient user. It is often a good idea to provide a mechanism for bypassing a lengthy animation.

3 Move the mouse over the notch where Nevada interlocks with Arizona. Click once when the mouse is over Nevada, return to the main sheet, and click again when the mouse is over Arizona.

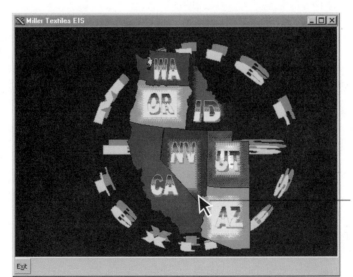

Click where Nevada and Arizona interlock.

You can click anywhere within the exact border of the state to show the data for that state.

This new screen with the table and the map is really a worksheet. Sometimes you want to use the features of an Excel worksheet but disguise that fact from the user.

4 Try selecting a cell on the worksheet.

This is a "look but don't touch" screen. The application makes use of a worksheet, but from the user's perspective it could be a completely custom application. Not only is the worksheet protected, you can't even see an active cell anywhere on it.

The data grid looks somewhat like a pivot table, but it also has some differences.

5 Look at the caption at the top of the application. The caption says Miller Textiles EIS, rather than Excel.

The caption contributes to the custom appearance of the application.

6 Look at the button at the bottom of the screen. It appears to be a toolbar or a menu bar, but unlike most toolbars, it doesn't have a double bar at the left, so you can't move it.

Many times in an EIS application, you want to limit the ways that the user can modify the environment.

7 Click the Exit button.

The Excel window returns to the way it was before: the same size and shape, with the same configuration of toolbars.

This EIS has many subtle features—features that you will build into your EIS as you go through this lesson.

Charting Data from a Database

Your first task is to build the core functionality of the application: the data sheet. This sheet will use a pivot table to retrieve the data from an external database. You will link a chart to the pivot table, and then format the chart and the pivot table to make a dramatic presentation.

IMPORTANT In order to retrieve data from an external database, you must install the Microsoft Query tool that comes with Microsoft Office. Please refer to "Installing All the Microsoft Excel Tools You Need," at the front of this book, for instructions on installing Microsoft Query and other database access tools.

285

Retrieve external data into a pivot table

When you retrieve data from an external database into a pivot table, Excel uses a separate program, Microsoft Query, to assist you in specifying what data you want. Microsoft Query does not actually retrieve the data from the database. Rather it returns the definition of the data you want and its location. The pivot table then uses that information to retrieve the data.

1   Save a new, blank workbook as Lesson12 in the folder containing the practice files for this book, and rename Sheet1 to **Data**.

2   From the Data menu, click Pivot Table Report. In Step 1 of the Wizard, select the External Data Source option, and then click Next.

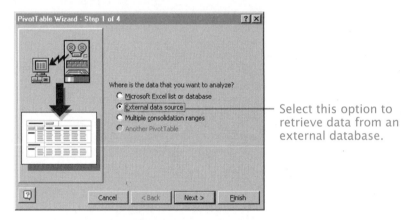

Select this option to retrieve data from an external database.

3   In Step 2, click the Get Data button.

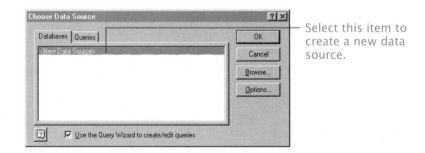

Select this item to create a new data source.

The Choose Data Source dialog box appears. You use a data source to tell Microsoft Query where the data is and what kind of driver to use to retrieve it.

4   Select the <New Data Source> option, and then click OK.

286

5   Type **Miller Textiles** as the name for the new data source, select the
Microsoft dBase Driver as the driver, and click Connect.

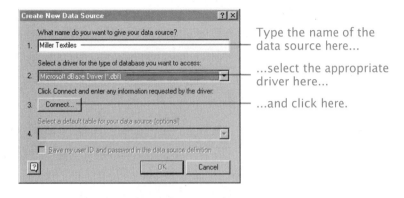

Type the name of the
data source here...

...select the appropriate
driver here...

...and click here.

> **NOTE**   ODBC is the abbreviation for "Open DataBase Connec-
> tivity," an industry-standard mechanism for letting applica-
> tions communicate with any database. All major database
> vendors distribute ODBC drivers with their databases. If you
> install the ODBC drivers for another type of database, such as
> Oracle or SQL Server, that driver will appear in the list.

6   Clear the Use Current Directory check box and click the Select
Directory button.

7   Select the folder containing the practice files for this book. The file name
orders.dbf appears in the File Name box, even though you can't select it.
Then click OK four times, moving through four dialog boxes.

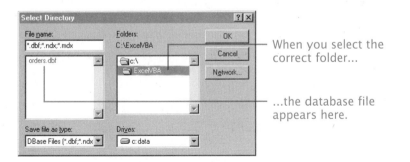

When you select the
correct folder...

...the database file
appears here.

This closes all the data source dialog boxes, selects the new data source,
and moves on to the Query Wizard.

A "column" in the Query Wizard is equivalent to a field in a pivot table.

8 In the Query Wizard - Choose Columns dialog box, click the plus sign next to the ORDERS table, and then double-click the DATE, STATE, CATEGORY, and NET columns.

Double-click an item in this list...

...to add it to this list.

These are the only fields you will need for the EIS.

9 Click Next to go to the Query Wizard - Filter Data dialog box. Select Date as the Column To Filter, select Is Greater Than Or Equal To from the first drop-down list box, and select 1996-01-01 from the second list box.

Select this option...

...and choose a starting date.

The EIS will display data for only the current and previous years.

10 Click Next twice, and then click Finish to return the definition of the data to the Pivot Table Wizard.

Query returns field names and instructions for retrieving the data.

At this point, you have returned to the Pivot Table Wizard the names of the columns and the instructions for retrieving the data.

> **NOTE** Even though you create a data source (Miller Textiles) in Microsoft Query in order to retrieve the data, the pivot table does not use the data source. Microsoft Query uses the data source to determine the connection information, and the pivot table stores only that connection information. If you will not need the data source for a different application, you can remove it once the pivot table is created.
>
> To remove a data source, use the ODBC data source administrator tool. Activate the Control Panel, and open the 32-bit ODBC item. Click the File DSN tab, select the data source name (here, Miller Textiles), and click Remove. You do not need the data source to refresh the pivot table, only to create it.

Define the pivot table

Once Microsoft Query has returned the information to the Pivot Table Wizard, you can specify how you want the pivot table to appear.

1   Click Next to go to Step 3 of the Pivot Table Wizard. Drag STATE to the page area, DATE to the column area, CATEGORY to the row area, and NET to the data area.

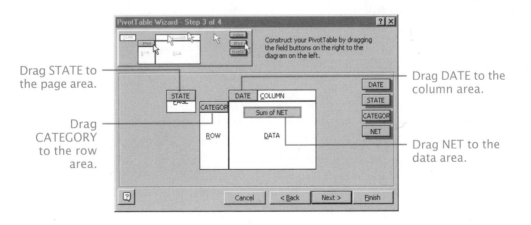

Drag STATE to the page area.

Drag CATEGORY to the row area.

Drag DATE to the column area.

Drag NET to the data area.

2 Double-click the DATE tile (in the column area), select the Show Items With No Data check box, and click OK.

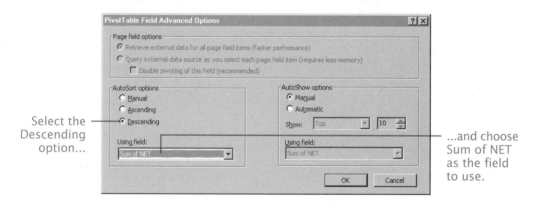

Select this option to always show all the items.

You want to show all the months for all the states, so by always showing items without data, the grid will always be the same size, and it will be easy to see which states have orders for only some of the months.

3 Double-click the CATEGORY tile (in the row area), again select the Show Items With No Data check box, and then click the Advanced button. Select Descending as the AutoSort option, and select Sum of NET from the Using Field list box at the bottom of the AutoSort group. Then click OK twice.

Select the Descending option...

...and choose Sum of NET as the field to use.

Once again, you don't want the grid to change size just because not all states sell products from all categories. The sort option will automatically sort the categories for each state, based on which category produced the most revenue.

4 Double-click the Sum of NET tile, and click the Number button. Select the Number category, specify no decimal places, and select the 1000 Separator check box. Then click OK twice.

Select the Number category.

Specify no decimal places.

Include the separator.

This formats the revenue values with commas, which makes the numbers easier to read.

5 Click Next to go to Step 4 of the Pivot Table Wizard, and click the Options button. Turn off grand totals for both columns and rows, and then click OK.

Turn off row and column grand totals.

Usually, when you chart a pivot table, you do not want to include grand totals.

6 In Step 4 of the Pivot Table wizard, type **B2** as the location on the existing worksheet where you want the top-left cell of the pivot table, and then click Finish.

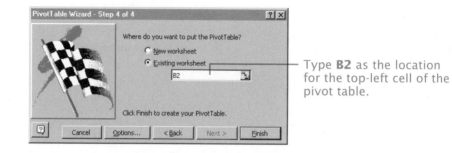

Type **B2** as the location for the top-left cell of the pivot table.

The pivot table finally retrieves the data from the external database and creates the table on the worksheet.

7 Save the Lesson12 workbook.

Format the pivot table

The table looks good, except that you want to display quarters instead of months. You also want to add a slightly more dramatic look to the sheet, and you want the columns to stay the same size, instead of adjusting as the data changes.

*Group
button*

1 Click the DATE tile, and on the PivotTable toolbar, click the Group button. In the By list box in the Grouping dialog box, deselect Months, select Quarters and Years, and click OK.

Deselect Months...
...and select
Quarters and Years.

When you group dates, you end up with two rows of labels. The chart can use one or more rows as labels.

Because of how Excel handles sizes internally, even if you set the column width to 6.5, Excel changes it to 6.57.

2 Set the width of column A to 3, the width of column B to 15, the width of columns C through J to 6.57, and the width of column K to 1.

To format the background of the pivot table, you can use Excel's AutoFormat command to take care of most of the work.

3 Select any cell in the pivot table. From the Format menu, click AutoFormat, and then click the Options button to extend the dialog box. Select Colorful 3 from the Table Format list, clear the Width/Height check box, and click OK. Select cell A1 to see the formatted table.

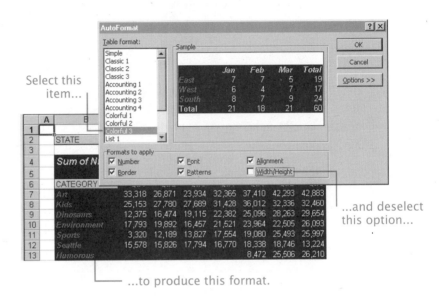

Select this item...

...and deselect this option...

...to produce this format.

AutoFormat would normally adjust the column widths as you change from state to state. By turning off the Column Width option, you can have AutoFormat do the formatting you want, while leaving intact the attributes you want to control.

While the rest of the table looks good, the pink labels are a little bit too strong for this application. Luckily, you can override specific portions of the automatic formatting.

Font Color
button

4 Click cell B6. (Excel selects B7:B13.) Click the arrow on the Font Color button on the Formatting toolbar, and then click the Sky Blue color.

Click cell B6
once...

...to select
the Category
labels.

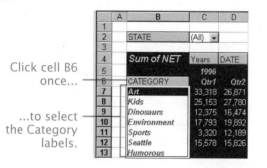

Bold
button

5 Click cell B6 again. (Because the range B7:B13 was already selected, this time Excel actually selects cell B6.) Click the Bold button and the Italic button. Set the font color to Black.

Italic
button

The pivot table looks pretty good (at least if you ignore the top three rows). The background of the sheet, however, is still white. One way to change the sheet background would be to select all the cells and change the fill color to black. A better way—particularly since you will want to change the background of all the sheets—is to redefine the Normal style. The Normal style is the default format for the workbook.

6 From the Format menu, click Style, select Normal, and click the Modify button. On the Patterns tab, select the color Black (the top-left color), and on the Font tab, from the Color list, click the color White. Then click OK twice.

Change the Normal
style to format all the
unformatted cells in
the workbook.

The entire worksheet changes to black. Changing the Normal style changes the background of all the worksheets in the workbook.

7 Save the Lesson12 workbook.

The pivot table is ready. Next you will create a chart to display the pivot table data.

Create and format a chart

A chart can make the numbers in the table easier to interpret. In order to show both the total orders for a state, and also show what portion of those orders came from each category, a stacked area chart is a good choice.

You will want the chart to be above the pivot table. Instead of inserting rows, you can enlarge the size of row 1 to make room for the chart.

1 Set the height of row 1 to 150.

Now create a chart to fill the row you just enlarged.

2 Click cell B4 to select the entire pivot table, and click the Chart Wizard button.

Chart Wizard button

3 In Step 1, select Area as the Chart Type, and click Next. In Step 2, click Next. In Step 3, select Category Major Gridlines on the Gridlines tab, select Left Placement on the Legend tab, and click Finish.

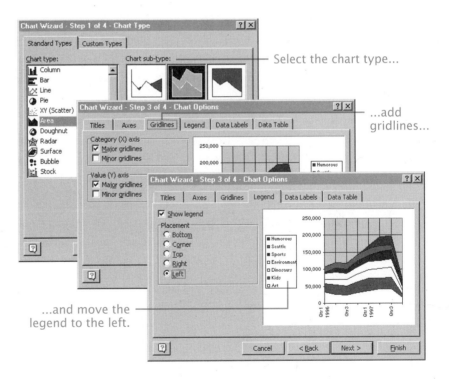

Select the chart type...

...add gridlines...

...and move the legend to the left.

4 Drag the chart up to the top left corner of the worksheet, and then hold down the ALT key as you drag the bottom right corner of the chart to the bottom right corner of cell K1.

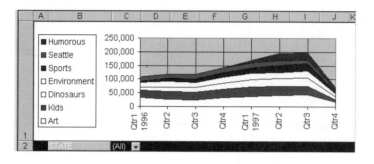

5 With the Chart Area still selected, click Selected Chart Area on the Format menu. On the Font tab, select Gray-25% for the Color and 8 as the Size. On the Patterns tab, select None for Border and None for Area. Then click OK.

Setting the pattern for the area to None makes the chart transparent. However, you won't see a dramatic change until you deselect the chart and the background changes to black. Setting the font for the Chart Area changes the font for all the elements of the chart at one time.

6 Move the legend down until its bottom almost touches the bottom of the chart. Then, with the legend still selected, click Selected Legend on the Format menu, and on the Patterns tab, select None for Border and None for Area. Then click OK.

7 Select the value axis, click Selected Axis on the Format menu, and on the Patterns tab, change the Color to Gray-40% and click OK.

8 Select the category axis, click Selected Axis on the Format menu, and on the Patterns tab, change the Color to Gray-40%, select None for Tick Mark Labels, and click OK.

You don't need category axis labels, because you will later make the tick marks line up with the labels in the pivot table.

9 Change the color of both sets of gridlines to Gray-50%.

10 Select the Plot Area, and format both the area and the border of the plot area as None. Drag the top size handle of the plot area as high as it will go, and then drag the bottom size handle as low as it will go. Drag the right size handle of the plot area to line up with the center of 1997 Qtr4 in the pivot table, and drag the left size handle of the plot area to line up with the center of 1996 Qtr1.

11 Press ESC twice to deselect the plot area and the chart. Then save the Lesson12 workbook.

This is the finished chart. The chart blends in nicely with the background. Next you can add some simple macros to control the pivot table.

Controlling the Pivot Table with Macros

You don't want the users to see the page field tile or to select a state from that tile. The user will use the map to change states. You can hide the rows that contain the page field, and then create a macro to change the state. You will also need to provide an alternative way to see which state is being displayed. In addition, you will need to create a macro to refresh the pivot table, so that new data will appear as it is available in the database.

Hide unwanted rows of the pivot table

You don't want the user to see the top three rows of the pivot table. They are ugly and unnecessary. You do, however, need a way to show which state is currently selected.

Text Box button

Be sure to type in the Formula Bar, not in the text box itself.

1 Select a cell outside the pivot table, and then, on the Drawing toolbar, click the Text Box button. Then click close to the top-left corner of cell A1.

2 Click in the formula bar, type **=C2**, and press ENTER.

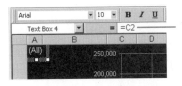

Type **=C2** here to link the text box to the cell.

Cell C2 is the cell in the pivot table that contains the state code. A text box can link to the contents of a cell.

Bold button

3 Change the font size of the text box to 36, click the Bold button, and change the font color to Sky Blue.

Font Color button

4 Select the range A2:A4, and hide the rows. (From the Format menu, click Row and then click Hide.)

5 Turn off the row and column headings. (From the Tools menu, click Options, click the View tab, and then clear the Row And Column Headers check box.) Click OK.

6 Save the Lesson12 workbook.

Who would guess that this glamorous worksheet has at its heart a simple pivot table? Now that the page field box is gone, you need to provide a new mechanism for selecting the state.

Make a macro change the pivot table

If you create a macro that takes an argument giving the state code, then you can use that one macro for any state. First create a macro that changes the pivot table to display orders for an arbitrary state, and then add the argument to generalize the macro.

*Run Macro
button*

1   On the Visual Basic toolbar, click the Run Macro button. Type **SetPivot** as the macro name, and click Create.

Visual Basic opens with a new macro named SetPivot.

2   Enter these statements as the body of the SetPivot macro:

```
Worksheets("Data").Select
ActiveSheet.PivotTables(1).PageFields(1).CurrentPage = "OR"
```

This macro changes the pivot table to display the orders for Oregon. The first statement selects the Data sheet, just in case it wasn't already the active sheet. The second statement changes the value of the CurrentPage property for the one page field of the one pivot table on the sheet. For now, the new state (OR for "Oregon") is a constant.

3   Press F5 to run the macro and change the state to Oregon. Change the state code in the macro to **NV** (for "Nevada") and try it again.

Next you can change the macro to accept an argument for the state code.

4   Insert **NewState** between the parentheses after the name of the macro. Then replace *"NV"* with **NewState**.

5   Press CTRL+G to display the Immediate window, and in that window type **SetPivot "AZ"** and press ENTER.

The state changes to Arizona. The SetPivot macro is ready to change the pivot table to any state.

6   Save the Lesson12 workbook.

The SetPivot macro is ready to use. Later you will create a graphical interface that calls the SetPivot macro, passing the appropriate state code as an argument.

Make a macro refresh the pivot table

A pivot table has an option named Refresh On Open. The purpose of this option is to automatically refresh the data in the pivot table whenever you open the workbook. Unfortunately, when you protect a worksheet that contains a pivot table (as you will do to this worksheet before you are through with it), the Refresh On Open option stops working. That means that you will need to create a macro to refresh the pivot table.

That's the bad news. The good news is that while you create a macro to refresh the pivot table, you can also make the connection to the data source more flexible. When you create the pivot table, Microsoft Query tells the pivot table where the database is located. The pivot table stores the entire location of the database. If you move the workbook or the database to a new location, the pivot table will not be able to find the database. By refreshing the pivot table in a macro, you can add some additional code to tell the pivot table that the database is in the same folder as the workbook. Then, if you move the workbook to a new location, as long as you move the database with it, the application will continue to work.

A pivot table stores its information in something called a *pivot cache*. Multiple pivot tables in a workbook can share the same pivot cache. A pivot cache has its own object, a PivotCache object. The PivotCache object has a Connection property that stores where to go to get the data. If the database is always in the same folder as the application workbook, you can set the Connection property to look at that folder.

1   In Visual Basic, add this new macro to Module1:

```
Sub RefreshPivot()
    Dim myConnect As String
    myConnect = "ODBC;"
    myConnect = myConnect &  _
        "Driver={Microsoft dBase Driver (*.dbf)};"
    myConnect = myConnect & "DBQ="
    myConnect = myConnect & ActiveWorkbook.Path
    ActiveWorkbook.PivotCaches(1).Connection = myConnect
    ActiveWorkbook.PivotCaches(1).Refresh
End Sub
```

> **IMPORTANT** Be especially careful to type semicolons after ODBC and the driver name. Do not put spaces around the equal signs. Watch out for the braces and the parentheses in the driver name. There is a space between *Microsoft dBase Driver* and the opening parenthesis.

This macro constructs a new connection string. Most of the string is constant. It is simply broken into three statements to make each one easier to read. The last part of the string retrieves the Path property of the active workbook, which gives the folder name where the workbook is stored.

Assuming that the active workbook is stored in the C:\ExcelVBA folder, the final connection string would be *ODBC;Driver={Microsoft dBase Driver (*.dbf)};DBQ=C:\ExcelVBA*. This is the minimal connection string necessary to connect to a dBase file database. After you create a database using Microsoft Query, you can look at the Connection property of the

PivotCache object to see what it created. The string returned by the Connection property can be very long. You can try leaving out parts to determine which are required.

Be especially sure to save the workbook at this time.

2 Save the Lesson12 workbook.

3 Press F5 to run the RefreshPivot macro.

You should see the message in the status bar showing that the data is being refreshed.

> **NOTE** If the macro produces an error, you have an error somewhere in the connection string. If that happens, the pivot table has become invalid. You must close the workbook without saving changes, open the copy you saved, and then try again to match the connection string listed above.

You have now created the core functionality of the application. The pivot table retrieves the data from the external database, and the chart presents the data in a visually appealing way. Your next task is to create an effective mechanism for interacting with the application.

Creating a Graphical Interface

A graphical interface, such as a map, can be an effective way of presenting choices. Instead of selecting the name of a state from a list, the user can simply click within the state boundary.

Insert a map

First you need to create a map on the worksheet. You can import pictures from Excel's clip art gallery or from a file in Windows. For this example, you will import the picture from a file.

1 Select Sheet2 in the Lesson12 workbook. Rename the sheet to **Main**.

2 Select cell D3, and from the Insert menu, Picture submenu, click From File.

3 Change to the folder containing the practice files for this book, select the Map.wmf file, and click Insert.

4 From the Format menu, click Picture, click the Size tab, set the height to 3.5 inches, and click OK.

Drawing button

5 If necessary, click the Drawing button to activate the Drawing toolbar. Click the Draw menu on the Drawing toolbar, click the Ungroup command, and click Yes when asked whether to convert the picture to a Microsoft Office drawing.

*Fill Color
button*

6 Click the arrow next to the Fill Color button, and choose Fill Effects.

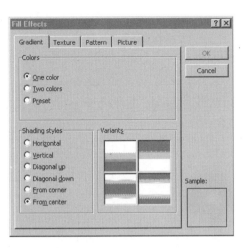

7 In the Fill Effects dialog box, select One Color as the Gradient and From Center as the Shading Style, and then click OK.

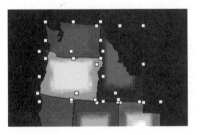

The new format
applies to each state.

The shading makes the states look something like jewels. Once you convert an imported picture to a Microsoft Office drawing, you can take advantage of the numerous impressive formatting features available to shapes.

8 Save the Lesson12 workbook.

The map is ready. You could have the user simply click on the state background, but adding the two-letter codes for the states will make it easier for people who get Nevada and Arizona confused.

Add state codes to the map

You could use command buttons to add the state code to the map, but buttons have very limited formatting capabilities. Instead, try using WordArt text, so you can make the state codes look attractive.

Insert WordArt button

1 On the Drawing toolbar, click the Insert WordArt button. Select the third style on the fourth row, and click OK.

Replace the default text with **WA**.

If you accidentally drag a state instead of the WordArt object, click the Undo button to move it back.

2 In the Edit WordArt Text dialog box, type **WA** as the Text, and click OK.

3 From the Format menu, choose Word Art, specify .35 inch as the Height, .5 inch as the Width, and click OK. Then drag the label for the state to the middle of the map of Washington state.

Drag the label to the middle of the state.

4 While holding the CTRL key, drag a copy of the WA label to each of the remaining six states.

5 Change the text of each WordArt object to the appropriate state code (OR, ID, CA, NV, UT, and AZ).

> **TIP** You can quickly change the text of a WordArt shape by using the keyboard. Press TAB to select the shape you want to change. Press ALT+X to execute the Edit Text command from the WordArt toolbar. Type the new text. Press TAB to activate the OK button and then press ENTER. Repeat for the next shape.

6 Click the WA label. Hold down the SHIFT key and click the map for Washington state. On the Drawing toolbar, click the Draw menu, and then click the Group command. Repeat for each of the other six states.

If the shapes are grouped, clicking the label selects the map of the state.

7 Double-check that each state map is grouped properly with its code, by clicking the code for each state. If the map becomes selected, then the objects are grouped.

8 Save the Lesson12 workbook.

By grouping the WordArt with the background picture, you can make it so that the user can click either the letters or the background to run the macro.

Link a macro to the graphical objects

Earlier in the lesson you created a SetPivot macro. That macro will display any state, provided that you pass it the appropriate state code. Coincidentally, the state code appears as the text of the WordArt object on each state. You therefore need to create a macro that can retrieve the text from the WordArt object for the state the user clicks.

In a macro, Excel's Application object has a property named *Caller*. The Caller property gives you the identifier of the object that the user clicked to run the macro. The identifier is the name that appears to the left of the Formula Bar when you select the object. In this example, the identifier for Washington State is something like Group 85. You can use the identifier that the Caller property returns to select the object from the Shapes collection on the active sheet.

The shape you will click is actually a group consisting of two parts: the map for the state and the WordArt label. A Shape object has a GroupItems collection, which you can index into to retrieve the WordArt object. It is a tortuous path to get from the identifier that Caller returns to the text in the WordArt object, but the benefit is that a single macro can handle all the states.

Select Objects button

1 On the Drawing toolbar, click the Select Objects button. Then drag a rectangle around the entire map. You should see sizing handles around each of the seven states. Click the Select Objects button again to turn it off.

2 Right-click on the map, and choose the Assign Macro command.

When you select multiple objects before assigning a macro, you assign the same macro to each object, the same as assigning the macros one at a time.

3 In the Assign Macro dialog box, type **ShowMe** as the macro name, and click New.

4 Enter these statements as the body of the ShowMe macro:

```
Dim myID As String
Dim myShape As Shape
Dim myName As String

myID = Application.Caller
Set myShape = ActiveSheet.Shapes(myID)
myName = myShape.GroupItems(2).TextEffect.Text
SetPivot myName
```

For some miraculous reason, when you group a WordArt object with a background object, the WordArt item is always the second item in the GroupItems collection, regardless of how you created the group. The TextEffect property returns a reference to the WordArt features of the shape.

Given that this one macro can handle any state, it is not all that complicated. (The macro would be even simpler if you hadn't been so insistent on allowing the user to click anywhere on the background of the map.)

5 Activate Excel and, with all states still selected, on the Drawing toolbar, click the Draw menu and the Group command, and press ESC to deselect the map.

This groups all the states into a single group, which will be convenient when it comes time to hide and show the map. Fortunately, even if you group the states, the Caller property still returns the identifier of the specific item that you click.

6 Save the Lesson12 workbook, and click anywhere inside the border of Nevada.

The Data sheet should appear and display the orders for Nevada.

The Application.Caller property is a very convenient tool for making a single macro handle any of several objects.

 NOTE When you use the Control Toolbox to add an object, you create an ActiveX control. Multiple ActiveX controls cannot share a single macro, because they use event handler procedures and an event handler can link to only a single object.

Add a background logo

You can also use WordArt to add an attractive logo for the EIS application. Later in the lesson you will animate the logo.

Insert WordArt button

1 Activate the Main worksheet, and click the Drawing toolbar's Insert WordArt button.

2 Select the fourth style on the fourth row and click OK. Type **Miller** and press ENTER, type **EIS** and press ENTER, type **Textiles**, and click OK.

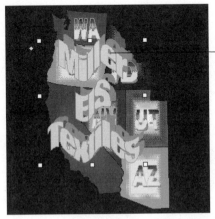

— Start with a built-in format.

The new WordArt object has the appropriate colors, but it has a very strange shape. You can easily change the shape.

WordArt Shape button

3 On the WordArt toolbar, click the WordArt Shape button, and select the Button (Pour) shape (the rightmost shape on the second row).

4 On the WordArt toolbar, click the WordArt Same Letter Heights button. Then click the WordArt Alignment button and choose the Stretch Justify option.

5 Drag the top-left sizing handle to the top-left corner of cell C3, and drag the bottom-right sizing handle to the middle of the bottom of cell H22.

Many shapes have an adjustment marker that allows you to modify the shape. It appears as a yellow diamond to left of center in the WordArt object. Later in the lesson you will see how a macro can change the adjustment.

6 Drag the adjustment marker to the left until it is about a quarter of an inch from the outside circle.

Drag the adjustment handle to change the shape.

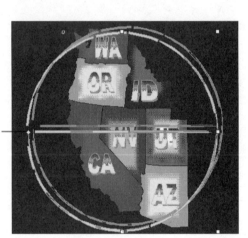

7 On the Drawing toolbar, click the Draw menu, choose the Order submenu, and click Send To Back.

8 Turn off the row and column headings. (From the Tools menu, click Options, click the View tab, and then clear the Row And Column Headers check box.)

9 Press ESC to deselect the logo, and save the Lesson12 workbook.

The logo looks good, but you can make it even more attractive by animating it.

Animate the logo

Animating a WordArt object is easy. The macro simply makes many small changes to the adjustment values that are available. When you adjust shapes in a macro, however, Windows does not refresh the screen until the macro has completed. In many cases, you will be glad that Windows does not refresh the screen, because your macro runs faster that way. When you are animating a shape, however, you want the screen to refresh each time the macro adjusts the shape.

1   Activate the Visual Basic Editor, and click at the bottom of the module. From the Insert menu, click File, change to the folder containing the practice files for this book, and double-click the Code12a file. This StartUpAnimation macro appears in the module:

```
Sub StartUpAnimation()
    Dim myLogo As Shape
    Dim myMap As Shape
    Dim i As Double
    Set myLogo = Worksheets("Main").Shapes(1)
    Set myMap = Worksheets("Main").Shapes(2)

    Application.EnableCancelKey = xlErrorHandler
    On Error GoTo StartUpAnimation_End

    myMap.Visible = msoFalse
    myLogo.Adjustments(1) = 91
    myLogo.Adjustments(2) = 0.5
    myLogo.TextEffect.Tracking = 0.1
    Worksheets("Main").Select
    Application.ScreenUpdating = True

    For i = 91 To 166 Step 5
        myLogo.Adjustments(1) = i
        DoEvents
    Next i
    For i = 0.5 To 0.18 Step -0.02
        myLogo.Adjustments(2) = i
        DoEvents
    Next i
    For i = 0.1 To 1.5 Step 0.1
        myLogo.TextEffect.Tracking = i
        DoEvents
    Next i
    For i = 0.2 To 0.455 Step 0.02
        myLogo.Adjustments(2) = i
        DoEvents
    Next i

StartUpAnimation_End:
    myLogo.Adjustments(1) = 166
    myLogo.Adjustments(2) = 0.455
    myLogo.TextEffect.Tracking = 1.5
    myLogo.Visible = msoTrue
    myMap.Visible = msoTrue
End Sub
```

This macro consists of five parts, separated by an extra blank line. The first part simply declares some variables and assigns references to the two shapes on the worksheet.

See Lesson 8 for more information about the On Error statement.

The second part and the fifth part work together to allow you to skip the animation by pressing CTRL+BREAK. The On Error Resume Next statement tells the macro to jump to the StartUpAnimation_End label if there is an error. The EnableCancelKey property tells Excel to consider it an error if the user presses CTRL+BREAK. The statements in the final part (after the label) simply set the shape adjustments to their final values and display both the shapes.

The third part sets the logo shape adjustments to their initial values, hides the map, and makes sure that screen updating has not been turned off by an earlier procedure. It then activates the Main worksheet, ready to show the animation. The Tracking property controls how much WordArt letters overlap.

> **NOTE** The constants *msoTrue* and *msoFalse* are identical to the ordinary Visual Basic constants True and False. The *mso* prefix stands for "Microsoft Office"; for some unknown reason, the designer of the Shape objects decided to create True and False values that are unique to Microsoft Office. You can use the True and False constants with Shape objects, but when you enter a statement using a Shape object, the Auto List offers only msoTrue and msoFalse.

The fourth part does the real animation. It consists of four loops, which change three different settings of the logo shape. You can find appropriate start and end values for an animation by turning on the recorder and making manual changes to the adjustments for a shape. Much of the process is simply trial and error. The DoEvents statement is the secret to making an animation work. This statement tells Windows to refresh the screen (refreshing is an "event" that Windows should "do"), without waiting for the macro to end.

See Lesson 8 for information about setting breakpoints.

2 Save the Lesson12 workbook, click in the StartUpAnimation macro, and press F5 to test the macro. You may want to set breakpoints in the macro and step through parts of the macro.

Your application now has both functionality and an effective user interface; however, it is still obviously part of Excel. Now is the time to package the application by removing any distracting toolbars, window features, and menu commands and by making the macros run automatically.

Packaging the Application

Packaging the application consists of bending the appearance and behavior of Excel's workspace to match your wishes. Many of the settings you will need to change—such as the window size and the appearance of the toolbars—can also be customized by the user. Excel stores changes to those settings. For example, after a user changes which toolbars are visible, Excel saves the settings when the program closes and restores them the next time the program starts.

If your application changes customization settings, it must restore them to the original state when the application closes. For example, if your application hides all the toolbars when it opens, it should redisplay the toolbars when it closes.

Replace and restore the menu bar

A Windows application can have many toolbars, but only one menu bar. The way to remove Excel's menu bar is to replace it with a custom menu bar of your own. When the application closes, removing the custom menu bar automatically restores Excel's standard menu bar. A menu bar is simply a command bar—just like a toolbar—that you designate as a menu bar. You give the menu bar a name when you create it, and you can then use that name to delete it. For this application, name the menu bar EIS.

1 In the Visual Basic Editor, add this procedure to the module:

```
Sub ZapMenu()
    On Error Resume Next
    CommandBars("EIS").Delete
End Sub
```

The On Error Resume Next statement allows you to use this macro to ensure that the custom menu is deleted, without worrying about whether it was ever created or not. When the application is working perfectly, the menu bar should never exist when the macro creates it, and it should always exist when the macro deletes it, but while you are developing and testing the application, you may sometimes run the ZapMenu macro when the menu has already been deleted. In that case, ignoring the error makes your life simpler.

The menu bar for this application will have two commands: Exit and Return To Main. Before creating the macro that adds the custom menu bar, you can create the sub procedures the commands will need.

2 Add this procedure to the module:

```
Sub ExitEIS()
    ZapMenu
    ActiveWorkbook.Close
End Sub
```

This procedure closes the active workbook. This is the macro that the Exit button will run.

3   Add this procedure to the module:

```
Sub ReturnToMain()
    Worksheets("Main").Select
End Sub
```

This procedure activates the Main worksheet. This is the macro that the Return To Main button will run.

Now you are ready to add the macro that adds the custom menu bar.

4   Click at the bottom of the module, and from the Insert menu, click File and double-click the Code12b file to add this procedure to the module:

```
Sub SetMenu()
    Dim myBar As CommandBar
    Dim myButton As CommandBarButton

    ZapMenu
    Set myBar = CommandBars.Add(Name:="EIS", _
        Position:=msoBarBottom, _
        MenuBar:=True)

    Set myButton = myBar.Controls.Add(msoControlButton)
    myButton.Style = msoButtonCaption
    myButton.Caption = "E&xit"
    myButton.OnAction = "ExitEIS"

    Set myButton = myBar.Controls.Add(msoControlButton)
    myButton.Style = msoButtonCaption
    myButton.Caption = "&Return to Main"
    myButton.OnAction = "ReturnToMain"
    myButton.Visible = False

    myBar.Protection = msoBarNoMove + msoBarNoCustomize
    myBar.Visible = True
End Sub
```

This macro consists of five parts separated by blank lines. The first part simply declares a couple of variables.

The second part runs the ZapMenu macro to make sure the EIS menu bar does not already exist, and then creates a new EIS menu bar. Passing True as the value of the MenuBar argument is what makes this new command bar into a menu bar. Putting the menu bar at the bottom of the screen makes it look less like a conventional menu bar.

The third and fourth parts add the two commands to the menu bar. Initially, the Return To Main command is invisible.

The final part protects the new menu bar. This property has an enumerated list of values that you can assign to it to control what you will and will not allow users to do to the menu bar. You can add values together to further control what you will allow. This macro does not allow the user to move or customize the new menu bar.

5   Save the Lesson12 workbook and run the SetMenu macro and the ZapMenu macro.

In summary, replacing Excel's menu bar is easy: you just create a new one of your own. Restoring Excel's menu bar is even easier: you just delete the one you created.

Show and hide a menu command

You still need to make the Return To Menu command visible whenever the Data worksheet becomes active, and to make it invisible whenever the Data worksheet becomes inactive. This looks like a job for event handler procedures—one to hide the command and one to show it. You can create a single procedure with an argument, and then you have the event handlers call that procedure.

1   Insert this procedure into the module:

```
Sub CommandVisible(IsVisible)
    On Error Resume Next
    CommandBars("EIS").Controls(2).Visible = IsVisible
End Sub
```

The On Error Resume Next statement again allows you to avoid inconveniences while building and testing the application; in case this procedure runs when the menu has not been created. The other statement makes the command visible or invisible, depending on the value of the argument.

Project Explorer button

2   Click the Project Explorer button, and double-click the entry for the Data worksheet.

3   Insert these two event handler procedures:

```
Private Sub Worksheet_Activate()
    CommandVisible True
End Sub

Private Sub Worksheet_Deactivate()
    CommandVisible False
End Sub
```

Whenever the Data worksheet becomes active, the Return To Menu command will become invisible. Whenever the worksheet becomes inactive, the command will disappear.

4 Reactivate the module, close the Project window, save the Lesson12 workbook, and run the SetMenu macro.

5 Activate Excel and switch back and forth between the Data and Main worksheets. Watch to see the command appear and disappear.

6 Run the ZapMenu macro.

Change and restore windows

You can package the application pleasingly by creating a window that is precisely the right size for the table and chart. When the application closes, however, you should restore the window back to the way it was. Restoring the window is harder than restoring Excel's menu bar, because you must make the macro remember the original size of the window.

You can store the size of the window in a variable, but when you use Dim to declare a variable inside a procedure, the variable lasts only as long as the procedure is running. You can keep a variable from disappearing by using the word *Static* to declare the variable.

1 Insert this partial procedure into the module:

```
Sub SetWindow(State)
    Const myWidth = 425
    Const myHeight = 320
    Static myOldWidth
    Static myOldHeight
    Static myOldState

End Sub
```

You will use this same procedure to change the window and to restore it. The State argument will determine which task the procedure will carry out. By using a single procedure for both tasks, you can store the old values right here in the SetWindow procedure using the Static keyword. The Const statements give the new custom values for the height and width. A *Const* is a constant value. You can use it like a read-only variable. Giving the width and height new values at the top like this makes them easy to change if you want to adjust your application later.

2 Click in the blank line before the End Sub statement of the SetWindow procedure, and from the Insert menu click File and double-click the file Code12c. That inserts the following part of the macro:

```
If State = xlOn Then
     myOldWidth = Application.Width
     myOldHeight = Application.Height
     myOldState = Application.WindowState
     Application.WindowState = xlNormal
     Application.Width = myWidth
     Application.Height = myHeight
     Application.Caption = "Miller Textiles EIS"

     ActiveWorkbook.Unprotect
     ActiveWindow.WindowState = xlMaximized
     ActiveWindow.Caption = ""
     ActiveWorkbook.Protect , True, True

     ProtectSheet xlOn, "Main"
     ProtectSheet xlOn, "Data"
     Application.DisplayFormulaBar = False
     Application.DisplayStatusBar = False
     ActiveWindow.DisplayHorizontalScrollBar = False
     ActiveWindow.DisplayVerticalScrollBar = False
     ActiveWindow.DisplayWorkbookTabs = False
```

This is the first half of an If...Else...End If structure. It runs if the value of the State argument is xlOn. The value *xlOn* is a built-in Excel constant. Using the constant makes the macro easier to read than using an arbitrary number, and using a built-in constant is easier than creating a custom constant.

Setting the window consists of three parts. The first part stores the old height, width, and window state of the Excel application window in the static variables. It then assigns new values to those properties. When you resize the application window, you should always set the WindowState property to xlNormal first, because if the application is maximized, you cannot change the width or the height. This part also customizes the Excel application caption.

The second part makes sure that the workbook window is maximized and protected. You must unprotect it before attempting to maximize it. Setting the caption to an empty text string keeps the workbook name from appearing in the caption bar. The final statement of this part protects both the structure and the windows of the workbook.

ProtectSheet is a procedure you will create shortly that protects or unprotects a sheet. You give it the sheet name and specify whether protection should be on or off.

The third part is mostly for your convenience as you develop the application. You could protect the worksheets interactively, but then you would always have to unprotect them interactively to make any changes. Likewise, you could hide the scroll bars, the sheet tabs, the formula bar, and the status bar interactively, but sometimes they are useful while you are developing the application.

3 Click before the End Sub statement of the SetWindow procedure, and insert the file Code12d to add this final part of the macro:

```
Else
    Application.Caption = Empty
    If Not IsEmpty(myOldWidth) Then
        Application.Width = myOldWidth
        Application.Height = myOldHeight
        Application.WindowState = myOldState
    End If
    ProtectSheet xlOff, "Main"
    ProtectSheet xlOff, "Data"
    ActiveWorkbook.Unprotect
    Application.DisplayFormulaBar = False
    Application.DisplayStatusBar = False
    Application.DisplayFormulaBar = True
    Application.DisplayStatusBar = True
    ActiveWindow.DisplayHorizontalScrollBar = True
    ActiveWindow.DisplayVerticalScrollBar = True
    ActiveWindow.DisplayWorkbookTabs = True
End If
```

These statements are the second half of the If…Else…End If structure. Basically, they undo everything the statements in the first half did. Again, checking whether the myOldWidth variable is empty is for your convenience while you are developing the macro. When you make certain changes in Visual Basic—such as adding or deleting a procedure—the value of static variables can be lost, effectively replacing the value with zero. Checking to see if the myOldWidth variable is empty keeps Visual Basic from shrinking the application window to a tiny block on the screen if you happen to do something that resets the static variables.

4 Click at the bottom of the module, and insert the file Code12e to add this macro:

```
Sub ProtectSheet(State, SheetItem)
    If State = xlOn Then
        Worksheets(SheetItem).EnableSelection = xlNoSelection
        Worksheets(SheetItem).Protect , True, True, True, True
    Else
        Worksheets(SheetItem).Unprotect
    End If
End Sub
```

This is the macro that the SetWindow macro calls to protect a worksheet. Setting the EnableSelection property to xlNoSelection prevents the user from selecting any cells when the worksheet is protected.

You now need a way to run the SetWindow macro with the appropriate arguments.

5 Insert these two macros in the module:

```
Sub InitView()
    SetMenu
    SetWindow xlOn
End Sub

Sub ExitView()
    ZapMenu
    SetWindow xlOff
End Sub
```

6 Save the Lesson12 workbook and test the InitView and ExitView procedures.

Static variables are a valuable tool for remembering values that must be restored later.

Remove and restore toolbars

The procedure for removing and restoring toolbars is very similar to that for changing and restoring windows: store the old values before making changes, and then use the stored values to restore the workspace. Storing toolbars, however, adds a new twist. Storing the size of the window always requires exactly three static variables for three and only three values (height, width, and state), but storing the list of visible toolbars can involve an unknown and varying number of toolbars.

As you know, Excel organizes multiple objects into collections. In fact, the toolbars themselves are in a collection. Visual Basic will actually allow you to create your own custom collection; you can make a collection of only the toolbars that need to be restored. Collections are powerful tools, and this example shows only a very simple (but extremely useful) way to take advantage of them.

1   Click at the bottom of the module and insert the file Code12f to create this procedure:

```
Sub SetBars(State)
    Static myOldBars As New Collection
    Dim myBar

    If State = xlOn Then
        For Each myBar In Application.CommandBars
            If myBar.Type <> 1 And myBar.Visible Then
                myOldBars.Add myBar
                myBar.Visible = False
            End If
        Next myBar
    Else
        For Each myBar In myOldBars
            myBar.Visible = True
        Next
    End If
End Sub
```

Once again, a single procedure handles both the changing and the restoring, so that a static variable can store the old values. This time, however, the static variable is declared as a *New Collection*. Declaring a variable as a New Collection tells Visual Basic that you want to create a collection of your own.

The first half of the If...Else...End If structure loops through each of the items in the application's CommandBars collection. If the command bar is a menu bar, its Type property is 1 and you should not hide or restore it. Otherwise, if the command bar is visible, you want to add it to your custom collection and then make it invisible. To add an item to a custom collection, you use the Add method followed by a reference to the item you want to add.

The second half of the If...Else...End If structure simply loops through the custom collection, unhiding every toolbar in it.

You can launch SetBars from the InitView and ExitView macros, the same as you did with SetWindow.

2   Insert the statement **SetBars(xlOn)** before the End Sub statement of the InitView macro.

3   Insert the statement **SetBars(xlOff)** before the End Sub statement of the ExitView macro.

4   Save the Lesson12 workbook and test the InitView and ExitView procedures.

This section did not give details about all the ways you can use a custom collection, but even if you use a custom collection only for storing items from a standard collection—essentially copying the code from this lesson—you will find it a valuable tool.

Complete the package

All the pieces are in place for the finished application. You just need to make it happen automatically when the workbook opens.

1 Activate the Project Explorer window, and double-click ThisWorkbook.

2 Insert this event handler for when the workbook opens:

```
Private Sub Workbook_Open()
    Application.ScreenUpdating = False
    RefreshPivot
    InitView
    StartUpAnimation
End Sub
```

Every time the workbook opens, you want to check for new data in the database, customize the environment, and play the initial animation. Setting ScreenUpdating to False restricts the amount of flashing you see on the screen.

3 Insert this event handler for when the workbook closes:

```
Private Sub Workbook_BeforeClose(Cancel As Boolean)
    ExitView
    ActiveWorkbook.Saved = True
End Sub
```

Every time the workbook closes, you want to restore the environment. You also want to keep Excel from asking whether to save changes. Setting the Saved property of the active workbook to True makes Excel believe that it has been saved, so it doesn't ask.

4 In the ExitEIS macro, insert the statement **ExitView** before the *ActiveWorksheet.Close* statement.

The Workbook_BeforeClose event handler needs to run ExitView in case the user closes the workbook by clicking Excel's Close Window button.

 NOTE   Theoretically, the ExitEIS macro should not have to run ExitView. ExitEIS closes the window, and the event handler should run when the window closes regardless of what causes it to close. For some reason, however, the event handler does not run the ExitView macro if the ExitEIS macro triggered the event. It's just another reminder that Visual Basic was created by humans.

5   In Excel, rename Sheet3 to **Blank**. Turn off the row and column headers. Select a cell several rows and columns away from cell A1. Save the workbook while the Blank sheet is active so that the user won't see anything when the workbook first opens.

6   Close the workbook, and reopen it. Test the application and close the workbook.

The application is beautiful. It is has functionality. It has an effective user interface. It is well packaged. Congratulations!

Lesson Summary

To	Do this
Import data from an external database into a pivot table	In step 1 of the Pivot Table Wizard, select the External Data Source option. In step 2, click Get Data, and create a new data source for the external database.
Keep a pivot table the same size, even if it has blank items	Double-click the tile of the field whose items you want to show, and select the Show Items With No Data check box.
Change the default format for the cells in a workbook	From the Format menu, click Style. Select the Normal style and change the formatting to the desired default.
Link a text box to the contents of a cell	Create the text box on a worksheet. Press ESC to select the container box. In the Formula bar, type an equal sign and the cell address you want to link to the text box.
Use a macro to refresh the data in a pivot table	Assign a new value to the Connection property of a PivotCache object.
Convert an imported picture into Office 97 shape objects	Select the picture, click the Draw menu on the Drawing toolbar, and choose Ungroup.
Determine which object launched a macro when the macro is attached to several objects	Use the Application.Caller property to find the identifier of the object.
Force the screen to refresh while animating a shape object	Include a DoEvents statement in the macro.
Make CTRL+BREAK trigger an error that you can trap	Assign xlErrorHandler to the Application.EnableCancelKey property.

To	Do this
Replace Excel's standard menu bar	Create a new menu bar using the CommandBars.Add method with True as the value of the MenuBar argument.
Make a variable retain its value from one time you run the macro to the next	Use the keyword Static to declare the variable instead of Dim.
Prevent the user from selecting any cells on a worksheet	Assign xlNoSelection to the EnableSelection property of a worksheet and then protect the worksheet.
Create a custom collection for storing references to objects	Declare a variable as New Collection. Then use the Add method on the collection variable to add new items to the collection.

For online information about	Ask the Assistant for help using the words
Retrieving data from an external data source	"External data" (in Excel's Assistant)
Automating shape objects	"Shape object" (in Visual Basic's Assistant)
Using custom collections	"Collection object" (in Visual Basic's Assistant)
Using static variables	"Variable lifetimes" (in Visual Basic's Assistant)

Preview of the Future

You have now completed all the lessons in this book. You have created simple macros using the macro recorder. You have explored the wealth of objects available in Excel. You have learned how to use Visual Basic commands and statements to control an application. You have made macros easy to run using forms, toolbars, menu commands, and ActiveX controls. And you have built a packaged application.

Excel and Visual Basic are both very powerful and complex tools. You can continue learning new skills with both Excel and Visual Basic for a long time. The concepts and skills you have learned in this book will enable you to write useful and powerful applications now, and they will also serve as a good foundation as you learn more about Excel and Visual Basic.

Appendixes

Alternative Techniques

Microsoft Excel typically provides several methods for accomplishing the same task. Some use menu commands, some use keyboard shortcuts, and some use toolbar buttons. This appendix contains one or more alternative methods for carrying out many of the tasks described in this book.

Lesson 1

Task	Alternatives
Show a toolbar.	■ Right-click any toolbar and click desired toolbar. ■ From the View menu, the Toolbars submenu, click the toolbar name.
Record a macro.	■ Click the Record Macro button. ■ From the Tools menu, the Macro submenu, click Record New Macro.
Stop recorder.	■ On the Visual Basic toolbar, click the Stop Recording button. ■ From the Tools menu, the Macro submenu, click Stop Recording.
Display the Macro dialog box to run a macro.	■ On the Visual Basic toolbar, click the Run Macro button. ■ From the Tools menu, the Macro submenu, click Macros. ■ Press ALT+F8.

Lesson 1, *continued*

Task	Alternatives
Show the Visual Basic Editor.	■ Display the Macro dialog box, select a macro, and click Edit. ■ On the Visual Basic toolbar, click the Visual Basic Editor button. ■ From the Tools menu, the Macro submenu, click Visual Basic Editor. ■ Press ALT+F11.
Run a macro from Visual Basic.	■ Press F5. ■ On the standard toolbar, click the Run Sub/UserForm button. ■ From the Run menu, click Run Sub/UserForm. ■ From the Tools menu, click Macros, select the macro, and click Run.

Lesson 2

Task	Alternatives
Delete the rows containing the selected cells.	■ From the Edit menu, click Delete, and choose Entire Row option. ■ Press CTRL+- (minus). ■ Press SHIFT+SPACEBAR to extend the selection to the entire row, and choose the Delete command from the Edit menu.
Step through a macro.	■ Press F8. ■ Show the Debug toolbar and click the Step Into button. ■ On the Debug menu, click the Step Into command.
Display the Goto dialog box in Excel.	■ On the Edit menu, choose the Go To command. ■ Press CTRL+G. ■ Press F5.
Select the current region.	■ Press CTRL+SHIFT+*. ■ Press CTRL+* (on the numeric keypad). ■ Click the Select Current Region toolbar button. (To add the Select Current Region button to a toolbar, right-click any toolbar and choose Customize. On the Commands tab, select Edit. Drag the Select Current Region button to a toolbar.)
Close a workbook file.	■ From the File menu, click Close. ■ Press CTRL+W. ■ Press CTRL+F4.

Task	Alternatives
Delete a worksheet.	■ From the Edit menu, click Delete Sheet. ■ Right-click the worksheet tab and click Delete.

Lesson 3

Task	Alternatives
Delete a line in a macro.	■ Select the entire line and press DELETE. ■ Press CTRL+Y.
Show the Locals window.	■ From the View menu, click Locals Window. ■ On the Debug toolbar, click the Locals Window button.
Change which statement will execute next.	■ Drag the yellow arrow in the left margin of the code window. ■ From the Debug menu, click Set Next Statement. ■ Press CTRL+F9.
Show the Immediate window.	■ From the View menu, click Immediate Window. ■ Press CTRL+G. ■ On the Debug toolbar, click the Immediate Window button.
Get help on a keyword.	■ Click on the keyword and press F1. ■ On the Help menu, choose Contents and Index. In Help, select the Index tab, type the keyword, and press ENTER.
Show the global list of methods and properties.	■ With the cursor on a blank line, press CTRL+SPACEBAR. ■ Press CTRL+J. ■ From the Edit menu, click List Properties/Methods. ■ On the Edit toolbar, click the List Properties/Methods button.
Show list of constants.	■ Use Auto List. ■ Press CTRL+SHIFT+J. ■ From the Edit menu, click List Constants. ■ On the Edit toolbar, click the List Constants button.
Show the Object Browser.	■ On the Standard toolbar, click the Object Browser button. ■ Press F2. ■ From the View menu, click Object Browser.

Lesson 4

Task	Alternatives
Change a cell to bold.	▪ Click the Bold toolbar button. ▪ Press CTRL+B. ▪ Press CTRL+1, and select the Font tab.
Change selected cell font to italic.	▪ Click the Italic toolbar button. ▪ Press CTRL+I. ▪ Press CTRL+1, and select the Font tab.

Lesson 5

Task	Alternatives
Activate a sheet in a workbook.	▪ Click the sheet tab. ▪ Press CTRL+PAGE UP, or CTRL+PAGE DOWN to move to next or previous sheet.
Select an item in a chart.	▪ Click the item. ▪ Select the item in the Chart Objects list on the Chart toolbar. ▪ Press the UP ARROW and DOWN ARROW keys to move between groups of objects. Press the LEFT ARROW and RIGHT ARROW keys to move from object to object.
Select a graphical shape on a worksheet.	▪ Click the shape. ▪ To select all shapes and other objects, press CTRL+G, click the Special button, select the Objects option, and click OK. ▪ To move from shape to shape, select one shape and then press TAB.

Lesson 7

Task	Alternatives
Set or remove a breakpoint.	▪ Click in the margin. ▪ Press F9. ▪ From the Debug menu, click Toggle Breakpoint. ▪ On either the Debug toolbar or the Edit toolbar, click the Toggle Breakpoint button.
Run to the statement containing the cursor.	▪ From the Debug menu, click Run To Cursor. ▪ Press CTRL+F8.

Lesson 8

Task	Alternatives
Edit a formula.	■ Click the Edit Formula button. ■ Press F2.

Lesson 9

Task	Alternatives
Move a control on the worksheet.	■ Drag the control with the mouse. ■ Press any of the arrow keys to "nudge" the control.
Select a property in the Properties window.	■ Click the property name. ■ Simultaneously press CTRL+SHIFT and the first letter of the property name.
Move between areas of the Properties window.	■ Click in the area. ■ Press TAB.
Exit Design Mode.	■ On the Visual Basic toolbar, click the Exit Design Mode button. ■ In Visual Basic, from the Run menu, click Exit Design Mode.
Show the Project window.	■ On the Standard toolbar, click the Project Explorer button. ■ Press CTRL+R. ■ From the View menu, click Project Explorer.

Lesson 11

Task	Alternatives
Insert a user form.	■ Click the Insert UserForm button. ■ From the Insert menu, clickUserForm. ■ In the Project window, right-click to show the shortcut menu. Then from the Insert submenu, click UserForm.
Show the Properties window in Visual Basic.	■ Click the Properties Window button. ■ Press F4. ■ From the View menu, click Properties Window.
Run a form.	■ Press F5. ■ From the Run menu, click Run Sub/UserForm. ■ On the Standard or Debug toolbars, click the Run Sub/UserForm button.

Lesson 11, *continued*

Task	Alternatives
Display the find dialog box in Excel.	■ From the Edit menu, click Find. ■ Press CTRL+F.
Hide a row.	■ From the Format menu, the Row submenu, click Hide. ■ Press CTRL+9.
Show a row.	■ From the Format menu, the Row submenu, click Unhide. ■ Press CTRL+SHIFT+9.
Hide a column.	■ From the Format menu, the Column submenu, click Hide. ■ Press CTRL+0.
Show a column.	■ From the Format menu, the Column submenu, click Unhide. ■ Press CTRL+SHIFT+0.

Lesson 12

Task	Alternatives
Show the Style dialog box.	■ From the Format menu, click Style. ■ Press ALT+' (apostrophe).
Move a field in the PivotTable Wizard to the page, column, row, or data area.	■ Drag the field tile. ■ Press ALT+P, ALT+C, ALT+R, orALT+D, respectively.
Show the PivotTable field dialog box.	■ Double-click the PivotTable field tile. ■ Select the field tile and press ALT+L.
Scroll to the next procedure in a module.	■ Use the scroll bars. ■ To scroll down, press CTRL+DOWN ARROW. To scroll up, press CTRL+UP ARROW.
Go to a specific procedure.	■ Scroll to the procedure. ■ Click on the name of the proceprocedure and press SHIFT+F2. ■ Select the procedure name from the Procedure list at the top of the code window. ■ Click outside of any procedure, press F5, select the procedure, and click Edit.

Checking Your Configuration

Microsoft Excel allows you to customize your work environment to a remarkable degree. You can decide which toolbars are visible, which commands are on a toolbar, how the gridlines are displayed, and countless other customizations. In fact, it is possible that you could customize your working environment so that some of the exercises might work differently from the way they are described in the book.

In general, this book assumes that your environment matches Excel's default settings. This appendix describes the settings that affect the way exercises work in this book. If you find that your copy of Excel or Visual Basic does not behave the way the book describes, compare your custom settings with those described here.

Microsoft Excel Environment

The settings for Microsoft Excel are separate from the settings in Visual Basic.

Windows

- The workbook window is maximized.
- The Microsoft Excel window can be either maximized or resizable.

Toolbars

- The Standard and Formatting toolbars are visible.
- After Lesson 1, the Visual Basic toolbar is visible.
- The menus and all toolbars contain the default commands.

To control which toolbars are visible, click Customize from the Tools menu, click the Toolbars tab, and then put a check mark next to only the toolbars you want to see.

To reset the toolbars, click Customize from the Tools menu and click the Toolbars tab. Select a toolbar or menu name, and click the Reset button.

Add-Ins

This book does not require any add-ins to be installed. For the most part, installing or removing the add-ins that come with Excel should not affect any of the exercises in this book (except that if you have installed the AutoSave add-in, you may occasionally be prompted to save the open workbooks). If you are uncertain whether an add-in may be affecting the way this book is working, you can safely disable all the add-ins you have installed.

To disable an add-in, click Add-Ins from the Tools menu, select the add-in name, and remove the check box next to the name.

View Options

This book assumes that the following View Options are set. View options that are not mentioned do not matter.

- Show formula bar.
- Show status bar.
- Show all objects.
- Do not show formulas.
- Show gridlines.
- Gridline color is Automatic.
- Show row and column headers.
- Show horizontal scroll bar.
- Show vertical scroll bar.
- Show sheet tabs.

To set the View options, click Options from the Tools menu, click the View tab in the dialog box, and select the desired options.

Calculation Options

This book assumes that the following Calculation Options are set. Calculation options that are not mentioned do not matter.

- Calculation is automatic.
- In the Workbook options group, "Accept labels in formulas" is selected.

To set the Calculation options, click Options from the Tools menu, click the Calculation tab in the dialog box, and select the desired options.

General Options

This book assumes that the following General Options are set. General options that are not mentioned do not matter.

- R1C1 Reference Style is turned off.
- Macro Virus Protection is turned off (after Lesson 1).

- Sheets In New Workbook is 3.
- User Name is set to your name.

To set the General options, click Options from the Tools menu, click the General tab in the dialog box, and select the desired options.

Visual Basic Editor Environment

The Visual Basic Editor environment has customization settings that are independent of Microsoft Excel. To display the Visual Basic Editor, click the Visual Basic Editor button on the Visual Basic toolbar in Excel.

Windows

- All windows are closed except the code window.
- The code window is maximized.

Toolbars

- The Standard toolbar is visible.
- The menu and toolbars contain the default commands.

To control which toolbars are visible, click Customize from the Toolbars submenu of the View menu and click the Toolbars tab, and then put a check mark next to only the Standard toolbar.

To reset the toolbars, click Customize from the Toolbars submenu of the View menu and click the Toolbars tab. Select a toolbar or menu name, and click the Reset button.

Editor Options

This book assumes that the following Editor Options are set. Editor options that are not mentioned do not matter.

- Auto Syntax Check is turned on.
- Require Variable Declaration is turned off (until possibly after Lesson 8).
- Auto List Members is turned on.
- Auto Quick Info is turned on.
- Auto Data Tips is turned on.
- Auto Indent is turned on.
- Default to Full Module View is turned on.
- Procedure Separator is turned on.

To set the Editor options, click Options from the Tools menu, click the Editor tab in the dialog box, and select the desired options.

Editor Format Options

This book assumes that the following Editor Format Options are set. Editor Format options that are not mentioned do not matter.

- Normal Text has Auto for Foreground, Background, and Indicator.
- Execution Point Text has Auto for Foreground, and is yellow for Background and Indicator.
- Breakpoint Text is white for Foreground, and dark red for Background and Indicator.
- Comment Text is green for Foreground, and Auto for Background and Indicator.
- Keyword Text is dark blue for Foreground, and Auto for Background and Indicator.
- The Margin Indicator Bar is turned on.

To set the Editor Format options, click Options from the Tools menu, and click the Editor Format tab in the dialog box. Select the desired type of text, and choose the options you want.

General Options

This book assumes that the following General Options are set. General options that are not mentioned do not matter.

- Notify Before State Loss is turned off.
- Error Trapping is set to Break In Class Module.
- Compile On Demand is turned on.
- Background Compile is turned on.

To set the General options, click Options from the Tools menu, click the General tab in the dialog box, and select the desired options.

Docking Options

This book assumes that the following Docking Options are set. Docking options that are not mentioned do not matter. (These window settings do not affect the way anything in the book works, but may make your screens appear different from the captured screens in the text.)

- All windows are Dockable. (The Object Browser is Dockable after Lesson 3.)

To set the Docking options, click Options from the Tools menu, click the Docking tab in the dialog box, and select the desired options.

Index

IMPORTANT—READ CAREFULLY BEFORE OPENING SOFTWARE PACKET(S). By opening the sealed packet(s) containing the software, you indicate your acceptance of the following Microsoft License Agreement.

MICROSOFT LICENSE AGREEMENT
(Book Companion CD)

This is a legal agreement between you (either an individual or an entity) and Microsoft Corporation. By opening the sealed software packet(s) you are agreeing to be bound by the terms of this agreement. If you do not agree to the terms of this agreement, promptly return the unopened software packet(s) and any accompanying written materials to the place you obtained them for a full refund.

MICROSOFT SOFTWARE LICENSE

1. GRANT OF LICENSE. Microsoft grants to you the right to use one copy of the Microsoft software program included with this book (the "SOFTWARE") on a single terminal connected to a single computer. The SOFTWARE is in "use" on a computer when it is loaded into the temporary memory (i.e., RAM) or installed into the permanent memory (e.g., hard disk, CD-ROM, or other storage device) of that computer. You may not network the SOFTWARE or otherwise use it on more than one computer or computer terminal at the same time.

2. COPYRIGHT. The SOFTWARE is owned by Microsoft or its suppliers and is protected by United States copyright laws and international treaty provisions. Therefore, you must treat the SOFTWARE like any other copyrighted material (e.g., a book or musical recording) except that you may either (a) make one copy of the SOFTWARE solely for backup or archival purposes, or (b) transfer the SOFTWARE to a single hard disk provided you keep the original solely for backup or archival purposes. You may not copy the written materials accompanying the SOFTWARE.

3. OTHER RESTRICTIONS. You may not rent or lease the SOFTWARE, but you may transfer the SOFTWARE and accompanying written materials on a permanent basis provided you retain no copies and the recipient agrees to the terms of this Agreement. You may not reverse engineer, decompile, or disassemble the SOFTWARE. If the SOFTWARE is an update or has been updated, any transfer must include the most recent update and all prior versions.

4. DUAL MEDIA SOFTWARE. If the SOFTWARE package contains both 3.5" and 5.25" disks, then you may use only the disks appropriate for your single-user computer. You may not use the other disks on another computer or loan, rent, lease, or transfer them to another user except as part of the permanent transfer (as provided above) of all SOFTWARE and written materials.

5. SAMPLE CODE. If the SOFTWARE includes Sample Code, then Microsoft grants you a royalty-free right to reproduce and distribute the sample code of the SOFTWARE provided that you: (a) distribute the sample code only in conjunction with and as a part of your software product; (b) do not use Microsoft's or its authors' names, logos, or trademarks to market your software product; (c) include the copyright notice that appears on the SOFTWARE on your product label and as a part of the sign-on message for your software product; and (d) agree to indemnify, hold harmless, and defend Microsoft and its authors from and against any claims or lawsuits, including attorneys' fees, that arise or result from the use or distribution of your software product.

DISCLAIMER OF WARRANTY

The SOFTWARE (including instructions for its use) is provided "AS IS" WITHOUT WARRANTY OF ANY KIND. MICROSOFT FURTHER DISCLAIMS ALL IMPLIED WARRANTIES INCLUDING WITHOUT LIMITATION ANY IMPLIED WARRANTIES OF MERCHANTABILITY OR OF FITNESS FOR A PARTICULAR PURPOSE. THE ENTIRE RISK ARISING OUT OF THE USE OR PERFORMANCE OF THE SOFTWARE AND DOCUMENTATION REMAINS WITH YOU.

IN NO EVENT SHALL MICROSOFT, ITS AUTHORS, OR ANYONE ELSE INVOLVED IN THE CREATION, PRODUCTION, OR DELIVERY OF THE SOFTWARE BE LIABLE FOR ANY DAMAGES WHATSOEVER (INCLUDING, WITHOUT LIMITATION, DAMAGES FOR LOSS OF BUSINESS PROFITS, BUSINESS INTERRUPTION, LOSS OF BUSINESS INFORMATION, OR OTHER PECUNIARY LOSS) ARISING OUT OF THE USE OF OR INABILITY TO USE THE SOFTWARE OR DOCUMENTATION, EVEN IF MICROSOFT HAS BEEN ADVISED OF THE POSSIBILITY OF SUCH DAMAGES. BECAUSE SOME STATES/COUNTRIES DO NOT ALLOW THE EXCLUSION OR LIMITATION OF LIABILITY FOR CONSEQUENTIAL OR INCIDENTAL DAMAGES, THE ABOVE LIMITATION MAY NOT APPLY TO YOU.

U.S. GOVERNMENT RESTRICTED RIGHTS

The SOFTWARE and documentation are provided with RESTRICTED RIGHTS. Use, duplication, or disclosure by the Government is subject to restrictions as set forth in subparagraph (c)(1)(ii) of The Rights in Technical Data and Computer Software clause at DFARS 252.227-7013 or subparagraphs (c)(1) and (2) of the Commercial Computer Software — Restricted Rights 48 CFR 52.227-19, as applicable. Manufacturer is Microsoft Corporation, One Microsoft Way, Redmond, WA 98052-6399.

If you acquired this product in the United States, this Agreement is governed by the laws of the State of Washington.

Should you have any questions concerning this Agreement, or if you desire to contact Microsoft Press for any reason, please write: Microsoft Press, One Microsoft Way, Redmond, WA 98052-6399.

The
Step by Step
Practice Files CD-ROM

The enclosed CD-ROM contains timesaving, ready-to-use practice files that complement the lessons in this book. To use the practice files, you'll need Microsoft Excel 97 (version 8) or Microsoft Office 97 and either the Microsoft Windows 95 operating system or version 3.51 Service Pack 5 or later of the Microsoft Windows NT operating system.

Most of the *Step by Step* lessons use practice files from the disk. Before you begin the *Step by Step* lessons, read the "Installing the Practice Files and Additional Microsoft Tools" section of the book. There you'll find a description of each practice file and easy instructions for installing the files on your computer's hard disk.

Please take a few moments to read the license agreement on the previous page before using the enclosed disk.

Register your Microsoft Press® book today, and let us know what you think.

At Microsoft Press, we listen to our customers. We update our books as new releases of software are issued, and we'd like you to tell us the kinds of additional information you'd find most useful in these updates. Your feedback will be considered when we prepare a future edition; plus, when you become a registered owner, you will get Microsoft Press catalogs and exclusive offers on specially priced books.

Thanks!

I used this book as
- ● A way to learn the software
- ● A reference when I needed it
- ● A way to find out about advanced features
- ● Other_____

I purchased this book from
- ● A bookstore
- ● A software store
- ● A direct mail offer
- ● Other_____

I consider myself
- ● A beginner or an occasional computer user
- ● An intermediate-level user with a pretty good grasp of the basics
- ● An advanced user who helps and provides solutions for others
- ● Other_____

I will buy the next edition of the book when it's updated
- ● Definitely
- ● Probably
- ● I will not buy the next edition

The next edition of this book should include the following additional information:

1•_____

2•_____

3•_____

The most useful things about this book are_____

_____

This book would be more helpful if_____

_____

My general impressions of this book are_____

_____

May we contact you regarding your comments? ● Yes ● No

Would you like to receive a Microsoft Press catalog regularly? ● Yes ● No

Name_____

Company (if applicable)_____

Address_____

City_____State_____Zip_____

Daytime phone number (optional) (_____)_____

Please mail back your feedback form—postage free! Fold this form as
described on the other side of this card, or fax this sheet to:
Microsoft Press, Attn: Marketing Department, fax 206-936-7329

TAPE SIDES (NO STAPLES PLEASE)

TAPE SIDES (NO STAPLES PLEASE)

FOLD HERE

NO POSTAGE
NECESSARY
IF MAILED
IN THE
UNITED STATES

BUSINESS REPLY MAIL

FIRST-CLASS MAIL   PERMIT NO. 53   BOTHELL, WA

POSTAGE WILL BE PAID BY ADDRESSEE

MICROSOFT PRESS
MICROSOFT® EXCEL 97/VISUAL BASIC®
STEP BY STEP
PO BOX 3019
BOTHELL WA 98041-9946

FOLD HERE

TAPE SIDES (NO STAPLES PLEASE)

TAPE SIDES (NO STAPLES PLEASE)